Know Your Fire

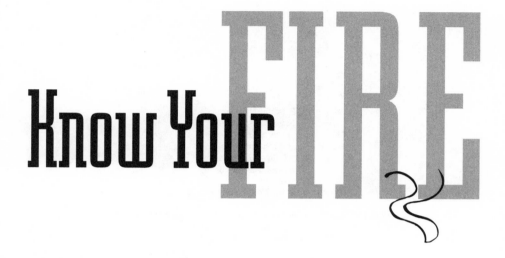

Know Your FIRE

George Hirsch

with Marie Bianco

G. P. Putnam's Sons
New York

G. P. Putnam's Sons
Publishers Since 1838
a member of
Penguin Putnam Inc.
200 Madison Avenue
New York, NY 10016

Library of Congress Cataloging-in-Publication Data

Hirsch, George.
Know your fire / by George Hirsch with Marie Bianco.
p.   cm.
Includes index.
ISBN 0-399-14288-6
1. Cookery. I. Bianco, Marie.   II. Title.
TX652.H557   1997   96-52934 CIP
641.5—dc21

Printed in the United States of America

1   3   5   7   9   10   8   6   4   2

This book is printed on acid-free paper. ∞

Book design by Richard Oriolo

For JoAnn, Dori,
Diane, Celine,
and Tom

Acknowledgments

Every creative project begins with an idea. Now that this book has been written, it's time for its birth. But between conception and birth there are many who have contributed to the words that have formed its personality.

I offer my heartfelt thanks to many people, and wish to acknowledge their importance in this project:

Marie Bianco, my co-author, who is the best thing that ever happened to the printed word. I'm fortunate in having her participation in this fourth book.

Our agent, Frank Bianco, the most persistent advocate and believer in the George-and-Marie team.

John Duff, our editor, who may say he has been stern with me to keep it moving, but he is the best person to have as the keeper of the word.

The people at Char-Broil, Hickory Specialties, WLIW 21 and Whitehawk, who mated image to the word and made the television series possible.

The people at Opryland USA, who define the word hospitality.

Arlene Wong, who in the daily process assured that all the words are tried and true on all levels. She will have forgotten more than most will ever know, and her dedication to the word is unparalleled.

But most of all, my love to everyone in my family, who will always be part of my words and deeds. Always, and especially, Mom and Dad.

Contents

A Personal Invitation   xi

Ingredients

Introduction	3	Pasta	81
Beef	5	Potatoes	90
Veal	16	Rice/Grains/Beans	97
Lamb	20	Salads	116
Pork	27	Sauces and Condiments	125
Poultry	34	Seafood	137
Herbs and Spices	49	Soups	157
Hot Peppers	62	Vegetables	167
Oils and Vinegars	71	Basic Recipes	185

Cooking Methods

Introduction	197	Roasting	240
Braising	199	Grilling	247
Frying	208	Smoking	257
Poaching	220	Baking	267
Sautéing	229	Preserving	284

Index   297

A Personal Invitation

You've gotta know when to hold 'em and know when to fold 'em. That's the savvy cardplayer's bottom line, a guide that draws on instinct as much as it does on thorough knowledge of the odds that govern the game. For me, "know your fire" says the same thing. People often ask me whether I have some secret, a style, or some special methods of cooking, and I always give the same answer. The biggest secret I have, the key to all my success, can be reduced to the three words with which I close every television show: "Know your fire." That phrase is my cooking credo, one that can play a big part in your everyday cooking. It's the reason for this book.

There's more to inspired cooking than recipes. The working chef does have technique. He must if he is to survive in the demanding arena that is his daily world. He knows how and what to choose and prepare. He knows what must take time and what can be done in a hurry. He knows how a dish must taste to be authentic. He knows the key ingredient that needs to be included and the contribution it will make, when and how it needs to be added during the preparation.

If you consider this book as a companion to my television programs, I'll show you the things I do before the camera starts rolling, the steps I take so everything flows smoothly. I'll show you how the food is chosen and prepared so that each component works with everything else. I'll also show you how to make a marriage of different ingredients so that they can live happily ever after in your and your guests' memories.

I served a long apprenticeship before I began sharing my fire on television. I've always believed that when I teach others, I become the beneficiary of my own passion. I learned a great deal when I directed restaurant kitchens. I learned even more after I helped found and direct a university-level culinary institute. All of what I had learned to that point, the things that I did instinctively, had to be dissected and reviewed before I could feed them into the minds of my aspiring assistants and student chefs.

In my years as a professional chef and as a teacher, I've observed that cooking neophytes always lack the same two skills. The first is cooking methods and procedures. The second is knowledge and understanding of seasonings and flavorings. This is why, for instance, I have given so much attention to spices and herbs for seasoning and flavoring in this book. Most people can read a recipe and cook an enjoyable dish, but once you have an understanding of the tiniest ingredient and what it does, you are able to cook with better results. The techniques you will learn in this book will seem new and perhaps strange only for the first few times you use them. Eventually, they will form your instinctive repertoire, your own special fire. As you read through these pages, I hope the sparks fly and land on the tinder of your own imagination. Perhaps something will remind you of grandma's way or one of her special dishes, or that treat you enjoyed as a child. Put it all in a pot. Stir in some adventure and season with the salt of your ancestry. This may be the makings of my fire, but I hope (and secretly know) that before long it will become the fuel for yours.

—CHEF GEORGE HIRSCH

Ingredients
What to Cook

Introduction

The Ingredients

I'm a strong believer that recipes are only guidelines, so it should be no surprise that when two people make the same recipe, the results are different. One dish is not better than the other; it is just different because each cook has brought to the dish a particular way of cutting an onion or slicing a carrot. One may use a cast-iron skillet so the fish gets crustier, while another may choose to add less stock to a soup to make it thicker.

There's a lot to learn in the kitchen and this first section will cover many of the essentials you'll need to know in order to have a better understanding of ingredients. You'll learn, for instance, why a tender beef fillet needs a different cooking treatment from the tough beef of a stew.

Most dinners center around meat, so this book begins with the chapters on meat. You'll notice that I like to marinate meat or pat it with a combination of aromatic spices called rubs to bring out the meat's full flavor and, in some cases, tenderize it as well.

People tell me they love to eat lobster but hesitate to cook it at home because they don't know how. I've included three recipes that I think you'll find easy and delicious. And carbohydrate lovers will find many ways to prepare pasta, potatoes, rice, grains and beans.

You'll find interesting soups that can be whole meals, and new ways of preparing vegetables and salads that make them exciting and nutritious additions to everyday meals.

Recipes are only guidelines, and sometimes you have to punt. Occasionally your market won't have a particular kind of fish you may need, so you'll need to purchase a substitute. No more green peppers for sale? Use a red one. Can't find pancetta? Use bacon. Recipes will give alternative ingredients when applicable.

I don't want you to be a slave to a recipe. Improvise, experiment, try something new. But, most of all, enjoy your time in the kitchen. Nothing shows love and affection like preparing a meal for someone you really care for. And then they can do the dishes.

Beef

Meat is the most expensive food item we buy and the one that confuses people the most. In this and the following sections you'll learn where various cuts of meat come from and why they require different cooking techniques. In years gone by, we could rely on the neighborhood butcher to steer us in the right direction, but today most of us never see a butcher at our local supermarket. In this section I'll show you how to read the label and to understand what cut you're buying. I'll give you tips on how to store it, freeze it, as well as cook it once you get it home.

Even if you rarely cook meat, one of your best kitchen investments is an *instant-read thermometer*. Buy one and you'll never serve an underdone or overcooked roast again. Just before you think the meat is done, insert the long thin probe into the meat and leave it in for about 10 seconds to get a reading. This type of thermometer should never be left in the meat while it's cooking. Look for one with a clear, readable face. Also, if you're only learning to bake with yeast, you can use an instant-read thermometer to check the temperature of the water, when proofing the yeast, which is critical in yeast baking.

Prime Choice, or Select: The Grades of Beef

Beef is graded by the U.S. Department of Agriculture into eight categories, but we only see three grades, U.S. Prime, U.S. Choice and U.S. Select, which come from animals usually less than two years old. The shield-shaped grade mark can be found on the carcass in edible purple dye in a long, ribbon-like imprint. Meat grading is a voluntary service, and firms pay a fee to the USDA for highly trained specialists to do the grading. When meat is graded, three factors are considered: conformation (ratio of meat to bone), finish (ratio of lean to fat) and overall quality.

On the other hand, mandatory meat inspection, which is different from meat grading, is also done by the USDA to determine meat's wholesomeness and safety.

When you order beef at a top-level steak house, you're probably served Prime beef which is grain-fed, well marbled with flecks of fat that break down during the cooking process, self-basting the meat and making it very juicy. It is the most tender of all beef cuts. Prime grade beef is sold by some small, private butchers at very high prices.

Choice grade beef is what you generally buy in the supermarket. It has slightly less marbling than Prime.

Select grade is lower-priced beef with less marbling and may not be as tender or as juicy as Choice.

Nutrition

All beef contains vitamin B_{12}, iron, zinc and a moderate amount of niacin, but no vitamin C or fiber. A three-ounce portion of cooked beef contains between 153 and 225 calories, 23 and 28 grams protein and 4 and 14 grams of fat, depending on whether the beef is broiled filet mignon or a lean well-done hamburger.

Cuts of Beef and Where They're Located on the Steer; The Most Tender and Flavorful Cuts of Beef

Rather than memorize the entire beef chart, remember that any cut labeled rib or loin is the most tender. Many beef lovers are of the opinion that the chuck is the most flavorful because it contains so much fat intertwined with tasty muscle, but it's a matter of preference.

How to Pick a Good Piece of Meat

Appearance is important when buying beef. Look at the color, the amount of marbling and the fat cover, which is the fat that covers the exterior of most beef cuts. It keeps beef from drying out because it acts as a self-baster on roasts. However, most of it is trimmed from steaks either before or after cooking. The lean portion of beef should be cherry red. When beef is first cut, it is a dark, purplish red. When exposed to air, the surface of the beef will react with oxygen and become bright red.

There's a growing trend in supermarkets to offer high-quality meats, especially beef. The prices are definitely higher, but the value is greater. I recommend buying meat in smaller quantities that you might prepare the same or the next day. This type of buying has been done for years by restaurants and it brings back how shopping for perishable groceries was done a few decades ago and how it's still done in many parts of Europe today. While shopping ahead may be convenient, when buying quality ingredients it's best to wait until the last moment.

Storing and Freezing Beef

Beef should be refrigerated at between 36° and 40°F. Many home refrigerators have a special meat drawer for this purpose. Plan to cook ground beef within 1 to 2 days, stew beef within 2 to 3 days, and steaks and chops within 3 to 4 days.

Freeze beef as soon as possible in specially coated freezer paper, aluminum foil or heavy duty plastic freezer bags at 0°F. It's necessary to remove as much air as possible from the package because air draws moisture to the surface of the meat causing the formation of a whitish layer known as "freezer burn." Although it doesn't affect the wholesomeness of the beef, it does affect its flavor.

If you're shopping for a new refrigerator/freezer, you may want to look at some of the new models that have a quick-freeze shelf.

Always defrost beef in the refrigerator in its original wrapping. A large roast will take 4 to 7 hours per pound, a small roast 3 to 5 hours per pound and a 1-inch steak about 12 to 14 hours. The time required for ground beef will vary according to the thickness of the package. Beef can be defrosted in the microwave, but using this method may cause the meat to lose a significant amount of moisture.

Completely defrosted beef should not be refrozen, but if the meat is partially thawed and still has ice crystals, it's safe to refreeze.

Grades of Hamburger Meat

Ground beef is labeled according to the ratio of lean to fat.

Ground beef, 73 percent lean/27 percent fat, is good when you can drain off the fat after browning meat for chili or spaghetti sauce.

Ground beef, 80 percent lean/20 percent fat, is for meatloaf, meatballs, casseroles and hamburgers.

Ground beef, 85 percent lean/15 percent fat, is used in combination dishes like casseroles and low-calorie recipes. However, when ground beef is very lean, it becomes dry and less palatable when cooked. A major fast-food burger chain recently removed its extra lean burger from the menu because it lacked the taste consumers wanted.

No More Rare Hamburgers

According to the Food and Drug Administration, the internal temperature of cooked beef checked with an instant-read thermometer should register 160°F. (Since beef will continue to cook while resting, cook it until the thermometer is 5 to 10 degrees less.) At this temperature all bacteria are destroyed. However, this amount of cooking may toughen and dry the meat, so I recommend marinating the beef to keep it moist. (See page 55 for a fuller discussion on marinades.)

Cooking Methods for Beef and Veal

Animals are made up of two kinds of muscles: suspension and locomotion. Suspension muscles do not get much exercise and have less connective tissue than locomotion muscles, which are used for movement.

The more movement the muscles perform, the tougher they become and the more flavorful they are. For example, legs and shoulders develop muscle, so the meat from these areas is not as tender as that from the center torso. Meat in the torso is protected by bone and fat so it does not develop much muscle. Take the example of a veal rib chop versus a veal shoulder chop. The rib chop is more tender because it is protected by rib bones and a layer of fat and these chops can be cooked using a dry heat method, such as grilling or broiling. The shoulder chop, which is found in the front of the animal above the leg, will be tougher and should be cooked using a moist heat method such as braising.

When you purchase meat already packaged, you'll see that most supermarkets have adapted an identification program called Uniform Retail Meat Identity Standards. At the bottom of the label are three classifications: the kind of meat (pork, beef, veal, lamb), the primal cut (shoulder, loin, leg) and the retail cut (blade steak, rib chop, sirloin roast, etc.)

Cooking Methods for Each Cut

The proportion of muscle to fat, the cut of meat, plus the age of the animal determine the preferred cooking technique. As meat is heated, the protein contracts causing the meat to toughen, so the cooking temperature is very important.

Roasting (dry heat): rib roast, rib-eye roast, boneless rump roast, round-tip roast, top-round roast, tenderloin roast, ground-beef loaf.

Broiling and grilling (dry heat): chuck-shoulder steak, rib steak, rib-eye steak, top-round steak, sirloin steak, porterhouse steak, tenderloin, flank steak, skirt steak, and ground-beef patties.

Sautéing (dry heat): rib-eye steak, eye round steak, round tip steak, top-round steak, sirloin steak, top loin steak, tenderloin steak, ground-beef patties.

Braising (moist heat): blade pot roast, arm pot roast, chuck roast, short ribs, round steak, flank steak.

Regardless of the cooking method, beef is rare with an internal temperature of 140°F, medium at 160°F, and well done at 170°F.

How to Slice a Roast

You need three things to slice a roast: a sharp knife, a cutting board and a knowledge of which way the muscle fibers run.

When meat is cooked, the muscle fibers are softened; when it's carved, the fibers are shortened. Most meat is cut across the grain, but some roasts have muscle fibers going in two or more directions. On a large piece of raw meat, these long muscle fibers are actually visible. To get a professional opinion, ask your butcher to point out which way the muscles run when you purchase your meat.

Always allow a rare roast to sit for 15 to 20 minutes, a medium or well-done roast for 7 to 10 minutes; it will be juicier and easier to carve. It may be necessary to cut off a small slice to determine which way the grain runs. While carving, you should hold down the roast with a two-pronged carving fork.

Slice roasts across the grain. Tender steaks should be carved with the grain, but carve less tender steaks, such as flank steak, diagonally across the grain into thin slices.

In addition to the recipes in this section, you will find additional recipes for beef as follows:

Steak and Bean Soup (page 163)

Beef Stock (page 191)

Grits and Grillades (page 202)

Swiss Steak (page 205)

Burgundy Pot Roast (page 206)

Stir-Fried Beef with Cashews (page 215)

Steak and Fusilli Salad (page 251)

Grilled Peppered Fillet of Beef

The cooking times for beef will vary according to the temperature of the fire as well as the temperature of the meat and the air. A beef fillet, or beef tenderloin, is the most tender of all beef cuts. It contains no bone or fat. Although the fillet is fork-tender, it lacks a real beefy flavor so it is often seasoned before roasting and served with a sauce.

2 pound beef tenderloin roast

2 teaspoons Tabasco

¼ cup prepared mustard

2 tablespoons coarsely crushed
peppercorns

I teaspoon coarsely chopped Italian
parsley

I recipe Vinaigrette Dressing II
(page 75)

Preheat the grill to high.

Rub the meat with the Tabasco and spread evenly with the mustard on all sides. Mix the peppercorns and parsley together and pat onto the meat.

Sear the meat on the grill until it's brown on all sides. Lower the heat to medium and finish cooking to desired doneness. For rare, the approximate time is 7 to 8 minutes per pound; 8 to 10 minutes for medium rare; 10 to 12 minutes for medium. Cool the meat slightly, refrigerate 1 hour and slice thin. Serve the beef at room temperature with sliced beefsteak tomatoes and grilled mushrooms on a bed of watercress.

Dress with a few tablespoons of the vinaigrette dressing.

Beef

Beef Tenderloin Tips with Curry Sauce

If you have a few extra dollars and want to treat yourself to filet mignon steaks, it's more economical to buy the whole fillet and have your butcher cut it up for you. You wind up with the Château or head for roasting (Grilled Peppered Fillet of Beef, page 11), steaks (Grilled Beef Fillet Steaks with Mushrooms and Red Wine Sauce, page 13), and the tips, traditionally used for Beef Stroganoff, which are used for this spicy curry dish.

If you don't want your curry too hot, add ½ cup unsweetened coconut milk. If you can't get it hot enough, add a generous pinch of ground cinnamon, coriander and a few hot, dry chile peppers.

1 pound beef tenderloin tips

2 tablespoons all-purpose flour

1 tablespoon olive oil

2 teaspoons curry powder

2 teaspoons ground cumin

1 green pepper, seeded and cut
   into strips

½ onion, sliced

6 cloves Caramelized Garlic
   (page 186)

¼ cup dry white wine

1 cup beef or chicken stock

1 teaspoon Tabasco

Freshly ground pepper to taste

FOR SERVING

Small dishes of shredded unsweetened coconut, raisins, sliced
   nuts, diced apples or mango.

Dredge the meat with the flour. Heat the oil in a large sauté pan or skillet over high heat and brown the meat on all sides. Stir in the curry and cumin and cook one minute, stirring constantly. Add the pepper strips, onion and garlic and cook 2 minutes, stirring frequently. Stir in the wine and cook 1 minute. Add the stock, Tabasco and pepper and cook 2 minutes longer. Serve immediately over hot cooked rice with dishes of coconut, raisins, sliced nuts, diced apples or mango.

Curry powder is not an individual spice, but rather a combination of up to 20 different spices. Cooks in India make their own version depending on the region. The two varieties available in local supermarkets are classified as standard curry powder, which is mild, and Madras, which is hotter.

Know Your Fire

Grilled Beef Fillet Steaks with Mushrooms and Red Wine Sauce

The ultimate prized piece of beef is the fillet mignon, the center of the beef tenderloin. Beef fillet steaks are cut from the tenderloin about an inch thick. The fillet mignon is a versatile cut of beef and it can be sautéed, broiled and, especially, grilled. Because the steaks have no fat on the surface, they're brushed with oil before cooking.

4 (6-ounce) beef fillet steaks	1 cup sliced shiitake mushrooms
2 tablespoons olive oil	2 shallots, finely chopped or 2
Freshly ground black pepper to	tablespoons chopped onion
taste	¼ cup dry red wine
2 tablespoons clarified (page 150)	½ teaspoon dried thyme
or regular butter	1 tablespoon sherry, optional

Preheat the grill until it's very hot.

Brush steaks with olive oil and season with black pepper on both sides. Place them on a very hot grill and sear for 2 minutes on each side. Move the fillets to the cooler edges of the grill and allow them to finish cooking, about 5 minutes longer.

Meanwhile, in a sauté pan melt the butter over medium heat and add the shiitake and shallots. Cook, stirring frequently, until the mushrooms begin to get a little color. Add the wine and thyme and cook 1 minute. If inclined, add the sherry.

To serve, garnish the steaks with the mushrooms and red wine sauce.

Beef

Texas Chili

Chili may have been introduced to the rest of America by the Texans, but its roots go back to the Aztecs. This Texas version is the ultimate and may not resemble what you have been eating up to now. The cooking technique calls for a very hot pan to sear the meat. After the cayenne pepper is added to the pot, the meat cooks gently for a couple of hours until it is nice and tender. Never allow the pot to boil or the meat will toughen.

I recommend using a large cast-iron skillet because it can get much hotter and holds the heat longer than aluminum or stainless steel. Cooking the chili the day before and reheating will improve its flavor.

The meat should be cut into small cubes and you'll have to set aside some time to do this by hand. Don't use ground meat. Besides beef, you can cook this chili recipe substituting pork, lamb, or chicken. Even rattlesnake.

You may wonder about the absence of tomatoes or beans in this recipe, but no self-respecting Texan would ever add these ingredients to a mess of chili.

3 tablespoons vegetable or canola oil

3 pounds beef round or chuck, cut into ½-inch cubes

1½ onions, chopped fine

1 head Caramelized Garlic (page 186)

1 tablespoon ground cumin

1 tablespoon sweet paprika

1 teaspoon ground coriander

1 teaspoon ground cayenne pepper or more to taste

2 cups water or stock

GARNISH

Bowls of sour cream, diced red onion, chopped scallions, shredded Cheddar cheese, avocado slices, guacamole, salsa, or crackers

Heat a large cast-iron skillet until it's very hot. Add the oil and, when it's hot, begin adding the meat in batches, just enough to cover the bottom of the pan. When you crowd the meat, it steams and the juices are not sealed inside. As each batch is finished, remove it from the pan and set aside.

When all the meat is browned, return it to the pan and add the onion, garlic, cumin, paprika, coriander and cayenne pepper. Cook the spices with the meat for about 5 minutes, stirring constantly, allowing the dry heat to intensify their flavors.

Add the water or stock, reduce heat to a simmer, and cook for 2 hours.

Serve with one or more garnishes of sour cream, red onion, scallions, Cheddar cheese, avocado, guacamole, salsa or crackers.

Veal

Veal is the meat from a calf under a year of age. The highest quality meat comes from a calf that is milk-fed up to about six months. The silky pinkish white flesh, a sign that it is very young, is underdeveloped so there are few muscle fibers and the meat is very tender. As it gets older and the calf is fed grain or chews on grass, the flavor and texture change. It becomes more flavorful, but the texture is a little chewier and dryer. When you find veal being sold that is reddish pink, it is really baby beef.

Veal has no marbling so it can be very dry when cooked, and very often it's served with a mild-flavored sauce. Save the barbecue sauce for chicken.

Storing and Freezing

Ideally, veal should be cooked the same day it's brought home. Otherwise, rewrap it loosely in wax paper and store in the coldest part of the refrigerator and use within two days. Veal can be frozen for up to two weeks in the retail packaging. For longer storage, rewrap in freezer paper, aluminum foil or plastic freezer bags and use within six to nine months. Ground veal should be used within 3 months.

Always defrost veal in the refrigerator, allowing 4 to 7 hours per pound for a large roast, 3 to 5 hours per pound for a small roast and 12 hours for 1-inch thick chops.

Nutrition

A 3-ounce serving of cooked veal contains 166 calories, 27 grams protein, 6 grams of fat and is a good source of niacin, zinc and vitamins B_{12} and B_6.

When to Roast and When to Braise

The best cuts of veal for roasting are the rump and the shoulder. Always let a veal roast rest about 15 minutes before slicing to set the juices, and since it will continue to cook, roast it to 155 to 160°F.

The best cuts of veal for broiling and grilling are the loin and rib chops, the arm and blade steaks, kabobs from the loin, and ground veal patties.

The best cuts of veal for sautéing are the cutlets, loin and rib chops, blade and arm steak, and ground veal patties.

The best cuts of veal for braising are the stuffed or tied boneless breast, riblets, arm and blade steaks, round steak, boneless shoulder roast and loin and rib chops.

In addition to the recipes in this section, you will find other recipes for veal as follows:

Veal Roast with Potatoes and Onions (page 243)

Veal

Veal and Pepper Stew

Cold, windy days call for comfort stew like this veal and pepper dish.

If you like meat on the bone, ask your butcher for veal breast, riblets, or shanks for this dish. Otherwise, look for boneless meat from the shoulder or leg.

1½ pounds veal stew, trimmed and
    cut into 1-inch pieces

2 tablespoons all-purpose flour

2 tablespoons olive oil

2 potatoes, peeled and cubed

2 red bell peppers, seeded and cut
    into 1-inch pieces

1 onion, sliced

8 cloves Caramelized Garlic
    (page 186)

2 cups chicken stock

1 tablespoon fresh rosemary leaves,
    chopped

½ teaspoon Tabasco

Dust the veal with the flour and tap off any excess. Heat a large sauté pan and heat 1 tablespoon of the olive oil. Brown the veal in the pan on all sides, remove and set aside.

Add the remaining tablespoon of olive oil to the pan and add the potatoes, red peppers, onion and garlic and cook 2 to 3 minutes, stirring constantly. Return the veal to the pan, add the chicken stock, rosemary and Tabasco and mix well. Bring to a boil, lower heat, and simmer until veal is tender, about 1 hour.

Add a loaf of crusty Italian bread and a salad and call it supper.

Grilled Veal Rib Chop

Most cuts of veal are expensive, so make it taste its very best by using only fresh herbs.

**2 pounds veal rib chops or a
30-ounce veal T-bone steak**

2 tablespoons olive oil

3 fresh sage leaves, finely chopped

2 basil leaves, chopped

I teaspoon crushed black peppercorns

I teaspoon lemon zest

Preheat the grill to high.

Brush the veal with the olive oil. Mix together the sage, basil, peppercorns and lemon zest and rub onto both sides of the meat. Grill the veal until brown, 4 to 5 minutes, turn, and grill until desired doneness, 4 to 5 minutes longer.

Veal

Lamb

How to Buy Lamb

You can tell the age of lamb by the color of its flesh. Baby lamb is pale pink, and the color darkens increasingly as the animal ages. The fat should be creamy white and the meat fine-grained. Bones should appear moist and porous; white bones indicate an older animal.

What Is Spring Lamb?

No longer is spring lamb available only in the spring. Because it's constantly being bred, spring lamb is now available year-round. Lamb slaughtered between 6 and 8 weeks of age is called baby lamb—technically, spring lamb is between 3 and 5 months. If packaged lamb is marked "genuine lamb" it means that the meat is from an animal less than a year old. Lambs between one and two years of age are called yearlings and any lamb older than that is designated as "mutton."

Lamb grown in the United States is fed on grain, has a milder flavor and is larger and meatier than imported lamb, which is fed on grass.

Cooking Lamb

Larger legs of lamb have a higher ratio of meat to bone and fat so they're a better buy. The thin parchmentlike covering on legs of lamb is called the fell. It helps to keep the meat juicy, so don't remove it before cooking unless so indicated in a recipe or if the lamb is to be coated with a rub.

Thick lamb chops are juicier than thinner ones. Before grilling or broiling, make small cuts 1 inch apart along the edges to prevent the chops from curling.

Lamb should never be overcooked, unless you like it tough and dry. When cooked medium (160°F) or medium rare (150°F), lamb is tender and succulent.

Before cooking, cut off most of the excess fat on chops and roasts and leave about ¼ inch fat to keep the meat moist during cooking. This can be trimmed off before serving.

Lamb benefits greatly from marinating and using dry rubs. Tender cuts pick up additional flavor and tougher cuts become tenderized as well as receiving extra taste.

Ideal Cooking Methods for Each Cut

Roasting (145° to 150°F for medium rare and 160°F for medium): leg (boneless or bone-in), bottom tied leg roast, boneless sirloin roast, top-round roast, boneless, tied shoulder roast, rack of lamb, crown roast.

Broiling or grilling: loin, rib and shoulder chops, sirloin steaks, top-round steaks, center leg steaks, kabobs from the leg or loin, lamb patties, butterflied leg.

Grilling: shoulder, rib and loin chops, top-round steaks, center leg steaks, lamb patties, butterflied leg, top-round roast.

Sautéing: loin, rib, sirloin and shoulder chops, round leg steaks, lamb patties.

Braising: shoulder cuts, breasts, riblets, shanks, stew.

Storing and Freezing

To store, rewrap the lamb in wax paper and store in the coldest part of the refrigerator. Cook large pieces within three to four days and ground lamb and lamb chops within two days.

To freeze, wrap in specially treated freezer paper, aluminum foil or heavy-duty plastic freezer bags. Large cuts of lamb can be frozen up to four months, but ground lamb and chops should be used within two months. Defrost lamb in the original wrapping in the refrigerator, allowing two to three days for a large roast and one to two days for ground lamb or lamb chops. To defrost lamb in the microwave, follow the manufacturer's instructions. Never defrost lamb at room temperature.

Nutrition

Most cuts of lamb have under 200 calories in a cooked 3-ounce serving, 7 to 17 grams of fat, and 21 to 30 grams of protein, depending on whether the meat is from the lean leg of lamb or fattier ground lamb.

Racks of Lamb with Couscous

This is a great one-pot dish and can be prepared on the stovetop in about 30 minutes. The juices from the lamb are absorbed by the couscous making it very flavorful. A rack of lamb is the rib section of a lamb containing 8 small chops.

4 racks of lamb or lamb fillets

Lamb Rub I (page 58)

2 tablespoons olive oil

½ onion, finely chopped

¼ cup finely chopped carrot

1 cup red wine

1 cup beef stock (page 191) or
    chicken stock (page 188)

1 cup couscous

Season the racks of lamb with the Lamb Rub and refrigerate for 1 to 8 hours.

Preheat a large saucepan with a tight-fitting cover. Heat the olive oil and sear the lamb on all sides, turning occasionally, for 8 to 10 minutes. Remove the lamb and set aside. Add the onion and carrot and cook until light brown. Stir in the red wine, bring to a boil and reduce by half, about 4 to 5 minutes. Add the stock and the couscous and bring to a boil. Return the lamb to the pot, cover tightly, and turn off the heat. The dish will be ready to serve in 5 minutes. The carry-over heat will keep on cooking the lamb while the couscous plumps up.

Lamb

Lamb-Stuffed Peppers

Peppers are often stuffed with beef and rice, but these peppers change course and get stuffed with an herby ground lamb and barley mixture. The lamb remains moist, and the barley contributes a nice texture.

2 tablespoons olive oil

½ onion, chopped

1 carrot, chopped

6 cloves Caramelized Garlic
    (page 186)

8 ounces ground lamb

1 teaspoon dried thyme

1 teaspoon dried oregano

1 teaspoon dried mint

1 teaspoon Tabasco

Freshly ground black pepper to
    taste

1 cup cooked barley

1 cup cream or half-and-half

1 egg

8 small or 4 large green bell
    peppers

1 cup tomato sauce

Heat a sauté pan and heat the olive oil. Add the onion, carrot and garlic and cook until the onion is transparent, about 5 minutes. Add the lamb and cook, breaking apart any clumps, until the meat is lightly browned. Season with the thyme, oregano, mint, Tabasco and black pepper. Remove the pan from the heat, stir in the cooked barley and cool.

Preheat the oven to 350°F.

Beat the cream and egg together and stir into the lamb mixture.

Cut the tops from the green peppers and remove the seeds and white ribs. Stuff the peppers with the lamb mixture and cover with the pepper tops. Place the peppers into a buttered casserole that just holds them and pour in the tomato sauce. Bake the peppers until they're tender, about 25 to 30 minutes.

Serve with buttered carrots and a green salad.

Know Your Fire

Lamb Shanks in Red Wine

Lamb foreshanks from the front of the animal are larger, meatier and sometimes cheaper than the smaller, more tender shanks from the hind leg. Your butcher may not always have lamb shanks on hand because there isn't much of a demand for them, so ask him to order them for you.

4 lamb shanks, about 1 pound each

1 head Caramelized Garlic
    (page 186)

1 onion, chopped

¼ cup tomato sauce or tomato
    puree

2 cups dry red wine

2 stems fresh rosemary

6 stems fresh thyme

1 teaspoon crushed black pepper-
    corns

1 to 2 cups chicken stock

2 bay leaves

Preheat the oven to 375°F.

Rub the lamb shanks with the caramelized garlic and place in a small roasting pan.

Place the shanks in the oven until they brown, about 20 minutes. Remove the pan from the oven, add the tomato sauce and return to the oven for 5 minutes. In a bowl, combine the red wine, rosemary, thyme and peppercorns. Stir the mixture into the tomato sauce, and cook 5 minutes longer in the oven. Remove the pan and add the chicken stock and bay leaves. Cover the pan with aluminum foil and poke a few holes in the top.

Reduce the oven temperature to 350°F and cook the shanks for 1 hour. Remove the foil and if too much stock has simmered away add the additional cup. Re-cover, return the pan to the oven and cook until the meat is fork tender and falling away from the bones, about 30 minutes longer.

Lamb

Roasted Leg of Lamb with Beer

Many great lamb dishes have originated in England, and when I prepared this dish for live audiences there, they were delighted at how their local ales flavored the meat. Most leg of lamb is served rare or medium, but this one is well done and so tender that it can be cut with a spoon instead of a knife. Or it can be shredded and eaten like southern barbecue pork. The lamb can be cooked indoors in the oven or outdoors on the grill. Both ways the lamb is tender, but on the grill it picks up a smoky flavor.

1 (6 pound) leg of lamb	1 (12 ounce) can or bottle of beer,
1 tablespoon Tabasco	ale or your favorite brew
1 recipe Lamb Rub II (page 58)	2 tablespoons brown sugar
Cloves from 1 head Caramelized	2 teaspoons dry mustard
Garlic (page 186)	1 tablespoon balsamic vinegar

Brush the leg of lamb with the Tabasco, season with the Lamb Rub and refrigerate for 2 to 24 hours. Remove the lamb 30 minutes before roasting so that the bones will warm and the meat will cook more evenly.

Preheat the oven to 375°F or preheat the grill to medium.

Rub the lamb with the caramelized garlic and place in a roasting pan. Place the pan in the oven and allow the meat to brown all over, turning it occasionally. This should take about 1 hour.

Remove the meat and add to the pan the beer, sugar, mustard and vinegar and mix well, loosening up any brown particles on the bottom of the pan. Return the lamb to the pan, cover with aluminum foil and poke a few holes in the top of the foil. Lower the oven temperature to 300°F and cook the lamb 1½ hours longer, or until very tender.

If grilling the lamb, brown it over medium heat about one hour, turning several times. Place it in a pan, add the beer, sugar, mustard and vinegar and cook over low indirect heat for 1½ hours, or until very tender.

Allow the meat to rest for 20 to 30 minutes before serving.

Know Your Fire

Pork

Hogs have always been an American favorite and it's believed they were the second animal domesticated by man, right after the dog. However, the pork we eat today is far different from the pork our grandmothers cooked. Nowadays lean is in and fat is out. Fat as a hog is no longer true. As compared with pork of even the 1980s, today's has 31 percent less fat and 17 percent fewer calories.

How to Buy Pork

The meat should be pale pink with a small amount of marbling. The lean portion should be firm, fine grained and free from excess moisture. The thin outside rim of fat should be white, not yellow. Dark pink flesh indicates that the animal was old.

Storing and Freezing

If you're not using the pork the same day, rewrap loosely in wax paper and store in the coldest part of the refrigerator for no longer than three to four days for large pieces and from one to two days for chops and ground pork.

Pork can be frozen for three to six months in special freezer paper, aluminum foil or heavy duty plastic freezer bags. As with most meats, ground meat cannot be frozen as long as large roasts. Defrost the pork in the refrigerator in the original wrapping, allowing 4 to 7 hours per pound for large roasts, 3 to 5 hours per pound for small roasts and 12 to 14 hours for 1-inch thick chops. The time to defrost ground pork will depend on the thickness of the package.

Ideal Cooking Methods for Each Cut

Regardless of which cooking method you choose, pork should be cooked to an internal temperature of 160°F (medium) to 170°F (well done).

Roasting: loin, crown, leg, Boston blade, tenderloin, backribs, country-style ribs, spareribs, ground pork loaf, meatballs.

Broiling or grilling: rib or loin chop, boneless loin chop, blade chop, shoulder chop, kabobs, tenderloin, ground pork patties, country-style ribs, spareribs, backribs.

I n addition to the recipes in this section, you will find other pork recipes as follows:

Cavatelli with Hot Sausage and Broccoli Rabe (page 87)

Ham and Mushroom Sauce (page 132)

Pork with Honey and Walnuts (page 233)

Ham-Stuffed Shrimp (page 254)

Cold-Smoked Pork (page 260)

Pork Salad Roti (page 262)

Center Cut Hot-Smoked Pork Chops (page 263)

Smoked Ribs (page 264)

Sautéing: loin or rib chop, boneless loin chop, sirloin chop, tenderloin, sirloin cutlet, cubed steak, ground pork patties, meatballs.

Braising: loin or rib chop, boneless loin chop, spareribs, backribs, country-style ribs, tenderloin, shoulder steaks, cubes, leg steaks, Boston blade, sirloin.

Ham

All hams come from the same place on the hog—the hind leg—but the coincidence ends there. There are fresh hams (unprocessed) and cured hams (dry cured, sweet pickle cured, injection cured) bone in, boneless and partially boned, partially cooked and fully cooked.

Always read the label so that you'll know what you're buying and whether the ham has to be cooked before eating.

Parma ham, or prosciutto, comes from Parma, Italy. These hams are seasoned, salt cured and air dried, but not smoked. They're usually sliced thin, and a little can go a long way in adding flavor to a dish.

Pancetta, or Italian bacon, is different from what we know as bacon because it is cured with salt and spices, but not smoked. It comes in a roll shape and is usually sautéed at the beginning of a recipe, and the rendered fat used to brown vegetables or meat.

Should I Worry About Trichinosis?

With modern meat packing plants and the feeding of hogs so closely controlled, trichinosis is rarely a problem. However, never taste pork raw or before it has been cooked to 137°F, the temperature at which the parasite causing trichinosis is killed. Always wash hands, knives and cutting boards in hot soapy water after they come in contact with raw pork.

Nutrition

Due to scientific breeding, this once-fatty animal has become lean and appealing to health-conscious consumers. A cooked 3-ounce serving of the loin has 172 calories, 6 grams of fat, plus protein, iron, zinc and the B vitamins.

Pork

29

Sautéed Pork Loin Chops with Shrimp

Today's pork loin is so lean that it tends to dry out during dry cooking such as sautéing. The rub acts like a barrier to keep moisture in. The flavors of the pork and shrimp are highlighted by the beer-based sauce.

4 (6 ounce) boneless pork chops
   from the loin
2 tablespoons Pork Seasoning Rub
   (page 57)
2 slices bacon
2 tablespoons olive oil, if the bacon
   is lean
1 pound shrimp, shelled and
   deveined

¼ cup chopped scallions
6 cloves Caramelized Garlic
   (page 186)
1 cup beer
1 teaspoon Tabasco
2 tablespoons steak sauce

Rub the pork chops with the Pork Seasoning Rub and refrigerate for 2 to 8 hours.

Preheat a sauté pan and cook the bacon to render the fat; if the bacon is lean, add the olive oil. Remove the bacon, drain on paper towel and crumble. Increase the heat and sear the pork on both sides for 2 to 3 minutes total. Add the shrimp, scallions and garlic. Cook for 2 minutes or until the shrimp begins to turn pink. Add the beer and Tabasco and simmer 4 to 5 minutes. Remove the shrimp so that it does not overcook. Stir in the steak sauce and simmer the pork for 5 minutes longer. Return the bacon and shrimp to the sauté pan and reheat. Serve with cooked rice and broccoli.

Pork Cutlet with Grated Horseradish

Pork cutlets are cut from the leg or loin. They cook up very quickly and are very lean, yet tender and flavorful.

1½ pounds pork cutlets cut from
    fresh ham or the loin
Grated Horseradish Rub (page 57)
¼ cup all-purpose flour
2 eggs, lightly beaten
1 cup fresh bread crumbs

2 tablespoons butter
2 tablespoons olive oil

GARNISH
Lemon wedges, celery sticks, and
    blue cheese dressing

Rub the pork cutlets with the Grated Horseradish Rub and refrigerate for 1 hour.

Dredge the cutlets in the flour, dip into the egg and coat with the bread crumbs.

Heat a saucepan over high heat and add the butter and olive oil. When they are hot, reduce heat to medium and pan fry the cutlets until golden brown, about 3 to 4 minutes on each side.

Serve with lemon wedges, celery sticks and blue cheese dressing.

Pork

Pork and Mushroom Stew

Stews are the saving grace of both the harried cook and the pot washer. One-pot meals are the soul and heart that warms us on the first cool Autumn evening. In this country, stews were traditionally made using water as the liquid. As Americans traveled abroad, especially after World War II, and experienced "foreign" food, wine and beer became a welcome addition to the stew pot. It's important to note that when alcohol is added to the stew, it not only flavors the meat, but also aids in tenderizing it. Although the recipe calls for red wine, using white wine will give the stew a whole different personality.

2 tablespoons all-purpose flour	2 tablespoons olive oil
1 tablespoon dried rosemary, crushed	1 onion, sliced
1 teaspoon dried thyme	2 cups sliced mushrooms, a mixture of white button and shiitake
Freshly ground black pepper to taste	1 cup dry red wine
3 pounds pork stew meat, cut into 1-inch cubes	1 cup beef or chicken stock
	2 bay leaves

Combine the flour with the rosemary, thyme and black pepper in a bowl and mix well. Dredge the pork in the flour mixture. Heat the oil in a large saucepan or Dutch oven over high heat. Sear the meat on all sides and add the onion and mushrooms. (To sear meat means to brown it on all sides quickly over high heat. This can be done on the grill, under the broiler or in a skillet.) Cook 1 minute, stirring constantly, add the wine and cook 2 minutes. Add the stock and bay leaves, cover, reduce heat and cook on low until the pork is tender, about two hours. The stew can also be cooked in a 350°F oven or on a grill over medium-low heat, for about the same time. Remove bay leaves before serving.

Know Your Fire

Gougère of Ham

A gougère is a ring of piped pâté à choux flavored with ham or cheese. This version is simplified from the classic because the batter is cooked in a tube pan. It can be served as an appetizer or with cocktails.

I recipe Pâté à Choux (page 274)

I cup smoked ham, diced

I cup shredded Swiss cheese

¼ cup grated Parmesan cheese

4 slices bacon, cooked and
   crumbled

½ onion, chopped

6 cloves Caramelized Garlic
   (page 186)

I teaspoon chopped fresh thyme

I teaspoon chopped fresh parsley

I teaspoon Tabasco

Freshly ground black pepper to
   taste

Preheat the oven to 400°F.

Combine the pâté à choux with the remaining ingredients and mix well. Scrape the mixture into a well-greased 10-inch tube pan and bake until the gougère begins to brown, about 20 minutes. Do not open the oven door, even a crack, during this baking period as even the slightest draft will cause the gougère to collapse. Lower the temperature to 350°F and cook until the gougère is firm, crisp and golden brown. It should sound hollow when tapped with your finger and a toothpick inserted in the center should come out clean. Cut into pieces and serve.

Pork

Poultry

Chicken, Cornish Hen, Capon, Turkey, Duck and Goose

There's poultry for every pot and there are probably as many ways to cook poultry as there are pots. Whether it's chicken wings or ground turkey or duck breasts, poultry claims the largest percentage of space at the meat counter in any supermarket.

With the exception, perhaps, of wild turkey, poultry is naturally tender and since it has little fat (with the exception of duck and goose) there is little shrinkage. It also is economical and high on the nutrition index.

Chicken is marketed under different names: a *broiler/fryer* is 7 to 9 weeks old and weighs 2 to 4 pounds. It's best roasted, sautéed, fried or broiled. An *oven-roaster* is older, 3 to 5 months, weighs 4 to 7 pounds and lives up to its name as it makes a wonderful bird for roasting. Over-a-year-old *stewing chickens* or fowl weighing 3 to 7 pounds are hard to find these days but make delicious soups and stews.

Cornish hens or Cornish game hens weighing between 1 and 2 pounds are sent to market at the age of 5 to 6 weeks. They are best roasted, sautéed or fried.

A *capon* is a 4- to 5-month-old castrated male chicken weighing between 6 and 9 pounds. In ancient Rome it was forbidden to eat large hens because they were needed to lay eggs. Poultry breeders got around the ban by castrating male chickens and force feeding until they doubled their weight while, at the same time, they retained the tenderness of a young chicken. Because it has a thick layer of fat beneath its skin, a capon is a self-basting roasting chicken. However, we don't find many capons in the stores these days because the oven-roaster has taken its place.

The *turkey,* according to Benjamin Franklin, deserved to become the symbol of this new country rather than the bald eagle because it was here first—almost 2 million years. Normal size turkeys range from 12 to 25 pounds but some have been bred smaller, weighing 5 to 9 pounds.

The most famous duck in my neck of the woods is the White Pekin or Long Island duck raised locally in New York as well as in other states. Its origins can be traced back to clipper ship captains who brought the first ones over from China where they had been domesticated for over 2,000 years. *Ducks* are 10 weeks old and weigh a minimum of 5 pounds. *Ducklings* are 7 to 8 weeks old and weigh between 4 and 5 pounds.

Throughout Central Europe, the roasted *goose* is the traditional Christmas bird. Those weighing from 6 to 14 pounds are from 4 to 6 months old. Bigger geese are usually braised because they are too tough for roasting.

How to Buy Poultry

Fifty or sixty years ago, we could go into a chicken market, pick out the bird we wanted, and it would be slaughtered and cleaned while we waited. Nowadays most of us have to rely on supermarkets or butcher shops. Nonetheless, the fresher the bird, the better it will taste.

Examine the packaging. The bird should be clean and pristine looking. The skin should be smooth and have no discoloration or punctures. The chicken case should be clean and fresh smelling.

Check the pull date on the label or the last day the poultry should be sold.

Look for telltale signs that the chicken has been frozen such as ice crystals along the wings.

Avoid any chicken with traces of feathers. It means the chicken wasn't cleaned properly.

Poultry

Pick out plump chicken and parts so that you're buying a larger proportion of meat to bone.

Storing and Freezing

If the poultry has been purchased with airtight wrapping, rewrap it lightly in wax paper and cook it within 24 hours. Ideally, it should be refrigerated between 38 and 40 degrees F. During hot weather, especially, bring along an insulated cooler and a couple of frozen ice packs to carry the chicken home.

Never attempt to freeze chicken if your freezer cannot maintain 0°F or −18°C. Wrap the whole bird or parts in airtight plastic freezer-quality bags or in special freezer wrap, following the directions on the box. Chicken can be frozen up to 6 months but their quality is best when used within 2 months. As with all meats, always defrost chicken in the refrigerator, and never on the counter.

How to Cut Up a Chicken

To cut up your first chicken, you'll need a sharp knife, a sturdy surface and confidence. The following technique is designed to cut the chicken into 10 pieces, and it's easier than it sounds.

Place the chicken on a flat surface, breast side up. Pull a leg away from the body and cut through the skin between the body and the thigh until you come to the bone. Bend the leg away from the body and cut between the ball and socket. Repeat with the other leg. Cut each leg in two at the thigh joint.

Pull the wing away from the body and, with a knife, feel for the thigh joint and cut through it. Repeat with the other side.

Stand the carcass up with the back facing you. Insert the sharp edge of the knife or a serrated knife on one side of the backbone, press firmly down, and cut through down to the bottom. Do the same on the other side.

Divide the backbone into two pieces by cutting across where the rib cage ends.

Place the breast skin side up, and cut into two pieces through the breastbone, or to one side of it.

How to Make Chicken Cutlets

In order to make chicken cutlets, it's necessary to pull off the skin and cut away the bone. You'll notice that chicken breasts are thicker on one side than the other and, depending on how they'll be prepared, they can cook unevenly.

There are two ways to make chicken cutlets. If you are adept with a knife, you can cut the breast horizontally into two equal slices. Or you can place a boneless, skinless chicken breast on a sheet of plastic wrap on a sturdy flat surface and cover it with another sheet of plastic wrap. Using a meat mallet, or meat pounder, hit the chicken at the large end, allowing the mallet to glide off. Continue pounding the meat, allowing the mallet to travel in various directions until the cutlet is the same thickness all over. Never use a mallet with teeth because it will rip the delicate cutlets.

How to Roast a Duck

Ideally duck should be roasted on a rack so that it sits above the grease. Tie or truss the duck (see page 38 on trussing a chicken). Roast the duck in a 375°F oven for 30 minutes. Lower the temperature to 350°F and roast 12 minutes for each pound. The duck will be cooked when an internal thermometer registers 150°F. When pierced with a fork, the juices from the leg and thigh will run clear, not pink, and the flesh on the leg will begin to shrink away from the bone. Allow the duck to sit 20 minutes before carving.

How to Roast a Turkey

The golden-brown roasted turkey we have come to know and to love gracing the Thanksgiving table has two drumsticks, and I know from my own family experience that the oldest people in attendance always had first choice, and you know what they picked. But I also know from personal experience that when you roast a whole turkey, the dark meat takes longer to cook than the white meat. The result is either underdone dark meat and perfectly done white meat or perfectly done dark meat and overdone white meat.

Truly, the only way to avoid this is to cook turkey in parts. Have your butcher remove the legs (or you can do this yourself at home using a cleaver or hatchet). Roast the breast and legs separately and then reassemble them on a platter to present at the table.

Poultry

Should you choose to roast a whole turkey, here is an approximate timetable.

12 to 16 pounds	3 to 3½ hours
16 to 20 pounds	4 to 4½ hours
20 to 25 pounds	5 to 5½ hours

To test for doneness, insert a meat thermometer into the thickest part of the breast. It should register 165° to 170°F. The thickest part of the drumstick will feel tender when pressed, and the drumstick should move up and down in the socket. Allow the turkey to rest 20 minutes before carving.

Roast turkey legs (1½ to 3 pounds each) at 325°F lightly covered with aluminum foil, removing the foil for the last 30 minutes. For whole turkey breasts with the skin and bone attached weighing from 4½ to 8 pounds allow 20 minutes per pound in a 325°F oven. Boneless turkey breasts (1½ to 2½ pounds) require 20 to 25 minutes per pound in a 350°F oven.

To carve a turkey, first remove the leg-thigh and cut in half at the ball joint. If they're from a small turkey, each can be one serving. On a larger bird, slice the meat from the drumstick and thigh into 2 or 3 lengthwise slices. Remove the wings. Slice the breast by removing the breast half in one piece and cutting crosswise into slices.

How to Truss a Chicken

Trussing a chicken helps to maintain its shape and makes it easier to handle. Begin with a 3- to 4-foot length of butcher's twine. Lay the chicken on a flat surface and place the twine under the tail. Bring up the twine and loop each end around the opposite ends of the drumsticks, pulling tight so that the legs are up against the body and the vent is closed. Turn the bird over and bring one end of the string between the thigh and the body, loop it around the wing and pull across the neck flap. Do the same with the other end of the twine. Pull both ends tight, tie securely and discard the excess twine.

How to Roast a Chicken

A 6- to 7-pound chicken is best for roasting. After trussing, place the chicken in a roasting pan with 2-inch sides. Preheat the oven to 450°F and massage the chicken with 2 tablespoons of softened butter or oil. Place the chicken on the rack if you have one, breast side up, and roast for 1½ to 2 hours, lowering the temperature to 350°F after 30 minutes. See the section on turkey carving (page 38), which is applicable to carving a chicken.

How to Tell if Poultry Is Cooked

The surest way to tell if poultry is cooked is to insert a thermometer in the fleshiest portion of the thigh, away from the bone. It should read 170 to 180°F. Or, when you puncture the thigh with a fork, the juices should run clear to indicate doneness.

The Dark Splotches on the Bones

These dark splotches indicate that the chicken has been frozen. Freezing causes the blood cells in the bone marrow of young chickens to rupture, and when the chicken is thawed, these ruptured cells leak out and cause the dark splotches. Most of the discolorations will turn black after cooking, but are harmless.

A Word About Salmonella

Fresh poultry is very perishable and every effort should be taken to avoid contracting salmonella, a strain of bacteria that is difficult to detect because it is odorless and tasteless.

Transfer of salmonella from poultry to other raw or cooked foods occurs immediately, so all cutting boards, knives, and even your hands, must be kept scrupulously clean. A common mistake is to cut up a chicken and then cut up vegetables using the same cutting board and knife without washing them first.

The solution to salmonella is to rinse poultry well and cook it completely (180°F). There should be no pink left in the interior. Wash all utensils, cutting boards and your hands in warm, soapy water after handling raw poultry.

Cutting Boards—Wood Versus Manmade

Until recently wooden cutting boards were considered to be breeding grounds for bacteria, so plastic cutting boards were given the nod. However, new research at the University of Wisconsin has proved that bacteria disappears from wooden surfaces within minutes, even in the case of raw chicken. Plastic boards on the other hand can harbor bacteria in knife cuts. Regardless of which cutting board you use, make sure it's kept spotlessly clean. Wooden boards can be washed with detergent and hot water, plastic ones can be placed in the dishwasher.

In addition to the poultry recipes in this section, you will find other recipes as follows:

Turkey and Walnut Salad (page 223)
Roasted Cornish Hen (page 245)

Turkey Pinwheels

These make a good company dish because they make a dramatic presentation. They can be served at room temperature and heated by pouring the gravy over them. Make sure to remove the toothpicks or twine before serving.

6 turkey cutlets, or half a boneless
    turkey breast cut into 6 slices,
    pounded thin
6 thin slices prosciutto or smoked
    ham
6 slices provolone
1½ cups cooked spinach, squeezed
    dry

12 sage leaves
Freshly ground black pepper to
    taste
12 thin slices pancetta
2 tablespoons olive oil
1 cup chicken stock

Lay the turkey cutlets on a flat surface with the narrow ends facing you and cover them evenly with the prosciutto, provolone, spinach, sage and black pepper. Roll up the turkey from the ends facing you, wrap each with 2 slices of the pancetta and secure with butcher's twine or toothpicks.

Heat the olive oil in a large sauté pan. Add the turkey rolls and lightly brown them on all sides. Add the stock, cover and simmer until the turkey is tender, about 15 to 20 minutes. (This cooking method, braising, does not require the rolls to be completely covered by the stock. When food is cooked completely covered with liquid, the technique is called poaching.)

Remove the turkey rolls and set aside 5 minutes. Remove and discard the twine or toothpicks. Cut the rolls into ½-inch slices on the diagonal to show off the pinwheel filling and place them on a serving platter.

Return the saucepan to the heat, bring the drippings to a boil and pour over the pinwheels.

Poultry

Boneless Stuffed Duck Roast

Boning a duck can be tricky so rely on your butcher to do the job. This hot version of a galantine, a traditional French dish, is roasted rather than poached and the aspic covering has been eliminated.

½ pound ground chicken

¼ pound diced smoked ham

¼ cup chopped onion

¼ cup green peas

6 cloves Caramelized Garlic
   (page 186)

1 teaspoon dried rosemary

1 teaspoon dried thyme

½ teaspoon Tabasco

¼ teaspoon ground nutmeg

Freshly ground black pepper to
   taste

1 egg

1 cup diced French bread

1 (5 to 6 pound) duck

4 slices bacon

Combine the chicken, ham, onion, peas, garlic, rosemary, thyme, Tabasco, nutmeg and black pepper in a medium bowl and mix well.

In a separate bowl beat the egg slightly, add the French bread, toss gently and set aside for 5 minutes to allow bread to absorb the egg.

Add the bread to the meat mixture and mix well.

Pick out any pin feathers from the duck. Remove the bone from the duck, or have the butcher do it. The duck should be kept in one piece with the skin intact.

Preheat the oven to 350°F.

Lay the duck, skin side down, on a flat surface and spread with the meat mixture. Roll up the duck tightly and place the bacon strips over the top. Tie the duck with butcher's twine and wrap in aluminum foil. Place the duck in the oven for 1 hour and 15 minutes. Remove the duck and let it rest for 10 minutes. Unwrap the duck from the foil and place it in a roasting pan. Increase the oven temperature to 400°F, and return the duck to the oven until it's light brown, about 10 to 15 minutes.

Let the duck rest 20 minutes before slicing.

Know Your Fire

Chicken Fricassee

A fricassee is a thick chunky stew often made with chicken and vegetables and flavored with wine. Despite its fancy name, this is really one of the simplest dishes you can make. Remember to keep the temperature at a low simmer, so the chicken doesn't become tough.

1 (3½ pound) chicken, cut into 8 or
    10 pieces
1 onion, chopped
2 carrots, diced
2 ribs celery, chopped
1 parsnip, diced
1 red bell pepper, seeded and diced
1 cup white wine

1 cup water
6 fresh sage leaves
Pinch ground nutmeg
Freshly ground black pepper to
    taste
2 cups unseasoned mashed
    potatoes

Place the chicken, onion, carrot, celery, parsnip and red pepper in a large soup kettle or casserole. Add the wine, water, sage, nutmeg and black pepper. Bring the mixture to a boil, reduce heat, cover and simmer until chicken is tender, about 45 minutes.

Turn off the heat and allow the ingredients to cool so that the fat rises to the surface and can be skimmed off. If time allows, prepare the dish early in the day or the day before and refrigerate. The fat will solidify at the top and be easy to remove.

Just before serving, reheat the fricassee, add the mashed potatoes and stir well until the potatoes blend in and make it creamy.

Poultry

Chicken En Croûte

En croûte means in a pastry crust. In this case the pastry is flaky sheets of filo dough. Since filo can be purchased in most supermarkets, even this two-step procedure is easy enough for a novice but creates a real sensation for family and guests. This dish can be prepared in the oven or on the grill.

2 tablespoons butter

½ onion, finely chopped

I cup sliced mushrooms

¼ cup dry white wine

2 tablespoons cider or tarragon vinegar

I tablespoon chopped fresh tarragon

I teaspoon chopped fresh parsley

½ teaspoon Tabasco

Freshly ground black pepper to taste

4 (8 ounce) skinless and boneless chicken breasts

2 tablespoons olive oil

4 sheets filo dough

6 tablespoons melted butter

¼ cup fresh bread crumbs

2 tablespoons prepared mustard

Preheat oven to 350°F or preheat grill to high.

Heat a sauté pan until it's very hot. Add the butter and immediately add the onions, stir once and add the mushrooms. Cook 30 seconds without stirring, then stir and cook 30 seconds longer. Add the white wine, cider or tarragon vinegar, tarragon, parsley, Tabasco and black pepper. Cook, stirring frequently, until no liquid is left. Set aside to cool.

Brush the chicken breasts with the olive oil and quickly sear on a hot grill or in a sauté pan until light brown. Remove the chicken before it is cooked through, and allow it to cool.

Brush 1 sheet of filo with the butter and sprinkle with some of the bread crumbs. Repeat, layering the filo sheets on top of each other. Cut the sheets into 4 equal pieces and place one of the chicken breasts in the center of each piece, brush with some of the mustard and cover with some of the mushrooms. Brush the edges of the filo with water and fold the filo over to enclose the chicken. Place the chicken on a baking sheet.

If using the oven, bake the chicken for 20 minutes. If using the grill, reduce the heat to medium/low, place 2 bricks on the grid, place the baking sheet holding the chicken breasts on the bricks, close the lid, and cook 20 minutes.

Filo dough Filo or phyllo dough is composed of tissue paper-thin layers of pastry especially popular in Greek cuisine. They can be used for both sweet and savory dishes. Filo is especially delicate, and once it dries out it becomes brittle and cannot be used. Work with a small portion of filo at a time and keep the rest under a damp paper towel to keep it moist.

Rarely is a single layer of filo used. As each sheet is brushed with butter, it's usually sprinkled with finely ground bread crumbs or nuts to keep the layers slightly separated.

Filo is sold in Greek markets and in the freezer section of most supermarkets. If you buy frozen filo, it should be defrosted in the refrigerator and used within 2 to 3 days.

Wood-Smoked Chickens on a Spit

It may be monotonous watching chickens go round and round on a spit, but the taste of a spit-roasted chicken, Cornish hen or turkey can never be duplicated. Give yourself plenty of time so that the chickens can cook slowly, basting themselves with their own juices.

2 (3 pound) chickens	Hickory Dry Rub (page 59)
1 tablespoon Tabasco	

Wash the chickens inside and out and pat dry. Brush the chickens with the Tabasco and rub all over with the Hickory Dry Rub ingredients. Refrigerate for 1 hour.

Preheat the grill to medium.

Remove chickens from the refrigerator, place the rotisserie spit bar through them and secure with prongs, making sure they're evenly balanced. Attach the spit to the electric motor and start it rotating. Place a small pan under the chickens to catch the drippings and baste occasionally with these drippings or cook using the indirect method. Cook the chickens for about 1½ hours. They will be done when the meat shrinks away from the bottom of the thigh bone and the juices run clear when the flesh is pierced with a fork.

Indirect grilling Indirect grilling means that the food is not placed directly over the heat source. In an electric or gas grill, it calls for lighting only one half of the grill and placing the food on the other side. With a charcoal grill, the food is placed in the center and the coals are arranged around the outside of the fire-box.

The advantage of indirect grilling is that the fat from the food doesn't fall into the fire, causing flare-ups.

Chicken Livers in Tomato Sauce

Chicken livers are one of the cheapest forms of protein around and a good source of iron and vitamin A. They're sold fresh, but check the expiration date. If you think you don't like chicken livers, try this sauce over spaghetti or gnocchi and then decide.

8 ounces chicken livers

½ cup milk

¼ cup all-purpose flour

Pinch of ground nutmeg

Freshly ground black pepper to
    taste

4 slices pancetta or bacon, chopped

1 tablespoon olive oil, optional

¼ onion, chopped

6 cloves Caramelized Garlic
    (page 186)

¼ cup dry red wine

2 cups canned plum tomatoes,
    coarsely chopped

1 teaspoon chopped fresh thyme

1 teaspoon chopped fresh rosemary

¼ teaspoon hot pepper flakes

Soak the chicken livers in milk for 30 minutes. Drain well and discard the milk.

In a medium bowl combine the flour, nutmeg and black pepper and dredge the chicken livers in flour, shaking off any excess.

Heat a medium saucepan until hot. Add the pancetta and cook over medium heat until it gives up its fat. (If the pancetta is lean, add the olive oil; if the pancetta is fatty, you won't require any oil.) Raise the heat, add the chicken livers and sear on all sides until brown. Add the onion and garlic and cook, stirring occasionally, 4 to 5 minutes. Stir in the wine. Add the tomatoes, thyme, rosemary and hot pepper flakes and stir well. Lower the heat to a simmer and cook uncovered 15 to 20 minutes.

Sautéed Chicken Fingers with Linguine

Surprise! Who would think that something so good to eat takes only 30 minutes to get to the table? The secret of this dish is the cumin. A chicken finger is the long strip of very tender white meat attached to the breast. It's also called chicken tenderloin because it's so tender.

Cooking pasta *al dente,* from the Italian "to the tooth," means cooking until it still has a bit of a bite to it and is not soft or mushy.

1½ pounds linguine	2 teaspoons ground cumin
1 pound chicken fingers or boneless	2 teaspoons Tabasco
chicken breasts cut into long	1 teaspoon dried basil
strips about ½ inch wide	1 teaspoon dried oregano
2 tablespoons flour	¼ cup dry red wine
2 tablespoons olive oil	2 cups canned tomatoes with
2 bell peppers, seeded and cut into	puree, chopped
½-inch strips	2 bay leaves
1 onion, cut into ½-inch strips	Grated Parmigiano Reggiano cheese
8 cloves Caramelized Garlic	Freshly ground black pepper to
(page 186)	taste

Bring a large stockpot of water to a boil.

Dust the chicken with the flour, brushing off any excess. Heat the olive oil in a large sauté pan. Add the chicken and brown on all sides. Add the peppers, onion and garlic and cook 2 minutes. Add the cumin, Tabasco, basil and oregano and cook 2 minutes longer. Add the wine and cook 1 minute. Add the tomatoes and bay leaves, reduce the heat and simmer 15 minutes.

While the sauce is simmering, cook the linguine *al dente,* drain it well, and place on a serving platter. Remove the bay leaves from the sauce, and pour it on top of the pasta. Serve with grated cheese and pepper.

Herbs and Spices

The Difference Between Seasoning and Flavoring

A seasoning will enhance, but not change, the natural flavor of food. For example, herbs and spices are seasonings. Tomatoes taste better with basil; cinnamon adds zip to apple pie. A flavoring adds a whole new dimension to the original taste such as squirting lemon on fish, adding a dash of vinegar to a bean soup, or adding sugar to whipped cream.

What's the Difference Between an Herb and a Spice?

Herbs are the fragrant leaves and sometimes tender stems of plants grown in temperate climates. They can be used fresh or dried.

Spices are made from the bark, root, stems, buds, fruit or seeds of mostly tropical plants and trees and are most often used dried.

The longer herbs and spices are left to marinate in foods like vinaigrettes, soups, stews and chilies, the better their flavor, which is one reason why foods cooked with herbs and spices taste better the next day.

How to Buy Herbs and Spices

Always buy the best quality herbs and spices you can afford *in small amounts.* Buying a large bouquet of parsley or a super-duper size jar of ground cinnamon isn't a bargain if you have to discard it later because it's lost its potency.

Look for herbs with bright fresh color and lots of fragrance. It's hard to determine whether spices are fresh because you can't smell them in a closed container so buy them at a store that has lots of traffic.

Which Spices Should Be Purchased Whole?

Spices lose their flavor and aroma once they've been ground. By all means, invest in a pepper mill for freshly ground black pepper and a small nutmeg grater for nutmeg. Other spices such as allspice, cardamom, cloves and cumin can be purchased whole and ground in a spice or coffee mill.

How to Store Herbs and Spices

You can store fresh herbs for several days wrapped in wet paper towels, then placed in plastic bags and refrigerated. Or you can place fresh herbs in a small jar filled with water, add a pinch of sugar and cover with a plastic bag secured with a rubber band. Keep on the counter out of direct sunlight.

Dried herbs and spices have a limited shelf life. The length depends, however, on how long the box sat on the supermarket shelf before you brought it home but, unfortunately, you have no way of knowing when they were stocked. Stored in a cool, dark place, dried herbs have a shelf life of about 6 months. However, a cool dark place does not mean the refrigerator. It means a cupboard with a door that is as far away from the stove as possible.

Dried spices like cinnamon will last about a year. To determine their acceptability, open the container and give a quick sniff. If you need to sniff twice to determine whether it's good or not, it's time to discard it. When buying spices, write the date on the bottom so you'll know when to replace them.

A good way to use up outdated herbs and spices is to add them to a water pan in a water smoker.

Fresh Versus Dry Herbs

Using fresh herbs instead of dried herbs is a matter of preference. If you have fresh parsley growing in the garden, certainly you would use that rather than dried parsley. Likewise, last summer's frozen basil is better than dried basil. Certainly you want to use fresh herbs for garnishes.

How to Dry (or Freeze) Fresh Herbs

To dry fresh herbs, tie small bunches and place in a paper bag. Twist the top of the bag around the stems and, with the herbs hanging inside the bag, leave undisturbed for several weeks to dry. Never dry herbs by leaving them out in the sun. Their oil will be lost, and their fragrance will dissipate.

To dry herbs in the microwave, place a single layer of washed and dried herbs on three thicknesses of paper towel and cover with three more paper towels. Microwave on high for 2 minutes or until dry.

To freeze herbs, place clean dry leaves in freezer-quality plastic bags or place in rigid containers and cover with oil. Herbs can also be placed in ice cube trays, covered with water and frozen.

When to Add Herbs and Spices During the Cooking Process

Generally, when a seasoning or flavoring is added to a liquid at the beginning, the flavoring becomes more concentrated as the liquid reduces. Most often, dried herbs are added at the beginning and fresh herbs at the end of the cooking process.

Most aromatic spices, such as fennel and cumin seeds, are sautéed in a small amount of fat at the start of cooking, in order for their full flavor to expand.

Often Middle Eastern, Southwestern, Mexican and Indian recipes will call for heating seeds in a skillet or oven to intensify their flavor.

I often add flavorings like lemon, vinegar, hot sauces and liquid smoke seasoning at the beginning so that their pronounced flavors can mellow while cooking.

Why Salt Is Unnecessary in Most Cooking

You'll notice that most of my recipes don't have any salt added. Our palates have been used to salt since childhood, but once you begin to taste flavors, and not salt, a whole new world opens up for your taste buds. But tastes are individual and that's why there are salt shakers on tables.

Characteristics of Common Spices

It's difficult to describe the taste of herbs and spices because their flavors are so unique, but here's a rundown of some of the more common ones and when to use them.

Allspice is sold as whole berries or ground. It's so named because the aroma smells like a melding of clove, cinnamon and nutmeg. Use whole dark brown allspice berries in meat broth, gravies and pickling liquid. Use ground allspice in cakes, pies, relishes and preserves as well as yellow vegetables and tomatoes.

Anise seed was used as a digestive at Roman banquets and as a charm against bad dreams. The small gray-brown seeds have an unmistakably licorice flavor and give the characteristic flavor of anisette.

Basil is a member of the mint family and so popular in Italy that a romantic young Italian wears a sprig to indicate being in love. The leaves are bright green and are a popular seasoning for pizza, pasta sauce and tomato dishes. Add basil to vegetable soup, meat pies and stews and vegetables such as peas, green beans or cucumbers.

Bay leaves, from the laurel tree, are used to season meats, potatoes, stews, soups, sauces and fish. One or two leaves are recommended, but should be removed before serving.

Caraway seeds belong to the parsley family, and the brown, hard, curved seeds are often found in rye bread and cheeses, and used in pork and sauerkraut dishes, soups, meats and stews.

Cardamom is a member of the ginger family, and each pod, about the size of a large pea, contains approximately 20 tiny aromatic black seeds. Cardamom is sold as seeds or ground. It is used in baked goods, apple and pumpkin pies and is one of the spices that go into curry powder.

Chives belong to the onion family and can be used fresh or freeze dried. Chives are important to vichyssoise and the sour cream dressing over baked potatoes as well as cooked vegetables, cheese and egg dishes, gravies and dips.

Cinnamon, one of civilization's first spices, was once used as a medicine, a perfume and an ingredient for a love potion. It comes from the dried bark of trees in the evergreen family. The bark is peeled back and rolled into long, slender sticks. Ground cinnamon is an important ingredient in baking and delicious in hot chocolate. Cinnamon sticks can be used in sugar syrups and pickling liquids.

Cloves are the fragrant nail-like buds of a tropical evergreen. Whole cloves are used for studding hams and pork, in pickling spices, stews and meat gravies. Ground cloves are used in baked goods and chocolate desserts and to enhance vegetables like beets, sweet potatoes, boiled onions and winter squash.

Coriander seed is another ancient spice going back to the Hanging Gardens of Babylon. It is one of the ingredients in curry powder, and its mild, delicately fragrant seeds flavor frankfurters and are included in pickling spices. The fresh leaves of the plant are called cilantro or Chinese parsley, which is particularly popular in Mexican, Latin American and American Southwestern dishes.

Cumin seed is another spice with biblical roots. Cumin seeds look and smell somewhat like caraway seeds. Ground cumin is widely used in chili powder and curry powder. Whole cumin seeds go into making pork and sauerkraut dishes and cheeses.

Dill seed is the dried fruit of dill weed, a member of the parsley family. The seeds are small, oval-shaped and tan in color. Dill seed is used in making dill pickles, meat and fish dishes, sauces, salads, cold slaw, potato salad and sauerkraut. Fresh dill weed is well suited to chicken soup, salads and fish dishes.

Fennel seed with its aroma and flavor similar to anise seed is reputed to have medicinal qualities. The seeds are yellowish brown in color and oval in shape. A member of the parsley family, fennel can be added to bread, sausages, seafood, pork and poultry dishes.

Ginger comes in many forms. The root form is used for cooking. Ground ginger is used for baking and in rubs for meat, fowl and fish. Crystallized ginger is used in baking and is eaten as a candy.

Marjoram, used to make perfumes and medicines, has always been the symbol of romantic love. Its gray leaves are first cousin to oregano; both are members of the mint family. Fresh marjoram is a seasoning for green vegetables, and dried marjoram enhances the flavor of lamb, poultry and Italian dishes. Marjoram is one of the seasonings used in liverwurst, bologna and head cheese.

Mint is a large family but the two types we're most familiar with are spearmint and peppermint. Their aromas are strong and sweet with a cool aftertaste. They can be used fresh or dried and are a popular flavoring for candy, frozen desserts, chocolate, fruits, salads, jam and jelly.

Nutmeg and *mace* are harvested at the same time. The nutmeg is the pit or seed of the nutmeg fruit, and mace is the red lacy network that surrounds it. The aroma of tan-colored ground nutmeg is sweeter and more delicate than orange-colored ground mace. Nutmeg is sold whole or ground and used in baking, puddings, sauces, vegetables and beverages. Mace is always sold ground and used in pound cake, cherry pie and fish dishes.

Oregano is also known as wild marjoram, winter sweet and the pizza herb. It's available fresh and dried. The oregano grown in the Mediterranean is used for Italian and Greek dishes while oregano grown in Mexico is best for Mexican and Southwestern cuisine. It's delicious in meat, fish, cheese, eggs and vegetables such as tomatoes, zucchini and green beans.

Paprika is made from ground dried red peppers with the seeds and veins removed. Most of the paprika found on supermarket shelves is the mild or "sweet" type, but there is a paprika with a slight bite that is not as popular. Paprika is brilliant red in color and often sprinkled over food as a garnish. A great deal of paprika is used in prepared foods such as sausage, salad dressings and condiments.

Parsley, probably our most common herb, is used both fresh or dried in a wide range of dishes. Curly parsley is frequently found as a garnish and has a mild taste. Flatleaf or Italian parsley has a decidedly stronger flavor.

Black pepper was so precious in ancient days that rent and dowries were frequently paid with bags of it. The pepper berries grow in bunches like grapes and, as they ripen, turn from green to yellow to red. As they dry the color changes to deep mahogany even though we call it *black* pepper. Black pepper is available ground, coarse ground or whole, and it is used in innumerable dishes, even in ice cream and cookies like pfeffernuesse.

Rosemary is an evergreen shrub member of the mint family. The leaves resemble pine needles and come fresh or dried. The flavor of rosemary goes well with chicken, lamb, shrimp, cauliflower, green beans, beets and summer squash. The flavor is potent, so use it sparingly.

Sage is a hardy perennial of the mint family and a mainstay in kitchens for pork and poultry stuffings, fish, salad dressings and chowders. It's available fresh, ground or rubbed (this form is especially popular with sausage makers).

Sesame seeds, also known as benne seeds, are used as a flavoring or ground for oil. These small, pearl-white seeds are grown in the tropics and have a rich, toasted-nut flavor when baked on rolls, buns, and bread. Sesame seeds are the major ingredient in halvah candy.

Tarragon is a member of the aster family and has an aroma that hints of anise. It's often used in chicken, eggs and seafood dishes and to make flavored vinegar.

Thyme was the ancient symbol of elegance. This member of the mint family has long been a favorite of North American cooks. It goes into New England clam chowder, Creole seafood dishes and Midwestern poultry stuffings. It's also good in cream chicken and cottage cheese and teamed with butter over vegetables like white onions, braised celery, asparagus, green beans, eggplant and tomatoes. Buy it fresh or ground.

Turmeric is best known as an ingredient in prepared mustard or pickles. The saffron-yellow color is used as a natural dye to color foods and is an ingredient in curry powder. Use sparingly in chicken, seafood or egg dishes, or with rice and potatoes.

Herb Vinegars

Any herb or herb combination can be used to enhance the flavor of vinegar. Here's one I like: combine a cup of cider vinegar, a stem of rosemary, 2 sprigs each of thyme and parsley, a clove of garlic, a teaspoon of crushed peppercorns and a jalapeño pepper. Store in a sterile, dark glass jar with a tight-fitting cap (or use a cork from a wine bottle). Place out of sunlight for 2 or 3 days before using.

Marinades

Marinades have two purposes: in some cases they're used to flavor food and in other instances to tenderize it. A marinade usually consists of an acid (lemon juice, vinegar, wine), a liquid (oil, juice, stock) and herbs and spices (garlic, onion, parsley, rosemary, etc.). Since a marinade contains an acid, the liquid should be placed in a nonreactive container such as glass, stainless steel or plastic, but never in an aluminum pan or dish.

Meat, fish and poultry should always be covered and marinated in the refrigerator.

How Long Should You Marinate?

Marinating time will depend on the thickness of the meat, fish or poultry and how tough it is. Fish can be marinated for as little as 30 minutes while chicken parts and thin cuts of meat may need two hours. Thick roasts, such as sauerbraten, often call for several days in the refrigerator.

Rubs

A rub is a mixture of herbs and spices that is rubbed onto the surface of meat. The only difference between a rub and a marinade is that the rub is dry or pastelike and a marinade is wet. Both add a great deal of flavor to meat, fish and poultry and very often tenderize them.

Pork Seasoning Rub

For Sautéed Pork Loin Chops with
    Shrimp (page 30)
8 cloves Caramelized Garlic
    (page 186)

1 teaspoon dried rosemary, crushed
1 teaspoon dried thyme
½ teaspoon cayenne pepper or to
    taste

Combine all ingredients and mix well.

Grated Horseradish Rub

The secret ingredient to this marinade is definitely the vodka. Be sure
that your bottled horseradish is fresh. If it has begun to darken, it's time
to replace it.

For Pork Cutlet with Grated Horse-
    radish (page 31)
2 tablespoons fresh horseradish
¼ cup vodka
Juice of 1 lemon
1 teaspoon dried thyme

1 teaspoon ketchup or barbecue
    sauce
½ teaspoon Tabasco
Freshly ground black pepper to
    taste
¼ cup all-purpose flour

Combine all ingredients and mix well.

Lamb Rub I

**For Racks of Lamb with Couscous
    (page 23)**
**6 cloves Caramelized Garlic
    (page 186)**
1 tablespoon dried rosemary

1 tablespoon dried thyme
1 teaspoon ground coriander
**1 teaspoon crushed black pepper-
    corns**
1 teaspoon lemon zest

Combine all ingredients and mix well.

Lamb Rub II

**For Roasted Leg of Lamb with Beer
    (page 26)**
1 tablespoon paprika
1 tablespoon garlic powder
**1 tablespoon dried rosemary,
    crushed**

1 tablespoon dried thyme
**1 tablespoon coarsely ground black
    pepper**
¼ teaspoon ground nutmeg

Combine all ingredients and mix well.

Caribbean Spice Rub

For Cold-Smoked Pork (page 261)
Cloves from 1 head Caramelized
    Garlic (page 186)
Juice from 2 limes
2 scallions, chopped
1 hot chili pepper, such as
    habanero, chopped

1 tablespoon chopped fresh ginger
1 tablespoon dried thyme
1 tablespoon dried oregano
1 teaspoon ground nutmeg
1 teaspoon ground allspice

Combine all ingredients and mix well.

Hickory Dry Rub

For Wood-Smoked Chickens on a
    Spit (page 46)
1 tablespoon sweet paprika
1 tablespoon garlic powder

1 teaspoon ground sage
1 teaspoon ground cinnamon
Pinch ground nutmeg

Combine all ingredients and mix well.

Marinade for Cold-Smoked Trout

For Cold-Smoked Trout (page 260)
1 cup beer, ale or light beer
½ cup granulated sugar

½ onion, sliced
1 tablespoon whole mustard seeds
2 teaspoons Tabasco

Combine all ingredients and mix well.

Cornish Hen Marinade

For Roasted Cornish Hen (page 245)
8 cloves Caramelized Garlic
   (page 186)
Juice of 2 lemons
2 tablespoons olive oil

1 tablespoon soy sauce
2 teaspoons Tabasco
Freshly ground black pepper to
   taste

Combine all ingredients and mix well.

Rib Rub

For Smoked Ribs (page 264)
2 tablespoons sweet paprika
1 tablespoon ground cumin
1 tablespoon garlic powder
1 tablespoon dried rosemary,
   crushed

1 teaspoon ground coriander
1 teaspoon cayenne pepper
1 teaspoon dry mustard

Combine all ingredients and mix well.

Smoked Turkey Rub

MAKES
ABOUT ¾ CUPS

1 head Caramelized Garlic
   (page 186)
2 tablespoons chopped fresh
   cilantro
2 tablespoons grated orange peel
2 tablespoons soy sauce
1 tablespoon finely chopped fresh
   ginger

1 tablespoon honey
2 teaspoons Tabasco
1 teaspoon chopped fresh thyme
1 teaspoon coarsely ground black
   pepper

Combine all ingredients and mix well.

Herbs and Spices

Hot Peppers
From the Tiny Incendiary Habaneros to the Larger Poblano

After salt, the capsicum peppers, both hot and sweet, are the most frequently used seasoning in the world. And we owe it all to Christopher Columbus, who discovered both hot and sweet capsicum peppers growing in the West Indies and brought them back to Europe. Intrepid explorers, especially the Portuguese, carried pepper seeds to the far-flung corners of the world.

Capsaicin, the oil that causes the burning sensation, releases endorphins, which promote a sense of well-being. Hot capsicum peppers add zip to bland or monotonous diets and stimulate the taste buds. They stimulate the body's own unique air-conditioning ability and make you want to sweat. You can also be pretty sure that before the days of preserving and refrigeration, these tongue-searing flavors masked the taste of rancid food. Capsicums contain more vitamin A than any other food, plus vitamins B and C. The membranes and seeds carry up to 80 percent of the heat so I recommend that you wear rubber gloves when working with chiles. The hotness is not diminished by freezing or drying, and the only way to reduce it is to discard the seeds and membranes. After working with hot chilies, wash your hands and make sure you don't touch your eyes.

Chile or Chili?

For the sake of simplification, a chile is the hot capsicum pepper; chili is the dish seasoned with fresh, roasted or dried chile peppers.

What Is Chili (spelled with an "i") Powder?

Chili powder, like curry powder, is a blend of spices. The original mixture was sold commercially by Willie Gebhardt, a Texan, in 1892 for making chili con carne. Chili powder is made from dried and ground chile peppers mixed with oregano, cumin, cayenne, garlic powder and paprika.

What Is Chile (spelled with an "e") Powder?

This is the ground powder of one or more particular chile peppers without the addition of other spices. Its pungency depends on the types of chile pepper.

Different Types of Capsicum Peppers

Here are some of the more popular capsicum peppers, both hot and sweet.

The *banana* pepper (sweet) or *Hungarian wax* (hot) pepper are both pale yellow, about 6 inches long and slightly curved. They're always used fresh in salads and stews.

The *sweet bell* pepper comes in yellow, orange, red, green and purple and ranges from 4 to 6 inches high and from 3 to 4 inches wide. Eat them roasted, stuffed, in salads and in casseroles.

The hot *cascabel* pepper is cherry shaped, dark green to reddish brown when fresh and dark reddish brown when dried. Dried ground cascabels are added to tamales, sausages and casseroles.

The *cayenne* pepper is green when immature, but later turns bright red. Growing to almost 8 inches, the cayenne is very hot. It is used throughout the world especially in Creole and Cajun dishes. Dried cayenne is available both as ground pepper or as seeds.

Cherry peppers are small round peppers, green or red, sweet or hot, and eaten fresh or pickled.

The green, red or almost black *chiltepin* pepper is a good example of how tiny is hotter. These incendiary ¼-by-¾-inch peppers are eaten fresh or dried.

Cubanelle or *Italian* peppers are used fresh in salads or fried and are often substituted for bell peppers. Their glossy skin can range from yellow to green to orange and red, on the same pepper.

On the heat scale, the *habanero* pepper goes over the top. Only about one inch long and an inch wide, these green to yellow-orange, orange or red fireballs pack a wallop. Most often they are sold fresh or used in bottled sauces.

Of all the hot peppers, the *jalapeño* is probably the most familiar to Americans. Some grow to 3 inches long and their bright green turns red when mature. Buy them fresh, canned, bottled or pickled. A *chipolte* is a smoked jalapeño.

The *New Mexican* chile or *anaheim* is a hot or sweet pepper about 7 to 10 inches long. It's sold fresh, dried, canned or powdered. The green to red flesh turns brown when dried.

When the dark blackish green *chilaca* pepper dries it turns black and its name changes to *pasilla*. A medium hot pepper, it can grow to 12 inches. It's essential to Mexican mole dishes and is used as a condiment.

Green to red, 3 to 5 inches long, *pepperoncini* are most often found pickled and a popular addition to Italian antipasto.

Dark green *poblano* peppers turn red when mature. These mild to hot peppers are about 4 inches long and are often stuffed or used in soups and sauces. When the pepper is dried, it changes its name to *ancho* and turns dark brown which changes to brick red when soaked. Anchos are used in enchiladas, chili con carne, and in chili powder.

Scotch bonnets get their name because they slightly resemble a Scottish tam-o-shanter, but they're only 2 inches in diameter. These are one of the hottest peppers known to man. Fresh Scotch bonnets are frequently found in West Indian dishes; dried ones are added to bottled sauces.

Two-inch long *serrano* peppers grow green to red and are very hot. They do not dry well and are used fresh in sauces, guacamole, relishes and as a seasoning.

A Short History of Tabasco

The true Tabasco pepper, or *Capsicum frutescens,* is grown exclusively on Avery Island in Louisiana where it's planted in sandy soil atop the world's largest salt mine. The hot sultry days and cool nights make it the best geographic area in the world for growing these 1-inch long, exceedingly hot Tabasco peppers. The peppers are used exclusively for Tabasco Hot Pepper Sauce.

William McIlhenny, an avid gardener, settled on Avery Island and found that one of the few surviving things on the island after the devastation of the Civil War was pepper plants.

The peppers can only be picked when they're red and ripe. In the field, the peppers are matched against a red stick to ensure their quality by way of color. They're immediately crushed and mixed with salt (they're above a salt mine, remember). When the mixture has marinated and aged for three years in oak barrels, vinegar is added and the Tabasco is bottled.

On the Scoville scale, a standardized measure of the hotness of food, most hot sauces measure about 3,000 units; Tabasco measures between 9,000 and 12,000, so a little goes a long way.

I've had some success in growing Tabasco peppers on Long Island. Paul McIlhenny, Tabasco's senior vice president, sent me a few Tabasco pepper seedlings which I planted in my father's garden. As the plants grew to about 2½ feet, the green peppers turned white, then yellow, then green. Finally, there was a colorful burst of red and it looked almost like Christmas in August.

I know it was the care my father, the Master Gardener, gave them. It was the last growing season he was alive and those hot pepper seedlings have grown into a fond memory.

How to Roast Chile Peppers

Roasting brings out more of the chile flavor. Rinse the chile peppers and pat dry. Heat a heavy skillet over medium heat, add the chile peppers and toast, turning frequently so they do not burn. When cool, remove the seeds from the larger ones.

Sometimes dried chile peppers such as *anchos* are soaked and pureed before being added to a dish.

What to Drink When Your Mouth Is on Fire

A hot pepper can set your mouth aflame, but never reach for a glass of water to quench the fire. Or a beer. The best antidote is milk or yogurt. Second best—a slice of bread.

Nacho Corn

This southwestern-style corn dish is a painless way to get your daily dose of vegetables. To make 3 cups of corn kernels, you'll need about 3 ears of fresh corn. To remove the kernels, stand the ear of corn up at an angle and, with a sharp knife, cut down from top to bottom.

2 tablespoons butter

1 onion, diced

1 red bell pepper, seeded and diced

2 jalapeño peppers, seeded and diced

1 teaspoon ground cumin

2 tablespoons all-purpose flour

1 cup milk

3 cups corn kernels, fresh or frozen

½ cup shredded Cheddar cheese

1 tablespoon chopped fresh cilantro

½ teaspoon Tabasco

Freshly ground black pepper to taste

1 scallion, chopped

Heat a medium saucepan and melt the butter over low heat. Add the onion, bell pepper, jalapeños and cumin and "sweat" the vegetables until tender, about 10 to 15 minutes. Stir in the flour and cook 2 minutes. Add the milk and stir in the corn. Add the cheese, cilantro, Tabasco and black pepper. Bring to a boil, lower heat and cook the corn in the sauce for about 5 minutes. Top with the scallions and serve.

Know Your Fire

Fiery Peppers

If you like hot foods, you'll love these peppers, but don't drink water to put out the fire. Instead reach for a glass of milk or a slice of bread.

3 bell peppers, I each: red, yellow, green

2 hot Italian peppers or 2 serrano peppers

4 tablespoons olive oil

I tablespoon chopped Italian parsley

Freshly ground black pepper to taste

Cut the peppers in half lengthwise and remove the seeds.

Preheat the grill to high.

Brush the peppers with 2 tablespoons of the olive oil. Grill the peppers 3 to 4 minutes on each side, remove and drizzle with the remaining olive oil. Place the peppers in a serving dish, sprinkle with the parsley and season with the black pepper.

Chili-Baked Clams

Serrano peppers give these clams just the right amount of oomph and the bacon adds a touch of smoke flavor. If you aren't adept at opening clams, have your fishmonger do it.

4 slices bacon

¼ onion, chopped

2 scallions, chopped

4 cloves Caramelized Garlic
　(page 186)

3 serrano peppers, seeded and
　chopped

¼ cup butter, softened

1 tablespoon chopped fresh parsley

½ teaspoon Tabasco

16 Little Neck clams, on the half
　shell

Preheat the oven to 375°F.

Cook the bacon until half done in a medium skillet. Remove the bacon, drain on paper towel and cut each strip into 4 pieces. Sauté the onion, scallion, garlic and serrano pepper in the bacon fat until tender, about 7 to 8 minutes, remove from pan and cool to room temperature. Combine the vegetables with the butter, parsley and Tabasco.

Spread a heaping teaspoon of the mixture on each clam, top with a piece of bacon and bake for 8 to 10 minutes. Serve hot.

Bucatini with Spicy Tomato Sauce

Bucatini is a long macaroni with a hollow center, like a drinking straw. The openings capture some of the sauce. *Bucatoni* is slightly fatter than bucatini. South of Rome, bucatini is called *perciatelli*.

2 tablespoons olive oil

¼ cup chopped pancetta

1 head Caramelized Garlic
　　(page 186)

½ chopped onion

¼ cup chopped prosciutto

2 cups canned plum tomatoes,
　　chopped

½ cup dry white wine

2 teaspoons hot pepper flakes, or
　　to taste

10 to 12 fresh basil leaves, chopped

Freshly ground black pepper

1 pound bucatini

Grated Parmesan cheese

Heat a saucepan and heat the olive oil. Add the pancetta and cook until it becomes light brown. Add the garlic, onion and prosciutto and cook 2 to 3 minutes. Add the tomatoes, white wine, hot pepper flakes, basil, and black pepper, stir well and bring to a boil. Lower heat and simmer for 10 minutes. You can regulate the spiciness of the dish by adding more or less hot pepper flakes.

Heat a large pot of water and cook the bucatini according to package directions. Make sure to drain the pasta very carefully, shaking the colander to discard any water remaining inside the bucatini.

Return the pasta to the cooking pot, add the sauce, mix well and serve in deep bowls. Sprinkle with grated Parmesan cheese.

Hot Peppers

Jalapeño Rolls

Once you taste one of these rolls, you're bound to reach for another. You may want to double this recipe if you have to share with anyone else. Use your favorite recipe for pizza dough or buy frozen pizza dough from the supermarket. If you want to make extra fancy rolls, sprinkle the dough with fresh cilantro, ground cumin or chopped sun-dried tomatoes before rolling it up.

Serve the jalapeño rolls with sangria before dinner and, should there be any left, include them in the bread basket.

1 pound pizza dough	2 teaspoons sweet paprika
3 tablespoons olive oil	Freshly ground black pepper to
4 cloves Caramelized Garlic	taste
(see page 186)	2 jalapeño peppers, seeded and
4 tablespoons grated Parmesan	chopped
cheese	

Preheat the oven to 375°F.

On a lightly floured surface, roll out the dough into an 8-by-16-inch rectangle with the long edge facing you and brush with half the olive oil. Leaving the inch of dough closest to you unseasoned, spread the rest of the dough with the garlic and sprinkle with 2 tablespoons of grated cheese, paprika and black pepper. Beginning at the top, roll the dough toward you, jelly-roll style, and seal the edges by pinching the dough together.

Using a sharp knife, cut the dough into 2-inch pieces and place them on a greased baking sheet, seam side down. Sprinkle the tops with the chopped jalapeño.

Bake the rolls for 10 to 12 minutes or until lightly brown. Remove them from the oven and sprinkle with the remaining grated cheese while they're still hot.

Oils and Vinegars

A Word About Fats

Fats are classified as saturated, monounsaturated and polyunsaturated. On the technical side, all fats are composed of carbon, hydrogen and oxygen, and the amount of each contained in the fat determines what kind of a fat it is.

Saturated fats include animal fats such as butter and lard, which are solid at room temperature, and vegetable fats such as palm oil, coconut oil and palm seed oil.

Monounsaturated fats—olive oil, canola oil, almond oil and peanut oil—are liquid at room temperature. These are believed to reduce the levels of low-density lipids or LDL, the "bad" cholesterol in the blood.

Polyunsaturated fats, also liquids—safflower oil, soybean oil, corn oil and sesame oil—are considered to be relatively healthy.

Olive Oil

Olive oils can range widely in taste and color, from light yellow-green to deep forest green. Generally, the deeper the color, the more intense the flavor. Their flavors depend on where the olives were grown and whether they were picked green or left on the tree to turn brown and mature. Spanish and Greek olive oils have a particularly strong olive taste and fragrance whereas oil from olives grown in Provence or Tuscany have a more delicate flavor and aroma. Olive oils made from olives grown largely in California vary.

Olive oil is graded by the amount of oleic acid it contains. All cold-pressed olive oils—those extracted without the use of heat or chemicals in huge circular stone presses—are low in acidity. Extra-virgin olive oil, which is the first pressing of the olives, contains 1 per cent acid. Virgin olive oil, the second pressing, has acidity between 1 and 2 per cent. The less expensive "pure" olive oil and generic olive oil have more acidity, are less flavorful and should be for frying and baking.

Use extra-virgin and virgin olive oil for salads made with robust greens or for dressing beans and soups when you want the oil's fruity flavor to stand out.

Don't be fooled by "light" or "lite" olive oil. This classification refers to olive oil that is light in color and flavor because it has gone through a filtration process. It contains the same amount of calories as regular olive oil, 120 calories per tablespoon.

Olive oil can become rancid, so purchasing a large bottle is not always a good buy. Store oil in a cool, dark place for up to six months, or up to a year in the refrigerator. Chilled olive oil will become cloudy and difficult to pour, but if the oil is left at room temperature for a short time, it will liquefy.

Other Oils

Almond oil is very low in saturated fats. It's pale brown in color and has an intense aroma. A few drops add lots of flavor to a salad, especially if the salad is sprinkled with a few toasted almond slices.

Hazelnut oil is low in saturated fatty acids. Its amber color and mellow flavor make it a good choice for salad dressings as well as for baking.

Peanut oil is low in saturated fat and high in monounsaturates and polyunsaturates. It has a pale golden color and almost no flavor so it's popular as a frying oil, especially in Asian countries.

Sesame oil has been used by Chinese cooks for ages. Cold-pressed sesame oil is straw colored and almost tasteless and is used for frying. When the oil is made from roasted sesame seeds, the oil is warm brown and has a nutty flavor.

Walnut oil is low in saturated fat and is very perishable, so it should be purchased in small amounts and stored in a cool, dry spot. Walnut oil is a favorite with French cooks, who use it for vinaigrettes. It's golden amber in color and has a decidedly walnut flavor. When cut by half with a flavorless oil and used for sautéing, it imparts a nutty taste to foods.

Substitutions for the Calorie-Conscious

In most salad dressings, you can substitute buttermilk, tomato juice, apple cider, chicken stock, wine, yogurt or puréed cottage cheese for all or part of the oil.

Vinegars

Vinegars vary as widely in flavor as oils or wines, depending on how they are made. But since they are relatively inexpensive, you can afford to have several different kinds on hand. Most have long shelf lives.

White distilled vinegar is made from grains such as corn, rye and barley and has a harsh flavor. It's used mainly for pickling and washing windows.

Fruity *cider* vinegar is produced from fermented apple cider and is probably the most popular all-around vinegar used in this country.

Wine vinegar, made from either red wine, white wine, sherry or Champagne, is mainly used for vinaigrettes and marinades.

Malt vinegar is made from malted barley. It's essential in Britain for fish and chips.

Balsamic vinegar, known in Italy as *aceto balsamico,* gets its dark brown color and pungent sweetness from long aging in wooden barrels, even though it starts out as white Trebbiano grape juice. Use balsamic vinegar in salad dressings and in cooking but use less because its flavor can be overpowering. Try a few drops of balsamic on strawberries.

Herb vinegars can be made at home by steeping fresh herbs in cider or wine vinegar. Use them in dressings and marinades.

Fruit vinegars are made by macerating fresh fruit such as raspberries and blueberries in cider or wine vinegar. Use in dressings, fruit salads and for deglazing pans.

Rice vinegar, which is so popular in Asian cuisine, is made from fermented rice. It has a clean taste and is not as sharp as distilled vinegar. It's used in cucumber salads and in sushi.

Salad Dressing

Like good wine, a dressing improves with age. A salad dressing is a combination of many elements—oil, vinegar, herbs, spices, salt, pepper—and for the best flavor, they need some time to get to know each other. As an experiment, make a dressing, use some of it immediately and set the rest aside, refrigerated, until the next day. Let it come to room temperature, pour it over some greens and taste the difference.

What's an Emulsion?

Mayonnaise is the classic emulsion. It combines elements such as oil and lemon juice that don't usually blend smoothly. Egg is used as the binding agent. Emulsifying has to be done slowly while mixing rapidly. In the case of mayonnaise, the oil is slowly added drop by drop to the egg yolks and lemon juice as they are whisked together. The egg absorbs and holds the fat, and the mixture thickens. Before the days of the food processor and blender, this was done by hand with a fork or a whisk, but with the advent of electrical appliances, emulsifying is as easy as flicking a switch. However, there's a caveat. Because of the danger of salmonella, the U.S. Department of Agriculture does not recommend making homemade mayonnaise with raw eggs.

Basic Vinaigrette

Use whichever vinegar appeals to you: red wine, white wine, or cider. If using balsamic, cut the amount in half. This is a basic or "mother" sauce to many cold sauces.

1¼ cups virgin olive oil

¾ cup vinegar

½ teaspoon freshly ground black
    pepper

¼ teaspoon dry mustard

¼ teaspoon Tabasco

Combine all ingredients in a small bowl and beat with a fork or a whisk to blend. Or place the ingredients in a jar with a tightly fitting lid and shake until they're well blended.

Allow the dressing to sit at room temperature for 24 hours to develop the flavor.

Vinaigrette Dressing II

for Grilled Peppered Fillet of Beef (page 11)

¼ cup olive oil

2 tablespoons balsamic vinegar

1 green olive, chopped

2 cloves Caramelized Garlic
    (page 186)

1 teaspoon dried thyme

½ teaspoon Tabasco.

Combine all ingredients and mix well.

**MAKES
2¼ CUPS**

Herb Vinaigrette

It's time to check the ages of your dried herbs. If they're older than six months, make a quick trip to the market. Buying a fresh supply of dried herbs is still cheaper than buying prepared salad dressings. And they taste a lot better, too.

I recipe Basic Vinaigrette (page 75)

I tablespoon prepared mustard

I teaspoon dried parsley

I teaspoon dried chives

I teaspoon dried basil

I teaspoon dried oregano

I teaspoon dried thyme

I teaspoon dried rosemary

4 cloves Caramelized Garlic

(page 186)

Combine all ingredients in a medium bowl and blend well using a fork or a whisk. Or place ingredients in a jar with a tightly fitting lid and shake until they are well blended.

Allow the dressing to sit at room temperature for 24 hours to develop the flavor.

Know Your Fire

Blue Cheese Vinaigrette

Each blue cheese comes from a different country and its flavor and texture vary according to the molds that form its blue or greenish blue veins. Blue cheese can be imported from Denmark or made in Wisconsin. Gorgonzola comes from Italy, Roquefort from France and Stilton from Great Britain.

If you're used to the taste of store-bought salad dressings, be prepared for the surprise that a homemade dressing with real blue cheese can deliver.

1 tablespoon dried chives	¼ cup heavy cream
1 teaspoon dried parsley	¼ cup crumbled blue cheese, Gor-
1 teaspoon capers or chopped	gonzola, Roquefort or Stilton
green olives	1 recipe Basic Vinaigrette
½ teaspoon lite soy sauce	(page 75)

Combine the chives, parsley, capers, and lite soy sauce with the cream and half the blue cheese and blend well. Add the vinaigrette and stir in the remaining blue cheese. Let the dressing stand at room temperature for a minimum of 1 hour before serving.

Oils and Vinegars

Creamy Blue Cheese Dressing

Salads made with creamy blue cheese dressing can be garnished with toasted walnuts or almonds for more flavor. Low-fat sour cream or plain yogurt can be substituted for the buttermilk. Serve over crisp greens or with roast beef sandwiches on rye bread.

I cup buttermilk

2 tablespoons sour cream, regular
   or low-fat

¼ cup crumbled blue cheese, Gorgonzola, Roquefort or Stilton

2 tablespoons chopped scallions

I teaspoon dry mustard

½ teaspoon Tabasco

Freshly ground black pepper to
   taste

Combine the buttermilk, sour cream and half the blue cheese in a small bowl and blend well with a fork. Add the scallions, dry mustard, Tabasco and black pepper and mix well. Stir in the remaining blue cheese and refrigerate overnight to allow flavors to blend. Let dressing sit at room temperature for 30 minutes before serving.

Thousand Island Dressing

The name Thousand Islands could come from all the bits of sweet pickle, green olive and pimiento floating in the "sea" of dressing or from the belief that it was first served on the Thousand Islands in the St. Lawrence River. Take your pick. You'll want to use this dressing with dark leafy greens or with a sandwich of sliced turkey on pumpernickel bread.

1 cup mayonnaise

2 tablespoons olive oil

2 tablespoons ketchup

1 tablespoon cider vinegar

1 tablespoon chopped sweet pickle
   or pickle relish

1 tablespoon chopped green olive

1 tablespoon chopped pimiento or
   red pepper

1 tablespoon dried parsley

1 tablespoon chopped fresh chives

1 teaspoon prepared mustard

2 cloves Caramelized Garlic
   (page 186)

Combine all the ingredients in a bowl and mix well. Refrigerate dressing 24 hours before serving to allow flavors to blend.

Smoky Ranch Dressing

MAKES
2 CUPS

There is no reason why this should be called ranch dressing, especially since I don't think cowboys ate much salad. Reduce the calories by using low-fat or fat-free sour cream.

1 cup plain unflavored yogurt

½ cup sour cream

Juice of 1 lime

¼ cup seeded, peeled and chopped
   tomato

2 slices bacon, cooked and
   crumbled

2 jalapeño peppers, roasted and
   chopped

1 tablespoon chopped fresh cilantro

1 teaspoon dried thyme

½ teaspoon Tabasco

Combine all the ingredients in a bowl and mix well. Refrigerate dressing 24 hours before serving to allow flavors to blend.

Fruit Dressing

Use Fruit Dressing over cold poached chicken, mesclun greens (see page 117) or even a fruit salad (omitting the garlic, of course).

1 cup apple juice	Juice and zest from 2 lemons
½ cup fruit purée made from soft fruit such as peaches, straw-berries, cherries, etc.	1 tablespoon balsamic vinegar
	1 tablespoon chopped fresh mint
	2 cloves Caramelized garlic
Juice and zest from 1 orange	(page 186)

Combine all ingredients in a nonreactive bowl and mix well. Refrigerate for 24 hours before serving to allow flavors to blend.

Zest The outer skin of citrus fruits (mostly lemons and oranges) without the white pith is called the zest. It contains aromatic oils and adds intense flavor to both sweet and savory dishes. You can remove the zest with a gadget called a zester, a vegetable peeler or a sharp knife. The secret is not to include any of the pith, which can be bitter.

Pasta

Pasta is loosely divided into two categories—dry pasta and fresh pasta.

Dry pasta is made from durum wheat or semolina and water and is machine extruded into long strands of spaghetti, short tubes and special shapes like bow ties and shells. These types work well with spicy, zesty, or olive oil–based sauces.

Although American-made pasta can be very good, the best dry pasta is imported from Italy and has become so popular that nowadays several imported brands are sold in supermarkets. The mark of a good dry pasta is that it's made from 100% durum wheat and it does not become soft and gummy after the sauce has been added. Rather, it should remain al dente, even when it's reheated the next day.

Dry pasta can be stored in a cool, dry spot for several months.

Fresh pasta is made with flour and eggs, and since the eggs allow the pasta to absorb sauces more readily, they are better suited to cream- and butter-based sauces or milder sauces.

Fresh pasta can be homemade or store-bought. Making pasta at home is time-consuming even when using a food processor for mixing the dough and a pasta machine for rolling it out. However, some people prefer its delicate texture and the time used for preparing fresh pasta is made up during cooking because it takes only a minute or two to cook in boiling water.

Whether dry or fresh, the consistency of the sauce determines the shape of pasta to use. If the sauce is thin or contains small pieces of vegetables, it calls for pasta with holes and crevices such as shells, bow ties or radiatori to catch the sauce so that it doesn't slide off. On the other hand, rich sauces, thick with cream or tomatoes, work best with ribbon pasta such as fettuccine or bucatini.

Long thin pasta such as spaghettini or linguine demand sauces such as pesto or aglio e olio, clinging sauces made with olive oil.

Soups call for small pastas called *pastine* such as orzo, acini de pepe or stelline.

Some Common——and Uncommon——Pasta Shapes

Acini de peppe—tiny bits of pasta used in soup; name means peppercorns

Bucatini or perciatelli—spaghetti with a narrow hole down the center

Capellini—very thin pasta strands; also called angel's hair

Conchiglie—medium-size seashells with ridged sides

Ditali—tubes about ¼ to ½ inch wide and ¼ inch long

Farfalle—bow ties or butterflies

Fettuccine—¼-inch-wide flat ribbons

Gemelli—two 2-inch strands of thick spaghetti twisted together; name means twins

Lasagna—2-inch-wide, flat noodle used for classic baked lasagna; the sides can be straight or curled

Linguine—narrow flat ribbons; the name means tongues

Linguine fini—very narrow flat ribbons

Mafalda—1-inch-wide ribbons with 2 rippled edges

Margherita—1-inch-wide ribbons with 1 straight edge and 1 rippled edge

Pappardelle—¾-inch-wide ribbons

Orecchiette—almost flat little discs that resemble ears

Orzo—pasta shaped like rice

Pastina—a star-shaped pasta, often made with egg

Penne or mostaccioli—1-inch-long tubes, ¼-inch-wide, but cut on the slant; means pen and mustache respectively. Sides can be smooth or ridged.

Radiatore—round, 1-inch-long shapes with ridges that resemble the fins in a baseboard radiator

Rigatoni—large, hollow tubes with ridged sides

Rotelle—shaped like wagon-wheels

Spaghettini—thin spaghetti

Tagliatelle—⅓-inch-wide ribbons

Vermicelli—fatter than capellini, but thinner than spaghettini

Ziti—similar to penne but cut straight across

How Large Is a Serving of Pasta?

Although pastaphiles and potential marathon runners might consider 8 to 12 ounces of uncooked pasta to be an adequate serving, most of us can't, or don't want to, consume that much. A serving size is usually determined by whether the pasta is to be an appetizer or an entree. If the pasta is used as an appetizer or first course, a 2- to 3-ounce uncooked portion is sufficient. If the pasta is used as the main course, it's more likely to be a 4- to 6-ounce serving.

Cooking Pasta in Advance

If pasta has to be cooked in advance, it should be slightly underdone, drained well and tossed with a few tablespoons of olive oil to prevent it from sticking. When ready to serve, heat the sauce in a pan, add the pasta and cook until heated through, stirring constantly.

How to Keep Pasta from Sticking While Cooking

The secret to keeping pasta from sticking is to use plenty of boiling water—at least 4 quarts to a pound of pasta—and stir it occasionally while it's cooking. Adding oil to the pot doesn't work because the oil and water don't mix.

How Much Sauce Is Needed for One Pound of Pasta?

Americans tend to sauce their pasta heavily, using as much as a quart of tomato sauce to 1 pound of pasta. Italians tend to use less sauce, certainly never more than 3 cups to a pound, and there is never a pool of sauce left in the bottom of the dish. But the amount of sauce depends on personal taste.

What Is the Correct Way to Eat Ribbon Pasta?

To eat long pasta, pick up a few strands with the tines of a fork and lift them about 6 inches above the dish to separate them from all the others. Then press the tip of the fork against the side of the dish and rotate the fork until all the pasta is rolled up.

Some pasta eaters will lift the pasta with one hand and twirl it against a tablespoon held in the other.

Whichever way you decide to eat your pasta, never cut it up into small pieces. Only children are permitted to do that.

Angel Hair Pasta with Smoked Salmon

Angel hair pasta cooks in about 2 minutes and, if you overcook it, you have a starchy tangle on your hands. You may want to cook the sauce first so that the pasta is hot when the sauce is added. Use smoked salmon rather than lox because lox is too salty.

If you love cream cheese and lox, you'll love this dish.

I pound angel hair pasta

2 tablespoons olive oil

I cup heavy cream or half-and-half

I cup seeded and chopped plum
   tomatoes

4 ounces thinly sliced smoked
   salmon, cut into strips

¼ cup chopped scallions

2 tablespoons sliced black olives

I tablespoon chopped fresh parsley

¼ cup sour cream

Cook the pasta according to package directions, taking care not to overcook it. Drain the pasta.

Preheat a sauté pan over high heat. Add the olive oil and when it's hot, add the heavy cream, tomatoes, and half the smoked salmon. Bring to a boil, lower the heat, add the scallions, olives, and parsley and simmer 2 minutes. Stir in the sour cream and the remaining smoked salmon, toss lightly and serve immediately.

Pasta

Orzo and Peas

This recipe is inspired by a Venetian specialty combining rice and peas called risi-bisi. Orzo, a rice-shaped pasta, is substituted for the rice.

1 pound orzo

2 tablespoons olive oil

1 onion, chopped

6 cloves Caramelized Garlic
(page 186)

1 cup tomato sauce, canned or
homemade

1 teaspoon fresh mint

½ teaspoon Tabasco

Freshly ground black pepper to
taste

1 cup frozen green peas, defrosted

2 tablespoons grated Parmesan
cheese

Cook the orzo according to package directions.

Heat the olive oil in a sauté pan over high heat. Add the onion and garlic and cook 3 to 4 minutes. Add the tomato sauce, mint, Tabasco, and black pepper, bring to a boil, lower the heat, and simmer 5 minutes. Add the peas and cook 5 minutes longer. Toss with the hot orzo, sprinkle with the Parmesan, and serve.

Know Your Fire

Cavatelli with Hot Sausage and Broccoli Rabe

Cavatelli are short, narrow curled pasta that come fresh, frozen or dry
and are traditionally coupled with sausage. Despite its bitter flavor,
broccoli rabe is fast becoming a favorite American green. To cook broccoli rabe, trim and discard the stem ends, peel any thick stems, cut into
2-inch pieces, cook in boiling water until tender, about 5 minutes, and
drain well.

1 pound cavatelli, fresh, frozen or dry	6 cloves Caramelized Garlic (page 186)
½ pound hot Italian sausage, removed from casing	1 cup chicken stock
2 tablespoons olive oil, optional	1 teaspoon chopped fresh rosemary
½ onion, chopped	1 cup cooked broccoli rabe
	Parmesan cheese shavings

Cook the cavatelli according to package directions. Drain well and keep
warm.

Heat a sauté pan over high heat, add the sausage meat, using the olive oil
if the sausage is lean. Cook the sausage until brown, breaking apart the clumps
with a wooden spoon. Add the onion and garlic and cook 2 minutes. Add the
chicken stock and rosemary and bring to a boil. Add the broccoli rabe, reduce
heat and simmer 5 minutes. Mix the sauce with the cooked cavatelli and toss
well. Top with shaved Parmesan cheese.

How to keep pasta warm If you're going to use the pasta within 5 minutes,
cook it until it's almost al dente and take the pot off the heat, but don't drain it
until you're ready to add the sauce. You can also heat a metal bowl with hot
water, drain out the water and place the pasta in the hot bowl and cover it. Or
you can drain the pasta in a colander and, when the sauce is ready, combine the
pasta with the hot sauce and cook them together until the pasta is hot.

Pasta

**MAKES
4 SERVINGS**

Cheese Ravioli with Pine Nuts and Basil

Using sheets of prepared fresh pasta dough or wonton skins, which are almost universally available in specialty stores and in many supermarkets, makes ravioli shaping a snap. Set everything out on the table or counter and make it a production line assembly.

FOR FILLING

1 cup ricotta

¼ cup grated Parmesan cheese

4 cloves Caramelized Garlic
   (page 186)

2 tablespoons pine nuts

1 tablespoon chopped fresh basil

Pinch ground nutmeg

Freshly ground black pepper to
   taste

1 pound fresh pasta sheets or 100
   wonton wrappers

Semolina or corn meal

Grilled Tomato Sauce (page 131)

For the filling: Combine the ricotta, Parmesan, garlic, basil, pine nuts, nutmeg and black pepper in a medium bowl and mix well.

For the ravioli: If using pasta sheets, roll 2 out at a time on a lightly floured surface until you can see your hand through the pasta, about ⅟₁₆-inch thick. Cover one of the two sheets with damp paper toweling so that it doesn't dry out.

Place teaspoons of the filling on the other sheet of pasta, spacing them so that each is in the center of a 2- by 2-inch square. (You may wish to draw a grid on the pasta with the blunt side of a knife. Using a brush or your finger, dampen the grid with water. Top with the second sheet of pasta and press down *between* the fillings to seal the ravioli. Cut out the ravioli with a round fluted cutter or a sharp knife.

If using wonton skins, make individual ravioli by using 1 skin for the bottom and another for the top. Place a teaspoon of filling on the bottom skin, brush the edges with water, top with the second skin and cut along the edge with a fluted cutter or a knife.

Dust each ravioli with cornmeal or semolina to prevent sticking during the cooking process.

In a large pot, bring water to a boil and cook the ravioli gently until they are al dente, about 5 minutes. Serve with your favorite tomato sauce.

Know Your Fire

88

Pasta with Broccoli and Caramelized Garlic

Broccoli is one of the cruciferous vegetables that researchers believe reduces your risks of cancer. It's also loaded with vitamin C. This zesty preparation is sure to wake up your taste buds and make a good side dish.

I pound pasta such as penne or ziti, cooked

I bunch broccoli (2 large or 3 small stems)

2 tablespoons olive oil

I head Caramelized Garlic (page 186)

¼ cup white wine

Juice and zest from I lemon

¼ teaspoon hot pepper flakes, or to taste

Freshly ground black pepper to taste

Grated Parmigiano Reggiano

Cook the pasta according to package directions.

Cut off the florets from the broccoli, peel the stems and slice ¼-inch thick. Fill a medium stockpot with water and bring to a boil. Add the broccoli and cook until al dente, about 5 minutes. Drain well.

Heat a medium sauté pan over high heat. Add the olive oil and when it's hot add the garlic and cook 1 minute. Add the drained broccoli, white wine, lemon juice and zest, hot pepper flakes and black pepper and cook 1 minute, stirring frequently. (Use caution when adding the broccoli. It will be wet and when it hits the hot oil, it may spatter.) Place the broccoli mixture in a large bowl, add the cooked pasta and toss lightly. Sprinkle with Parmigiano Reggiano and serve at once.

Pasta

Potatoes

The Potato, a Powerhouse of Nutrition

The fruitful potato is ready for harvest in 90 to 120 days and gets high marks for nutrition. One medium potato contains only 118 calories and is virtually free from both fat and salt. Boiled in its skin, the potato contains 3 grams protein, 2 grams of dietary fiber, 27 grams carbohydrate, vitamin C, B_6 and a host of minerals. Since many of its nutrients are stored directly below the skin, whenever possible, eat potatoes with the skins on.

Choosing the Best Potatoes for the Job

Although some varieties of potatoes are labeled "all purpose," many cooks prefer one potato over another. After all, we use different types of apples and tomatoes, so why be limited to one type of potato.

Potatoes come in four basic varieties: russet, long white, round white and round red. Most potatoes taste the same. Their difference is mainly in their texture and color. When you cut into a potato and the knife sticks, it's because the potato is high in starch.

Russet potatoes are brown and rough with a scaly and netted skin. They are best used when you want potatoes to keep their shape when fried or sautéed. Russets are low in moisture and have a high starch content, making them excellent for baking and mashing. However, when mashed in a food processor, they tend to become gluey.

Russet Burbanks, the original potato developed by Luther Burbank, are chiefly grown in Idaho. When this variety of potato is grown outside Idaho, it's called a russet.

Long whites are light buff in color, thin skinned and waxy. They are good for frying and make perfect potato salad because they do not break apart when boiled.

Round whites are brown in color, round or elliptical in shape and are often called boiling potatoes. They have less starch and more moisture and are best for mashing or in soups or stews when you want a mealy potato.

Round reds are red-skinned and good for boiling or in potato salads.

"New" potatoes are not a variety of potato but small, immature potatoes of any variety with a papery skin that come to market directly from harvesting and skip storage altogether. They can be boiled or roasted whole.

"Colored" potatoes such as *Yukon gold* and purple *Peruvian* potatoes have become popular recently. When Yukon golds are mashed, their yellow color gives the illusion that they're prepared with lots of butter. When Peruvian purples are cooked, they add a faint purplish blue color to the plate.

Storage

When potatoes are stored in the refrigerator, the starch turns to sugar and they tend to become sweet and will turn brown after cooking. Store your potatoes above 50 degrees, where there is good air circulation.

When immature potatoes are exposed to light, a green tinge caused by alkaloid solanine will develop on the surface. If eaten, this portion of the potato can cause discomfort in the digestive tract, but once this bitter section is discarded, the potato is safe to consume.

Recommended Cooking Techniques

To boil potatoes: Any type of potato can be boiled, but if you're making potato salad you would choose a potato that will keep its shape such as round red or long white; if you want to mash it, use an all-purpose potato. If the potatoes are destined to be mashed, start them in cold water so that they cook more evenly. (Otherwise add the potatoes to boiling water.) Leave the skins on. When the potatoes are cool enough to handle, remove the skins unless you want to mash them, skin and all.

To fry potatoes: Wash 4 to 6 russet potatoes and peel, if desired. Slice lengthwise into ¼-inch slices. Stack slices and cut lengthwise into ¼-inch fingers. Soak in cold water for 20 minutes. Remove and wipe dry. Heat vegetable oil to 350°F 1-inch deep in a skillet and fry the potatoes, a few at a time, for 4 to 5 minutes. Remove and drain on paper towel. Just before serving, reheat the oil to 390°F and fry the potatoes a second time until they are crisp and golden brown. Drain well on paper towel and sprinkle with salt. A thermometer or electric deep fryer is critical for determining the correct temperature.

To microwave potatoes: Wash potatoes and pat dry. Prick the surface in several places with a fork or make ½-inch slits with a sharp paring knife. Place the potatoes in the microwave oven and cook on high allowing 4 minutes for one potato, 7 to 9 minutes for 2 potatoes and 11 to 13 minutes for 4 potatoes. Reverse potatoes halfway through the cooking period, unless your microwave has a turntable. Let stand 3 minutes after they're removed from the microwave.

To bake potatoes: Wash russet potatoes and pat dry. Prick the surface in several places with a fork or make ½-inch slits with a sharp paring knife to allow moisture to escape. Omitting this step could result in a potato literally exploding like popcorn. Rub potatoes with melted butter or olive oil and season with salt and pepper. This keeps the skin soft and helps control shrinkage. Bake the potatoes in a 500°F oven for 15 minutes, lower the temperature to 400°F and cook until done, from 35 to 45 minutes, depending on their size. Test for doneness by squeezing a potato gently with a towel or inserting a sharp paring knife in the center. There should be no resistance. Never bake a potato in aluminum foil; it will be steamed, not baked.

To roast potatoes: Peel 2 to 3 pounds of potatoes, cut into 1-inch pieces, place them in a saucepan and cover with water. Bring to a boil and cook 2 minutes. Drain well and place in a large greased baking pan. Add 2 to 3 tablespoons of olive oil and toss gently. Place the pan in a 375°F oven and cook approximately 45 minutes, turning the potatoes 3 or 4 times with a pancake turner. To brown the potatoes, raise the heat to 500°F for the last 15 minutes. Season with salt and pepper and serve. These potatoes will come out crispier if they're not crowded in the pan.

Perfect Mashed Potatoes

This is the quintessential potato recipe, but by all means be creative and add your favorite spices or other embellishments. It can only get better. Mashing the potatoes with their skins on increases their nutritive value. (When potatoes are placed in cold water and brought to a boil, they cook more evenly throughout than when placed in boiling water.)

10 medium new potatoes, about
   2½ pounds, well scrubbed

2 slices bacon, chopped

4 tablespoons butter

¼ cup chopped scallions

1 head Caramelized Garlic
   (page 186)

1 cup heavy cream

½ teaspoon Tabasco

Dash ground nutmeg

Finely ground black pepper to taste

2 tablespoons grated Parmesan
   cheese

1 tablespoon chopped fresh parsley

1 tablespoon chopped fresh chives

Place the potatoes in a large pot and cover them with water. Bring the water to a boil, lower the heat to a simmer and cook the potatoes until very tender, about 25 to 30 minutes.

While the potatoes are simmering, cook the bacon over medium heat in a large skillet. Leaving any drippings in the pan, remove the bacon, drain on paper towel, and crumble. Add the butter, scallions and garlic to the skillet and, when the butter melts, add the cream, Tabasco, nutmeg and black pepper and heat until very hot.

Mash the potatoes with their skins on. Add the hot cream mixture, Parmesan cheese, parsley and chives and beat with an electric mixer or by hand until smooth and creamy. Of, if you like, leave in some lumps. Garnish with the cooked bacon.

Potatoes

Potato and Rutabaga Mash

The much ignored rutabaga deserves better. After tasting it in this adaptation of mashed potatoes, you'll like it so much you'll want to prepare it alone because rutabagas have the same creamy texture as potatoes. Rutabagas are available year-round, but this member of the cabbage family is best from July through April.

3 russet potatoes, peeled and
    cubed
1 rutabaga, peeled and cubed
3 tablespoons melted butter
¼ cup hot half-and-half or milk

¼ teaspoon Tabasco
Pinch ground nutmeg
Pinch freshly ground black pepper
½ cup chopped **Caramelized Onion**
    (page 238)

Place the potatoes in a medium saucepan, cover with cold water, and bring to a boil, cooking until tender, about 20 minutes, and drain well. In a separate pot, cook the rutabaga in boiling water until tender, about 25 minutes, and drain well. Mash the potatoes and the rutabaga together, add the melted butter, half-and-half, Tabasco, nutmeg and black pepper and mix well. Stir in the caramelized onion and serve.

Gnocchi

MAKES 4 SERVINGS

These Italian dumplings are served like pasta. Dress them with Chicken Livers in Tomato Sauce (page 47), Ham and Mushroom Sauce (page 132), Pesto (page 133) or with a mixture of ¼ cup melted butter combined with ¼ cup grated Parmesan cheese.

The gnocchi can be flavored with 2 tablespoons finely chopped basil, or 2 tablespoons tomato puree and 2 tablespoons chopped sun-dried tomatoes, or ¼ cup toasted, chopped walnuts.

1 pound russet or baking potatoes, peeled and cut into cubes	Freshly ground black pepper to taste
½ cup all-purpose flour	Pinch ground nutmeg
1 egg, lightly beaten	

In a pot of lightly salted water, boil the cubed potatoes until tender, about 20 minutes. Drain the potatoes and mash using a ricer or heavy-duty mixer. There should be no lumps.

Add the flour, egg, black pepper and nutmeg and mix well. Turn mixture out onto a lightly floured surface and knead until the mixture forms a smooth dough. Divide into 4 portions and roll each portion into a ½-inch rope with the flat of your hand. Cut into 1-inch lengths, and press down in the center of each piece with your thumb until the ends curl up slightly.

Heat a large pot of water to a rolling boil. Add the gnocchi, a few at a time so they do not crowd, and cook until they rise to the surface and are tender, about 5 minutes. Drain and serve with one of the sauces suggested above.

Potatoes

Pierogi

Many cuisines feature stuffed dough specialties. Italians make ravioli, the Chinese make wontons, and the Polish make pierogi, a half-moon dumpling stuffed with mushrooms, potatoes or cheese. In this version, the stuffing is sauerkraut. The potatoes that go into the dough should be baked, as boiling will render them too moist.

DOUGH

I pound (2 to 3) russet potatoes

I cup all-purpose flour plus additional for rolling dough

I egg, lightly beaten

I teaspoon chopped chives

Pinch of ground nutmeg

Freshly ground black pepper to taste

FILLING

I tablespoon olive oil

½ onion, chopped

4 cloves garlic, chopped

I tablespoon all-purpose flour

I teaspoon sweet paprika

½ cup canned sauerkraut, rinsed and drained well

Pinch of ground nutmeg

Freshly ground black pepper

GARNISH

½ cup butter, melted, and ½ cup toasted bread crumbs

Wash the potatoes and pat dry. Prick them on all sides with a fork or the point of a sharp paring knife. Bake the potatoes until tender in a 350°F oven, about 1 hour. While the potatoes are still warm, remove the skins and mash potatoes in a ricer or through a strainer. In a large bowl mix the potatoes with the flour, egg, chives, nutmeg and pepper until a smooth dough is formed. Set dough aside.

To make the filling, heat a saucepan on high and add the oil. When the oil is hot, add the onion and garlic and cook 30 seconds. Stir in the flour and paprika and lower the heat. Add the sauerkraut, nutmeg and black pepper and mix well. Cook 1 minute, remove from heat and cool to room temperature.

On a lightly floured surface, roll out the dough ⅛-inch thick. Cut out circles using a round 3-inch cookie cutter and place a scant teaspoon of the filling in the center of each. Moisten the edge of the dough with water, fold in half and, using a fork, seal the edges. Bring a large pot of water or stock to a rolling boil and gently slip the pierogi into the pot a few at a time. Remove them as soon as they float to the surface and drain well. Place the pierogi on a serving platter. Pour the melted butter over them and sprinkle with the bread crumbs.

Rice/Grains/Beans

Simply put, carbohydrates are sugars and starches, the fuel the body runs on. Complex carbohydrates are polysaccharides, an elaborate chain of glucose molecules combined with dietary fiber, vitamins and minerals that digest slowly. All carbohydrates have 4 calories per gram. Complex carbohydrates, which take longer to digest, are found in potatoes, pasta, rice and other grains, beans and peas. Carbohydrates fill you up and curb your appetite. According to the USDA food pyramid, Americans should be consuming 55 to 60 percent of their calories in carbohydrates.

Rice——It Feeds the World

The story of rice is as old as civilization itself. Some archeologists claim that rice has been consumed for over 5,000 years. Even today almost half the world's population uses rice as its number one food. Annual consumption worldwide is 143 pounds per capita, but in Southeast Asia it's 300 pounds. In fact, the United States exports two-thirds of its production to more than 100 countries.

Different Types of Rice and Their Uses

It's hard to believe that there are over 40,000 different varieties of rice grown in the world today. Rice kernels are either long, medium or short and each of these groups comes in both white and brown.

Long-Grain rice is four to five times longer than it's wide. When cooked, the grains are separate and fluffy. Long-grain rice is all-purpose rice and the most popular type in this country. Carolina brand rice is an example of long-grain rice.

Medium rice is short and plump. Cooked grains are moist and tender and have a tendency to cling together. Use medium rice for risotto, molds and dessert when you want the rice to be sticky.

Short-grain rice is rich in amylopectin, a starch that tenderizes the grains and at the same time makes them sticky. This type of rice is sold in Asian and Hispanic markets and is a favorite accompaniment to sushi.

Parboiled rice or *converted* rice is white long-grain rice that has been soaked, pressed, steamed and dried before milling. Once cooked, the grains are separate and never sticky. Uncle Ben's is one brand of converted rice.

Brown rice is the entire rice grain with the inedible outer husk removed. Because it still contains the nutritious, high-fiber bran, brown rice is likely to become rancid if stored longer than 6 months. However, the uncooked grains can be refrigerated, or even frozen, for longer storage.

Waxy rice, also called sweet or glutinous rice, is short, plump and chalky white. Once cooked, it loses it shape and becomes very sticky. Its starch and flour are used as a binder for frozen gravies and sauces because they do not break down after freezing and thawing.

Aromatic rices are long-grain types that give off an aroma similar to nuts or popcorn as they cook. "Wild pecan" rice and "popcorn" rice, both grown in Louisiana, are available in limited quantities.

Basmati rice is a curved, long-grain aromatic variety originating in India. A favorite with curries, basmati rice is frequently aged for a year to improve its flavor. A form of basmati rice called Texmati is successfully grown in Texas, and Wehani, a hybrid of basmati and brown rice with a nutty flavor and aroma, is cultivated in California.

Short fat grains of *arborio* rice, from the Piedmont and Lombardy areas of Italy, are used chiefly for making risotto. Arborio rice is often sold in 1-pound cloth bags.

Although it is called rice, *wild* rice is not a true rice, but an aquatic grass grown in Minnesota, Canada and, most recently, California. It's chewy, dark brown and nutty in flavor. It has become much more affordable in recent years thanks to expanded cultivation and the development of more efficient harvesting methods. Depending on how long it's been in storage, wild rice can take up to 1 hour to cook.

"Instant rice" began life as real rice but it has been cooked and pressed through a machine that reforms it back into the shape of rice so that when water is added it will plump up and resemble rice in flavor and texture. It doesn't.

How to Cook Rice

Every country has its own surefire way of cooking rice, and it all has to do with the ratio of rice to water.

The Chinese like to rinse rice until the water runs clear, then simmer it in twice the volume of water, tightly covered, for about 18 minutes. The Japanese boil rice in a covered pot for 10 minutes, simmer it for 10 minutes longer and then leave it off the heat for 10 minutes. In Singapore, you are apt to find rice boiled in three to four times its volume of water for 12 minutes, drained and dried out in the oven. Indians generally cook rice for 20 minutes before rinsing it in cold water. Italians cook rice like pasta, in large amounts of rapidly boiling water.

Adding ½ teaspoon salt and a tablespoon of butter or margarine to the pot is optional. Instead of cooking it in water, you can add a lot of flavor to rice by using beef or chicken stock, water left over from cooking vegetables, diluted tomato juice, unsweetened coconut juice, even clam broth, depending on what the rice is going to be served with.

The timing depends on the shape of the pot, how tightly the lid is secured and the age of the rice. Even altitude can affect the cooking time. If you always make your rice in the same pot, you will soon have it down to a science.

	LIQUID	COOKING TIME	YIELD
I cup long-grain rice	1¾ cups	15–18 minutes	3 cups
I cup medium or short-grain rice	1½ cups	15 minutes	3 cups
I cup brown rice	2–2½ cups	35–45 minutes	3–4 cups
I cup parboiled rice	2–2½ cups	20–22 minutes	3–4 cups
I cup wild rice	3 cups	30–60 minutes	2 cups

Grains

Wonderful dishes can be made with grains, a staple of the vegetarian diet. They don't contain saturated fat or cholesterol, so they're a healthy way of getting protein. And they're inexpensive, so they help the pocketbook. Grains may seem a bit exotic to us but they're "meat and potatoes" in many parts of the world.

Barley and Bulghur

Some historians believe that barley is the world's oldest cultivated grain and surely there wouldn't be a Scotch whisky or beer industry without it. Most barley sold today has been "pearlized," which means that the nutrient-rich husk is removed and the grains are steamed and polished. Barley is sold in small-, medium-, and large-pearl sizes and used chiefly in soups and stews.

Bulghur

Bulghur or bulghur wheat is whole wheat kernels that have been steamed, dried and crushed. It is often mistaken for cracked wheat. This nutritious Middle Eastern staple is tender and chewy and comes in coarse, medium and fine grinds. Bulghur is already cooked and only has to be soaked in boiling water for 10 minutes to make it edible, allowing 2 cups water to 1 cup bulghur. It is used to make Middle Eastern dishes like tabbouleh and kibbeh.

Cracked wheat is whole wheat berries broken into coarse, medium and fine particles. It is used in pilafs, breads or cooked as cereal. It has a strong and distinctive grainy flavor and is often mixed with other grains and starches to add a contrasting texture and flavor. It is high in fiber.

Couscous

Couscous is granular semolina popular in Northern Africa and parts of the Middle East. To cook, either steam the tiny pale yellow couscous grains or soak in a hot liquid. It can be used in salad, as a substitute for rice and as a porridge. Couscous is also the name of a dish that is prepared in many parts of the Mediterranean and, depending on the area, includes lamb, fish or vegetables.

Beans

The dried bean is more than just a passing fancy. With the rapid growth of ethnic restaurants around the country, beans are no longer considered "poor man's food." Beans are full of soluble fiber, an excellent source of protein and iron and rich in vitamins, potassium and calcium, low in fat, and they contain no cholesterol. And there are about 10,000 varieties, so you can never become bored with beans.

Buy dried beans in stores such as ethnic markets where beans are a way of life and turnover is constant. The color should be bright. A dull finish indicates the bean has been sitting on the shelf for a long time. Look for beans of approximately the same size so that they cook evenly.

Store beans in an airtight container. They have a shelf life of about one year. Old beans should not be mixed with a new batch because the older the bean the longer it takes to cook.

Dried beans have a better texture and a better flavor than canned beans, which tend to be overcooked. Some brands are better than others, so try different brands until you find one that's best.

To Soak or Not to Soak

Dried beans should be soaked to soften them, to prevent their skins from splitting, to shorten cooking time and to leach out the indigestible sugars that cause bloating and gas.

The only beans that should not be soaked are dried split peas and lentils.

Before soaking, the beans should be rinsed in cold water and examined for bits of foreign matter. For long soaking, place the beans in a bowl and cover with water, about four times their volume. Set aside for 7 to 8 hours. Drain the beans, rinse in clear water, and proceed with recipe using fresh water.

If you don't have the time, try this short soak method: Place the beans in a medium saucepan and cover with water. Bring to a boil, and boil 2 minutes. Cover the beans, remove from the heat, and set aside for 1 hour. Drain off the water, rinse the beans, and proceed with the recipe using fresh water.

Never add salt or baking soda to the soaking or cooking water. Salt causes the skins to split and baking soda will make them mushy.

Some of the More Popular Kinds of Beans

Black beans—small, shiny black kidney-shaped beans about ⅝ inch long with an earthy mushroomlike flavor. Black beans, also known as *turtle beans,* are used chiefly in Latin American and Southwestern cuisine.

Black-eyed peas—creamy in color with a purplish black dot on the keel, these ½-inch, kidney-shaped beans have a buttery smooth texture. Also called *cow peas* or *purple eyes,* they are frequently found in Southern cuisine and in African dishes.

Cannellini beans—oval, white, ½-inch-long beans with a smooth creamy texture and a nutty flavor. Also known as *haricot blanc* or *white kidney beans,* cannellini beans are used extensively in Italian dishes.

Chick peas—buff-colored, round, firm-textured beans, which are about ⅜ of an inch in diameter. Also called *garbanzo* or *ceci,* chick peas are very popular in Mediterranean and Middle Eastern cooking.

Cranberry beans—dried cranberry beans are tannish pink with beige spots but turn a pinkish brown when cooked. These plump, oval, ½-inch beans, sweet and nutty in flavor, are popular in Italian dishes.

Great Northern beans—mild with a slightly mealy texture, Great Northern beans are small and oval, and about ½-inch long. They're used for soup and bean casseroles.

Kidney beans—these ½-inch beans come in three colors: the *red kidney bean* is the one we know from Southwestern chili; *pink kidney beans* are used in New Orleans rice and beans and the *white kidney bean* is the cannellini bean used in Italian cuisine.

Lentils—round, flat and small (about ¼ inch in diameter) lentils come in green, brown and red (really orange) and their history goes back to the Bible when Esau sold his birthright for a dish of lentils. They cook fairly quickly and tend to disintegrate when overcooked.

Pinto beans—the name comes from the bean's resemblance to a pinto pony—beige with streaks of brown. Pintos, about ⅜ inch long, have a mealy texture and are popular in Mexican and South American cooking. They're also called *appaloosa beans* or *Mexican strawberries.*

Split peas—both yellow and green split peas are small in size, only ¼ inch. Once they are husked and dried, they actually split in half. Split peas are used mostly in soups.

MAKES 4 SERVINGS

Arancini or Rice Balls

In Italy these rice balls are called arancini, or little oranges. These are stuffed with mozzarella and ham and make a nice addition to a hot antipasto. Long-grain rice may be used, but arborio rice is traditional.

3 cups cooked rice, cooled

2 eggs, lightly beaten

I teaspoon chopped fresh basil

½ cup mozzarella, cut into ½-inch
    cubes

¼ cup smoked ham, cut into
    ¼-inch cubes

I cup dry bread crumbs

Vegetable oil for frying

Spicy Tomato Sauce (page 69)

Combine the rice, eggs and basil in a medium bowl and mix well.

Take a heaping tablespoon of rice and place it in the palm of your hand. Place a piece of mozzarella and ham in the center of the rice and top with another tablespoon of rice. Press the rice together with both hands and roll into a ball.

Roll the rice balls in the bread crumbs, covering them on all sides, and refrigerate 1 hour.

Fill a deep fat fryer or deep skillet with 2 to 3 inches of vegetable oil and heat to 375°F. Fry the rice balls a few at a time until they are golden on all sides. Remove, drain on paper towels and keep warm until all are cooked. Serve with Spicy Tomato Sauce.

Tomato Risotto

A classic risotto calls for olive oil or butter and Parmesan cheese. The resulting fat count can prevent those who are counting calories from enjoying this Italian rice specialty. In this version, wine is used in place of the fat, and the vegetables, sage, nutmeg, and tomato juice add to its richness. This labor-intensive dish requires continuous attention at the stove until the rice becomes tender and creamy, but it's well worth the effort. Add the stock and juice slowly so that the rice has the opportunity to absorb them in stages. The risotto can be finished off with a sprinkling of low-fat cheese, if you wish.

Some people like their risotto soupy, yet others do not want to see any liquid around the edges. If you like it wet, add all the chicken broth. If you like it on the dry side, start with 1¼ cups chicken broth before adding the tomato juice. Then add as much chicken broth as it takes to reach the correct consistency.

¼ cup dry white wine	1¾ cups hot chicken stock (page 188)
½ onion, chopped fine	1 teaspoon chopped fresh sage or
¼ cup finely chopped carrot	¼ teaspoon dried sage
4 cloves Caramelized Garlic	Pinch dried nutmeg
(page 186)	Freshly ground black pepper
1 cup arborio rice	1 cup tomato juice

Pour the wine into a medium nonstick skillet and bring to a boil over medium heat. Add the onion, carrot and garlic and simmer gently for 5 minutes, stirring frequently. There will be very little, if any, liquid left in the skillet. Add the arborio rice and cook, stirring constantly, for 2 to 3 minutes. The mixture will be dry, but the rice will pick up flavor as the kernels dry roast in the pan.

Add the hot stock ¼ cup at a time and cook, stirring constantly, until the liquid is absorbed by the rice. Season with the sage, nutmeg and black pepper. Begin adding the tomato juice ¼ cup at a time and cook until the risotto is creamy yet the grains remain separate and firm. The total cooking time can range from 20 to 30 minutes.

Rice/Grains/Beans

Arborio Croquettes

The first portion of this recipe makes a classic risotto, the traditional Italian rice dish so popular in the northern part of that country.

Make your own bread crumbs at home using a hand grater, a food processor or blender. Use fresh or day-old bread to make fresh, or soft, bread crumbs. To make dry bread crumbs, toast the bread in a 350°F oven until dry. Although any bread—white, whole wheat, rye— can be used to make bread crumbs, Italian and French bread make the best.

THE RICE

2 tablespoons olive oil

¼ small onion, chopped

I carrot, chopped

I rib celery, chopped

6 cloves Caramelized Garlic
   (page 186)

2 tablespoons pignoli or pine nuts

I cup arborio rice

I¾ to 2 cups hot chicken stock

¼ cup heavy cream

3 tablespoons grated Parmesan
   cheese

To make the rice: Heat a large sauté pan and heat the olive oil. Add the onion, carrot, celery and garlic and cook over medium high heat until the onion is translucent, about 5 minutes. Add the pignoli nuts and cook 30 seconds. Add the arborio rice and cook 2 minutes, stirring occasionally. Add ¼ cup of the chicken stock, stirring constantly. When the rice has absorbed the stock, add another quarter cup and so on until the stock has been used up and the rice is creamy. This will take about 20 to 25 minutes. After 15 minutes of cooking, add the cream and the Parmesan cheese. When the rice is done, it should be tender, yet al dente. Refrigerate the rice until it's well chilled.

THE CROQUETTES

¼ cup fresh bread crumbs

3 ounces prosciutto, thinly chopped

I egg, lightly beaten

I tablespoon chopped fresh basil

½ teaspoon Tabasco

Pinch ground nutmeg

Freshly ground black pepper to
   taste

To make the croquettes: combine all the ingredients with the chilled rice and mix well

Know Your Fire

TO COOK THE CROQUETTES

½ cup flour seasoned with black
   pepper, nutmeg, and cayenne
   pepper

3 eggs, lightly beaten

2 cups dried bread crumbs

Vegetable oil for frying

Using a medium-size ice cream scoop, pick up some rice mixture and pack it hard into the scoop. Release it into the seasoned flour and roll it so that it's completely covered in the seasoned flour. You can keep the round shape or form the croquettes into ovals. Dip them into the egg and then into the bread crumbs.

Pour several inches of oil in a deep fryer or skillet and heat to 360°F. Fry the croquettes until light brown on all sides and drain well on paper towels. If making the croquettes in advance, heat them in a 375°F oven until warm, about 10 minutes.

MAKES 6 SERVINGS

Two-Rice Pilaf

Combining expensive wild rice with less expensive long-grain rice stretches the budget. Also, the strong flavor of the dark wild rice is tempered by the subtler taste of the white rice. This is a great side dish to serve with duck or grilled meats.

2 tablespoons butter or margarine	3 tablespoons pecans, toasted
½ onion, chopped	1 teaspoon dried parsley
½ cup wild rice	½ cup long-grain rice
2½ cups stock	
1 teaspoon fresh thyme or ½ teaspoon dried thyme	

Heat a medium saucepan with a tight-fitting cover and melt the butter. Add the onion and sauté until transparent, 4 to 5 minutes. Add the wild rice and cook 1 minute, stirring constantly. Add the stock, thyme, pecans and parsley and bring to a boil. Then lower heat and cook 20 minutes. Stir in the long-grain rice, cover and simmer until the rices are tender, about 20 minutes longer.

Know Your Fire

Wild Rice Pilaf

A pilaf is a method of preparing rice that originated in the MIddle and Far East. The traditional pilaf (from the Turkish) is spiced and usually includes vegetables.

The somber brown color of the wild rice is brightened by the sweet potato in this original version of a classic pilaf. Sweetened with the apple, this is a good accompaniment for pork, chicken or duck.

2 tablespoons butter	½ cup chopped pecans
½ onion, chopped	2½ cups chicken stock
¼ cup chopped celery	I Granny Smith apple, peeled,
I sweet potato, peeled and diced	cored and chopped
very small	I tablespoon chopped fresh sage
I cup wild rice	½ teaspoon Tabasco

Melt the butter in a sauté pan. Add the onion and celery and cook until the vegetables are translucent, about 5 minutes. Add the sweet potato and cook until it's light brown. Add the wild rice and pecans and cook, stirring constantly, 2 minutes. Stir in the stock, apple, sage and Tabasco. Bring to a boil, lower heat, cover and simmer until the rice is tender, about 35 to 40 minutes.

**MAKES 6
SERVINGS**

Wild Rice Salad

Toasting the almonds increases their flavor. To toast almonds, place them in a single layer in an ovenproof dish and cook in a 350°F oven for about 5 to 8 minutes.

I cup wild rice, cooked and chilled
   (2 cups cooked)
½ cup long-grain rice, cooked and
   chilled (1 ½ cups cooked)
I cup green peas, cooked
I plum tomato, peeled, seeded and
   chopped

I cup Thousand Island Dressing,
   (page 79)
2 tablespoons sliced almonds,
   toasted
2 tablespoons chopped scallions

Combine the wild rice, long-grain rice, green peas, tomato and Thousand Island Dressing and mix well. Place in a serving bowl and top with the almonds and scallions.

Ginger Bulghur Pilaf

Tofu is a popular ingredient in Asian cooking. Very rich in vegetable protein, it is now widely available in many supermarkets in sealed or aseptic packaging. Tofu is quite neutral in taste, readily picking up the flavors of the other foods and spices while adding a fine texture, as well as nutritive value, to the dish.

1 square tofu (16 ounces)	4 cloves Caramelized Garlic
2 tablespoons lite soy sauce	(page 186)
1 teaspoon sesame oil	1½ cups bulghur
2 tablespoons butter	3 tablespoons chopped walnuts
¼ cup chopped scallions	3 cups chicken stock
¼ cup finely diced carrots	2 bay leaves
1 tablespoon chopped fresh ginger	½ teaspoon Tabasco

Marinate the tofu in the soy sauce and sesame oil for 10 minutes. Remove the tofu and cut into small cubes.

Heat a large sauté pan and melt the butter. Add the scallions, carrots, ginger and garlic and cook 1 minute. Add the bulghur, walnuts, chicken stock, bay leaves and Tabasco. Stir well and simmer 25 to 30 minutes. Add the tofu after 20 minutes of cooking. Remove the bay leaves before serving.

Semolina Fritters

Semolina is coarsely ground durum wheat that is used to make the best pastas. You can buy it at Italian food stores, upscale markets and from catalogs selling baking ingredients. Most fritters are deep-fried, but these are poached and then sautéed. Serve these dumplings as a first course or as a side dish with roasted or grilled meats.

½ cup (1 stick) butter, very soft

1 teaspoon chopped fresh sage or
    basil

½ teaspoon Tabasco

Freshly ground pepper to taste

2 eggs

1 cup semolina plus a few extra
    tablespoons for dusting the tray

2 tablespoons olive oil

Grated Parmesan cheese

Chopped fresh sage or basil for
    garnish

Combine the butter, sage, Tabasco and pepper and mix thoroughly. Add the eggs, one at a time, and stir until well combined. Fold in 1 cup semolina and stir until a smooth thick paste is formed.

Using 2 teaspoons, form the semolina into 2-inch dumplings and place on a semolina-dusted tray. Refrigerate dumplings for 1 hour.

Bring a large pot of water to a boil. Gently lower the dumplings into the water, bring the water back to a boil, lower heat, cover and simmer for 10 minutes. Remove the dumplings and drain well.

Heat a sauté pan and heat the olive oil. Add the dumplings and cook over medium heat until brown, turning them once. Do not crowd the dumplings. You may have to cook them in two batches. Serve immediately with Parmesan cheese and sage or basil.

Spoon Bread

Called spoon bread because it's usually eaten with a spoon, this corn-meal pudding is a traditional dish of the Deep South. I've boosted the flavor with sun-dried tomatoes, and the garlic-lemon butter adds a wonderful, smooth touch. This dish is a good alternative to rice or potatoes. If you don't have buttermilk on hand, mix 3½ cups whole milk with 1 tablespoon white distilled vinegar and set aside for 5 minutes before using.

¼ cup sun-dried tomatoes	¼ teaspoon ground nutmeg
3½ cups buttermilk	¼ teaspoon cayenne pepper
1¼ cups fine cornmeal	3 eggs, separated
¼ cup butter	Garlic and Lemon Butter
1 teaspoon salt	(page 132)

Preheat the oven to 350°F and grease a deep 9-inch baking pan.

Combine the sun-dried tomatoes with ¼ cup boiling water for 5 minutes. Drain, discard water and chop the tomatoes coarsely.

Place the buttermilk in a large saucepan and bring to a boil. Stirring constantly, slowly pour in the cornmeal and simmer for 3 minutes. Remove the pot from the heat and stir in the butter, sun-dried tomatoes, salt, nutmeg and cayenne pepper. Beat the egg yolks until light and fluffy and stir into the corn-meal mixture.

Beat the egg whites until stiff and gently fold into the cornmeal mixture. Scrape the batter into the prepared pan and bake until golden brown, about 35 to 40 minutes.

Serve with garlic and lemon butter.

Rice/Grains/Beans

Hoppin' John

This is a Southern beans-and-rice dish that is traditional fare on New Year's Day. It is said that anyone who eats Hoppin' John on the first day of January will have good luck all year. Supposedly, the name came from inviting guests to eat by saying "Hop in, John."

Serve Hoppin' John with a side of stewed tomatoes and a hearty salad followed by fresh fruit and frozen yogurt and you have a complete and nutritious meal.

1 pound dried black-eyed peas	2 cups chicken stock
½ pound slab bacon, chopped	1 ham bone, smoked ham hock or
1 onion, finely chopped	smoked sausage, optional
1 head Caramelized Garlic	½ cup chopped scallions
(page 186)	2 bay leaves
1 cup long-grain rice	

Place the beans in a colander, rinse in cool water and discard any that are broken. Place the beans in large bowl, add water until it is 2 inches above the beans and soak for 8 hours. Drain off the water, place the beans in a 4-quart pot and cover with fresh water, 1 inch above the beans. Cook the beans over medium heat until they're tender, about 1 hour. *Do not add salt.* Replenish the water if it evaporates.

Heat a large pot or Dutch oven and add the bacon, onion, and caramelized garlic. After the bacon has rendered its fat and the onion is lightly browned, add the rice and cook 2 minutes, stirring constantly. Add the stock, the ham bone, scallions and bay leaves. Bring to a boil, lower heat, cover and cook until the rice is very tender, about 25 to 30 minutes. Remove the bay leaves. Pick off any meat from the ham bone and mix it in with the beans.

Know Your Fire

Pasta with Beans

It's a cold and miserable night. You arrive home after an exhausting day without a clue about what to make for dinner. Take a look in the pantry and if you find some pasta, a can of beans, a can of tomatoes and some sun-dried tomatoes, a hearty, soul-satisfying dinner can be ready in moments. The pasta and bean combination provides complete protein, and the tomatoes offer a good amount of Vitamin C.

The sauce is a snap to make while the water for the pasta is coming to a boil. Don't worry if you don't have a whole pound of the same pasta. Use a combination of shells, ziti, penne and leftover pieces of spaghetti or linguine broken into two- to three-inch lengths.

This sauce is moist but not soupy. If you wish to change its character and serve the pasta in soup bowls, add 2 cups chicken broth and scatter some shredded spinach on top.

1 pound pasta, a combination of any shape or size	½ cup white wine
8 sun-dried tomatoes	1 teaspoon hot pepper flakes or to taste
4 tablespoons olive oil	2 cups canned white cannellini beans, washed and drained
1 onion, chopped	Grated Parmesan cheese to taste
1 head Caramelized Garlic (page 186)	2 tablespoons chopped fresh basil
2 cups tomatoes, canned or fresh, peeled or chopped	Freshly ground black pepper to taste
2 scallions, chopped	

In a large stockpot bring 4 quarts of water to a rolling boil and cook the pasta according to package directions. Place the sun-dried tomatoes in a small bowl, add boiling water to cover and let sit 10 minutes. Drain well and chop.

Preheat a sauté pan or a saucepan. Heat the olive oil, add the onion and garlic and sauté until the onion is transparent, about 2 minutes. Add the tomatoes, the presoaked sun-dried tomatoes, scallions, white wine, hot pepper flakes and cook 2 minutes. Add the beans and, when they're heated through, stir in the basil and pepper. Combine the sauce with the pasta and serve.

Salads

Thirty-five years ago food writer Paula Peck wrote the following warning: "To make it (a salad) all wrong, take some iceberg lettuce—the heart, never the outer green leaves. Pour over it a concoction which is an orangey color (popularly known as 'French' dressing), toss briefly, and you will have what is known as a tossed green salad."

Today's salads are a far cry from iceberg with an orange topping. In fact, it's hard to define salad. Some salads are simple; some are highly complicated. A salad could be green leaves, which could be served cold or warm. And those green leaves might include a red leaf and perhaps an edible flower or two. Add grains like rice, bulghur or pasta, or sliced meat or chunks of chicken.

The Versatile Salad

Ideas about when to serve the salad during a meal are ever-changing. Ancient Romans served lettuce at the end of dinner, whereas later in the first century it was served as an appetizer. There's a theory that, in the United States, salads jumped to the beginning of the meal when dieting became fashionable and it was dubbed eating California-style. It was thought that a heaping bowl of greens would dull the appetite for what came later. Others believe it was served first so that mothers could get greens into their children while they were hungry. Some believe that if a salad is served with the entrée, the vinegar in the dressing would clash with the wine. This could easily be remedied by using lemon juice instead of vinegar or serving a creamy salad dressing.

A salad can have its own "course" and be served separately after the entrée, with cheese, bread and the rest of the bottle of wine.

Nonetheless, people are eating more salads today, and they're eating them all day long.

A Perfect Balance of Texture, Color and Flavor

Any salad, green or otherwise, should be a mixture of textures, colors and flavors. Combine crisp romaine, buttery Boston and tender ruffled green leaf lettuce for texture. For color, match the pale inner leaves of escarole and deep dark green spinach with red radicchio. Mix the flavors of sweet iceberg lettuce with peppery watercress.

And then there are the accents: chick peas, sliced radishes or carrots, wedges of ripe red tomatoes, a few black olives, some crumbled feta cheese, crisp bacon or crunchy croutons. There are also almonds, walnuts, pumpkin seeds, pine nuts, hulled sunflower seeds, and crumbled Chinese noodles.

Designer Greens: Are They Worth the Price?

As with so many foodstuffs, the choices we now have in greens are limited only by our imaginations. Almost every supermarket carries a "gourmet" green or two. They can be pricey, but because many of them are strongly flavored, they can be used in small amounts as accents. Here are some you'll find in the market.

Mesclun: This is not one lettuce, but a combination of many baby lettuces—a concept that originated in southern France. There the greens would be part of a kitchen garden grown close to the house. The plants grow in rows next to each other and are harvested at the same time. The mixture varies, blending soft and sweet varieties. A few herbs and an edible flower or two are often included. Mesclun greens are delicate and need only a light dressing of vinaigrette.

The mesclun mix sold in the market may include the following:

Radicchio: Originally an Italian import, radicchio grows in small round compact heads with ruby-red leaves and thick white veins. It is somewhat chewy in texture and has a bitter flavor.

Arugula: A favorite green of Italians, arugula looks like radish leaves, is slightly bitter and has a distinctive peppery flavor. Used sparingly, it provides a particularly notable accent to the mix.

Belgian endive: These long, slender, creamy white leaves with pale yellow tips have a slightly bitter flavor. This lettuce is often used in appetizer dishes, stuffed with cheese or other fillings.

Mizuna: A member of the mustard green family originating in Japan, its delicate feathery leaves are bright green and mild flavored.

Frisee: A member of the chicory family, this bitter flavored green is pale yellowish white to pale green in color, with crisp feathery leaves.

Mache or *lambs lettuce:* Also called corn salad because it's frequently found growing wild in cornfields, mache has long, narrow, dark green leaves that have a tangy, almost nutty, flavor.

Red oak leaf: The leaves are loose and deeply cut, similar to the leaves of the oak tree. They are crisp yet tender with a delicate flavor.

Lolorosa: These loose green leaves with red edges are soft, tender and delicately flavored.

Other Salad Greens

Beet greens: These are rarely found on beets these days because they tend to be delicate and often don't survive the trip to the market. But if you're lucky enough to find some still attached to young beets, shred them thin and add to salad greens.

Chicory, also known as *curly endive:* The leaves are long and slender with very curly notches. Sometimes the outer leaves tend to be tough and take best to cooking, but the inner, almost white, heart is perfect for a salad.

Escarole: This is a broad-leaf member of the chicory family. The outer leaves are usually steamed and served as a side dish while the tender pale white to yellow inner leaves are added to salad.

Mustard greens: These have a very tangy flavor and young ones less than 4 inches long can be used in salads. (Cook larger leaves as you would spinach.)

Romaine: Also known as *Cos* lettuce, it's probably the most popular of all the lettuces because its leaves are crisp, flavorful and more nutritious than all the other lettuces.

Spinach: Both the crinkly and the flat-leaf kinds add a sweet touch to salads. Just make sure you wash it thoroughly to get rid of the dirt.

Swiss chard: This is usually steamed or boiled and served in soups, with pasta or eggs, but the tender inner leaves can be added to salad. The stems are never eaten raw.

Watercress: An aquatic green with a peppery taste, watercress can be found growing wild alongside streams. The small, round, dark green leaves can be added to soups as well as salads.

Storage

Store unwashed greens in dry paper toweling. Greens are mostly water and as they age they gradually give up their moisture, which will be absorbed by the toweling.

Keep delicate greens near the bottom of the refrigerator, preferably in a vegetable drawer. The temperature in most refrigerators is between 38 and 40 degrees, which is too cold for most salad greens.

How to Wash Greens

Whenever possible, clean only the greens you will be using immediately. Even with the best care and handling, greens bruise easily. Place the greens in a sink filled with cold water. Gently push the leaves up and down in the water to loosen the sand and dirt. Let them sit for a few minutes and scoop out the greens. Drain the water and repeat the process until there is no grit remaining in the sink. Some greens will need only one dunking, but others like spinach, Bibb lettuce, and arugula carry secret pockets of soil and require a thorough cleaning.

To Tear or to Cut

Some believe that breaking or tearing tender lettuce leaves by hand rather than cutting them avoids bruising and browning the leaves. Of course, greens cut with a carbon steel knife with a touch of rust will turn brown but greens cut with a stainless steel knife will never "rust." Several greens, such as romaine, Belgian endive and radicchio, are best cut with a knife. And, when faced with preparing salad for a large number of people, everyone will resort to a knife. However, if you like the look of torn greens, the choice is yours.

Hearty Green Salad

Hearty greens are a far cry from iceberg lettuce. Their robust flavor is only part of their popularity. They are delicious, versatile and low in calories, as well as high in vitamins and minerals. As a rule of thumb, the darker the green, the higher the amount of vitamin C.

Romaine	Spinach
Escarole	Mustard greens
Swiss chard	1 cup Creamy Blue Cheese Dress-
Watercress	ing (page 78) or Thousand
Chicory	Island Dressing (page 79)
Beet tops	

Mix together 8 cups of greens from the above list. Follow directions for washing greens on page 119. Place the greens in a salad bowl and serve the dressing on the side.

As a main dish, serve the salad on chilled, oversized plates and include one of the following to enhance the salad's eye appeal, texture and taste:

- cooked beans such as kidney beans, chick peas or black-eyed peas
- orange segments (when tomatoes are cottony and high priced)
- toasted tortilla wedges instead of croutons

Know Your Fire

Salmon and Onion Salad

This recipes calls for sweet onions such as Vidalia, Maui or Texas. Use whichever is available and in season. When the onions are caramelized, their natural sugars intensify their sweet flavor. If you prefer, the salmon can be poached in 2 cups fish stock. (See page 189.)

4 (5 to 6 ounce) salmon fillets

2 sweet onions, sliced very thin

1 cup Basic Vinaigrette (page 75)

4 tablespoons reduced-calorie
    cream cheese, at room
    temperature

8 plum tomatoes, peeled, seeded,
    and chopped

1 teaspoon chopped chives

4 lettuce leaves, such as Romaine
    or Chicory

4 slices toasted rye bread

1 orange, peeled and cut into
    segments

Prepare the salmon by cold or hot smoking (page 257).

Place the onions in a nonstick sauté pan and slowly heat the pan without stirring the onions. When the onions begin to brown, stir them slightly and allow them to cook a few minutes without disturbing them. Keep repeating until the onions are golden brown. Remove the onions and allow them to cool.

Slowly blend the vinaigrette and the cream cheese with a spoon until smooth. Stir in the tomatoes and chives.

Place a lettuce leaf on each slice of rye toast. Top with a smoked salmon fillet and some of the caramelized onions and orange segments. Pour a tablespoon or two of the dressing over each and serve the rest on the side.

Shrimp Curry Salad

Curry powder is not one spice but a blend of up to 20 different spices, herbs and seeds that can include cardamom, chilies, cinnamon, cloves, coriander, cumin, fennel seeds, fenugreek, nutmeg, red pepper, sesame seeds, saffron, tamarind and turmeric. For the purposes of this recipe, I suggest using a standard curry mix or, on a hot afternoon, make this really spicy by using hot Madras curry powder that will open your sweat glands and let you really cool off.

2 tablespoons butter

1 scallion, chopped

2 teaspoons curry powder

1½ pounds large shrimp, peeled
   and deveined

¼ cup dry white wine

1 teaspoon Tabasco

2 Granny Smith apples, peeled,
   cored and sliced

1 tablespoon lemon juice

1 tablespoon raisins

1 cup Smoky Ranch Dressing
   (page 79)

Lettuce leaves

1 tablespoon sliced almonds

1 tablespoon shredded coconut

Heat a sauté pan and melt the butter. Over high heat, cook the scallion and curry powder for 1 minute. Add the shrimp and cook 2 to 3 minutes, or until they become opaque. Stir in the white wine and remove the pan from the heat. Add the Tabasco, stir well, and set aside to cool. In a separate bowl, toss the apples with the lemon juice. Plump the raisins in ¼ cup boiling water for 5 minutes and drain well. Combine the apple slices, dressing, raisins and shrimp and mix well. Line a serving platter with lettuce leaves and arrange the shrimp mixture on top. Sprinkle with the raisins, almonds and coconut.

Tomato Tarragon Salad

This salad is so simple, yet it calls for perfectly ripe tomatoes. If you can only locate the pale cottony ones, wait until August when you can feast on "real" tomatoes. If you can't locate shallots, substitute ¼ cup finely chopped onion.

1 ½ cups Basic Vinaigrette (page 75)

2 shallots, chopped fine

3 tablespoons chopped fresh tarragon

4 to 5 large red ripe beefsteak tomatoes

1 head Boston lettuce, washed and dried

Freshly ground black pepper to taste

Combine the vinaigrette, shallots and tarragon in a small saucepan, bring to a boil, and cook until reduced to 1 cup, about 8 minutes. Cool to room temperature and strain, discarding solids. Do not refrigerate.

Slice the tomatoes and arrange on the lettuce leaves. Pour the dressing over the tomatoes and sprinkle with the remaining tarragon and the black pepper.

Salads

Celery Root Slaw

Celery root, or celeriac, is the knobby brown root of a special celery grown for its root. It can be eaten raw or cooked, but if you're eating celery root in a salad, soak it briefly in acidulated water to prevent discoloration. The flavor of celery root is somewhere between strong celery and parsley.

1 medium onion, thickly sliced
Olive oil
1 cup chicken broth
2 celery roots, shredded, about
    2 cups
1 tablespoon cider vinegar
1 tablespoon granulated sugar
1 carrot, peeled and shredded

2 to 3 cloves Caramelized Garlic
    (page 186)
¼ cup sour cream or mayonnaise,
    optional
Freshly ground black pepper to
    taste
1 teaspoon chopped Italian parsley

Preheat the grill or side burner.

Brush the onion with olive oil and grill over high heat for 3 to 4 minutes on each side. Cut into small pieces.

In a small saucepan, bring the chicken broth to a boil. Add the celery root, vinegar and sugar and simmer until the celery root is tender, 4 to 5 minutes. Remove the pan from the heat and cool. Drain the celery root, reserving the liquid. In a small bowl combine celery root with the onion, carrot and caramelized garlic. Moisten the vegetables with some of the cooking liquid, or for a creamier consistency, add the sour cream or mayonnaise. Season with black pepper and sprinkle with parsley.

Sauces and Condiments

Sauce making has always been a mark of creativity, and a chef's star could rise or fall on the sauce scale—the better the sauce, the better the food. Sauce making was so important in the classical kitchen that the chef's most valued assistant was the "saucier" (*Larousse gastronomique* calls the position *vinaigriers*) whose exclusive domain was making sauces under the chef's tutelage.

Antonin Careme, the nineteenth-century father of classical French cuisine, codified sauce making and established five common denominators called the "mother sauces": espagnole (brown sauce made with stock), velouté (light sauce made with stock), béchamel (basic white or cream sauce), hollandaise and mayonnaise (emulsified sauces), and vinaigrette (oil and vinegar). Later tomato sauce was added to the list.

Sauces are never eaten alone. Some sauces are meant to offer a contrasting flavor, such as a spicy tomato sauce over bland pasta, and other sauces, to enhance the dish, such as a brown gravy made with meat drippings.

As the trend seems to be moving away from sauces containing cream, eggs and butter, more food now tends to be served with salsa, the Mexican word for sauce. The original salsa contained tomatoes, onions, jalapeños, garlic, red bell pepper, avocado, lots of cilantro moistened with lime juice and a dash of olive oil. But salsa is a generic term and it has come to mean any mixture of raw, seasoned, finely chopped fruits or vegetables. Because salsas contain little fat and are highly seasoned, they go well with grilled foods.

Sometimes the only thing a sauce needs is the judicious addition of chopped fresh herbs, freshly grated black pepper or a drop or two of Tabasco. Some sauces start out as basics and get gussied up along the way. You probably won't make all these sauces at home, but here are some of the more familiar ones you'll find on restaurant menus based on the five "mother" sauces listed above:

Sauce Mornay: béchamel sauce with grated Gruyère and Parmesan cheeses

Sauce Soubise: béchamel sauce with sweated onions

Sauce Allemande: velouté sauce thickened with egg yolks

Sauce Aurora: velouté sauce flavored with tomato

Sauce Bercy: velouté sauce flavored with shallots, white wine, fish stock and herbs

Sauce Béarnaise: hollandaise sauce with shallots, tarragon, parsley and white wine

Sauce Bordelaise: a brown sauce made with red wine, bone marrow, shallots, parsley and herbs

Sauce Chausseur: brown sauce flavored with mushrooms, shallots, white wine, tomatoes and parsley

Sauce Estragon: velouté sauce flavored with fresh tarragon leaves

Sauce Marguery: a white sauce of white wine, fish stock, butter and egg yolks

Sauce Nantua: béchamel sauce flavored with crayfish butter

Sauce Perigueux: a brown sauce flavored with madeira and truffles

Sauce Rémoulade: mayonnaise flavored with mustard, capers, gherkins, anchovies and herbs

Sauce Rouille: mayonnaise flavored with hot chilies, garlic, bread crumbs and olive oil

Here are some of the more familiar Italian sauces based on tomato:

Fra Diavolo: a tomato sauce flavored with hot pepper flakes

Marinara: a simple tomato sauce flavored with onion, garlic and basil

Puttanesca: tomato sauce with anchovies, capers, black olives and hot pepper flakes

Sicilian: tomato sauce with eggplant and marsala; also called Norma sauce

Bolognese: a tomato sauce with beef, chicken liver and red wine

At a Chinese restaurant you might find:

Dark soy sauce: made from fermented black beans, wheat, salt and yeast. Used with beef and lamb

Light soy sauce: made from beans, wheat, salt and yeast. Used with fish and chicken

Hoisin sauce: A reddish brown paste made from soybeans, garlic, flour and spices

Oyster sauce: A thick brown sauce made from oysters, sugar, and soy sauce

Fish sauce: A light-brown liquid made from extracts of fish, water and salt

Hot brown bean sauce: A very hot, thick brown bean paste made with chili and garlic

Thickeners

Flour is the most common thickener for sauces but it must be cooked in the sauce for several minutes to lose its starchy flavor. It's very stable and will not break down.

Many dishes are thickened with a roux made by combining flour with an equal weight of clarified butter or oil. To make a brown roux, mix the flour and fat in a pan and cook slowly for 10 to 15 minutes, stirring constantly. To make a white roux, the flour and butter are blended together and whisked into a hot liquid and cooked for 4 to 5 minutes, stirring constantly.

Although arrowroot is not a popular household item, it can be used to thicken sauces at the last minute and will remain stable.

Cornstarch, used especially in Asian dishes, can be used as a last-minute thickener. However, it breaks down when the food is reheated.

Egg yolks are used to thicken "sauces" such as pastry cream. Make sure to whisk some of the hot liquid into the yolks before adding them to the pot to avoid curdling.

Heavy cream is not used in the kitchen the way it once was but it will thicken sauces, especially if the cream has been reduced.

Whisking butter into a hot liquid forms an emulsion that works similarly to egg yolks, but the sauce has to be used almost immediately or it will separate.

A slurry is a combination of flour and milk used to thicken gravies and sauces. For 2 cups of sauce, combine a tablespoon of flour with ¼ cup milk and mix well. Add some of the hot liquid from the gravy or sauce with the slurry, mix well, and pour back into the hot liquid, bring to a boil, lower the heat, and cook 3 to 4 minutes.

Yogurt can be used in place of butter or egg yolks to thicken sauces.

Some fresh cheeses will thicken sauces but can give it a grainy texture.

Natural thickeners like mashed potatoes, puréed beans, rice and root vegetables can also be used as thickeners without adding any fat to the dish.

How to Make Pan Gravy

Always make your gravy in the pan in which you roasted the meat, because those little bits and pieces stuck to the bottom have a great deal of flavor. First, skim off the fat and separate it from the pan juices. (For 2 cups of gravy you'll need 2 tablespoons fat, 2 tablespoons flour, 2 cups stock, and pan juices combined.) With the pan on medium heat, return the 2 tablespoons of fat to the pan and slowly whisk in the flour. Cook the flour until it becomes light brown, about 3 minutes. Slowly add the stock and cook a few minutes, whisking occasionally. Season according to the recipe or to your own taste.

How to Save a Sauce That Has Separated

Excessive heat can cause emulsion sauces to curdle or break down. Sometimes a hollandaise or béarnaise can be rescued by whisking in a tablespoon of cold water or heavy cream or an ice cube.

Cutting the Calories

Although traditional sauces have the reputation of being high in calories, the average serving is only a few tablespoons. But for the calorie- and fat-conscious cook, here are a few suggestions to reduce the calorie count without sacrificing the flavor:

- Skim off the fat, reduce pan juice and use as gravy
- Substitute yogurt for heavy cream.
- Use fortified skim milk in place of cream.
- Use a low- or non-fat mayonnaise as the basis of a sauce.

Turning Fruit into Sauces

Combine a cup of chopped fresh fruit such as strawberries, raspberries or peaches with a cup of corresponding preserves and simmer 4 to 5 minutes. Add a dash of citrus juice such as lemon, orange or lime. Use as is or press the sauce through a strainer for a smoother texture.

Ketchup

Two hundred years ago condiments were made at home from scratch. All this changed when H.J. Heinz began producing ketchup, a tomato-based condiment flavored with vinegar, sugar, salt and spices, in the 1880s. The original ketsiap, a pickled fish condiment, is believed to have come from China. It made its way around the world where the formula changed to include everything from nuts to mushrooms. Some clever New Englanders added tomato and it evolved into today's ketchup.

In spite of American's love of ketchup with french fries and hamburgers, recent sales have slipped while sales of salsa have soared.

Mustard

Mustard comes three ways: as seeds, as dry mustard powder and as prepared mustard. The name mustard comes from "mustum ardens," which means burning wine, a likely title since its formula was originally based on the Roman custom of combining crushed mustard seed with a fermented grape juice called must.

Mustard seeds come in two colors: large, mild, white ones favored by Americans and the smaller, sharper-flavored brown (sometimes called black) or Asian mustard seeds used in European and Chinese mustards.

Whole mustard seeds are used for pickling and flavoring foods. Dry mustard powder is finely ground mustard seeds and used for making prepared mustard.

The flavors of prepared mustards change the world over. American mustard such as French's is made from the mild white seeds and flavored with sugar, vinegar and turmeric, which gives it the distinctive yellow color. Chinese mustard is powerful stuff and should be used very sparingly. Breathing its vapors can burn sensitive mucous membranes. English mustards such as Coleman's are zesty and flavorful. Dijon mustard is made with white wine and comes from Dijon, France. German mustards, on the other hand, range from mild to sharp; some are even sweet.

You can make your own mustard very easily at home. Buy some dry mustard and dilute it with water, beer, wine, or lemon juice. Flavor the mustard with horseradish, garlic, herbs like chives or tarragon and spices like cloves and coriander seed. For texture, add some crushed whole mustard seeds. Blend well and season with salt to taste.

Grilled Tomato Sauce

Grilling the tomatoes enhances their flavor. I prefer plum tomatoes for this sauce because they have more flesh and less water and produce a thicker sauce than salad tomatoes. The basic sauce can be used just the way it is or you can add a few shrimp or black olives. This recipe makes enough sauce for 1 pound of pasta, but the recipe can be safely doubled.

2 pounds vine-ripened plum
 tomatoes
½ onion, thickly sliced
¼ cup olive oil
6 cloves Caramelized Garlic
 (page 186)

3 fresh basil leaves, coarsely
 chopped
Freshly ground black pepper

Preheat the grill on high.

Wash the tomatoes and cut in half through the stem. Brush the tomatoes and the onion lightly with 2 tablespoons of the olive oil and place on a very hot grill for 3 to 4 minutes on each side. Remove them and place in a saucepan with the remaining olive oil, garlic, basil and black pepper. Bring to a boil, lower heat, simmer 30 minutes and run through a food mill.

Garlic and Lemon Butter

This is a quick, all-around sauce for vegetables, seafood, pasta and chicken or with Spoon Bread (page 113).

¼ cup butter

1 head Caramelized Garlic
   (page 186)

Juice and zest of 2 lemons

1 teaspoon dried oregano

½ teaspoon Tabasco

¼ cup olive oil

Melt the butter in a small saucepan over medium high, add the Caramelized Garlic, and cook until the butter just begins to brown. Quickly add the lemon juice and zest and stir well. Add the oregano, Tabasco and olive oil and stir until blended. Serve warm.

Ham and Mushroom Sauce

Here's a fast and easy sauce to make while the pasta is cooking or to use over grilled pork chops.

2 tablespoons olive oil

1 onion, chopped

1 head Caramelized Garlic
   (page 186)

1 cup chopped smoked ham

1 cup mushrooms, sliced

8 plum tomatoes, peeled, seeded
   and chopped

½ cup white wine

3 tablespoons chopped fresh basil

Freshly ground black pepper

Heat the olive oil in a saucepan over high temperature. Add the onion and garlic and cook until the onions are light brown. Add the ham and mushrooms and quickly sear them. Add the tomatoes, wine, basil and black pepper. Bring to a boil, lower heat and simmer 20 minutes.

Pesto originated in Genoa, Italy, and although its traditional ingredient has always been basil leaves, pestos are made from a myriad of different ingredients including sun-dried tomatoes or cilantro. Pignoli, or pine nuts, can be used instead of the walnuts. If you double the recipe, store it in a jar, cover the top with ½ inch of olive oil and it will keep for several weeks refrigerated. After removing the amount you need, make sure the pesto is covered again with oil or it will become moldy.

I don't recommend freezing pesto unless you plan to use it within a month or two because the garlic, cheese and nuts can become rancid if frozen for an extended period. Pesto should be placed in ice cube trays before freezing. Then remove the cubes and place in a resealable plastic bag. For longer storage, purée only the basil and oil, place in resealable, freezer-quality, plastic bags, lay flat on freezer shelf and freeze. Break off the amount you need, defrost it, place in a food processor and process with the garlic, cheese and nuts.

1 cup packed fresh basil leaves	2 tablespoons chopped walnuts
1 head Caramelized Garlic (page 186)	¼ cup olive oil
4 tablespoons grated Parmesan cheese	

Combine the basil, garlic, Parmesan and walnuts in a food processor. With the machine running, slowly pour in the olive oil and process until the ingredients form a paste. Remove pesto and store in a tightly covered container until ready to use.

Garlic Horseradish Butter

Flavored or compound butters can be spread onto slices of Italian bread and lightly browned under the broiler. Or form the butter into a log the diameter of a quarter, wrap in plastic and store in the refrigerator. Once it's chilled, cut off a slice and place on top of grilled or broiled steaks.

2 tablespoons grated horseradish

4 ounces butter, softened

1 head Caramelized Garlic, pureed
   (page 186)

Juice of 1 lemon

1 tablespoon chopped fresh chives
   or scallions

1 teaspoon chopped fresh parsley

Squeeze all the moisture out of the horseradish. Whip the butter with a fork or whisk until smooth and fluffy. Stir in the horseradish, garlic, lemon, chives and parsley and blend well.

Bread and Butter Sauce

Definitely, this is the dish of the hour on the night before payday. Serve over spaghetti or linguine or even over cauliflower.

½ cup (1 stick) butter

1 head Caramelized Garlic
   (page 186)

¼ cup bread crumbs

1 tablespoon chopped fresh parsley

1 teaspoon fresh or ½ teaspoon
   dried oregano

Juice of 2 lemons

2 tablespoons grated Parmesan
   cheese

Freshly ground black pepper to
   taste

Heat a saucepan and melt the butter over medium-high heat. Add the garlic and cook 1 minute. Add the bread crumbs, parsley and oregano, lower the heat and cook until the crumbs begin to brown. Immediately stir in the lemon juice, Parmesan cheese and black pepper and blend well.

Know Your Fire

Fruit Sauce

MAKES ABOUT 3 CUPS

If you don't have a fresh lemon, use orange juice, but never resort to bottled lemon juice. This sauce is good over pound cake or ice cream.

1½ pounds fresh soft fruit, such as strawberries, raspberries, blueberries, peaches or apricots

Juice and whole rind of 1 lemon

1½ cups granulated sugar

1 cup water

1 to 2 ounces brandy, optional

Wash the fruit and drain well. Toss with the lemon juice in a bowl.

Combine the sugar, water and lemon rind in a nonreactive saucepan, bring to a boil, and boil 7 to 8 minutes. Remove from heat and cool to room temperature.

Place the fruit in a food processor or blender along with any accumulated juices and process until pureed. Slowly add the sugar syrup and blend well. Pass the sauce though a strainer to remove any seeds. Stir in optional brandy.

Apple-Raisin Sauce

MAKES ABOUT 2 CUPS

Fruit always goes well with pork, and this sweet-sour sauce is a good contrast to smoky foods.

1 tablespoon butter

¼ cup chopped onion

3 tablespoons cider vinegar

3 tablespoons steak sauce

1 cup chicken stock

1 apple, peeled, cored and diced

¼ cup raisins

Heat a small sauté pan and melt the butter over high heat. Reduce heat to low, add the onion and slowly sauté until light golden brown. Add the vinegar and steak sauce and simmer until the liquid is reduced by half, about 4 minutes. Stir in the stock, apple and raisins and simmer for 4 to 5 minutes.

Sauces and Condiments

MAKES
1 ¾ CUPS

Chocolate Sauce

Make this chocolate sauce and you'll never buy that stuff in a jar again. Chocolate melts very quickly at 90°F. That's why at a body temperature of 98.6, such as in your hand, it melts. Be sure not to overheat the chocolate, as the cocoa liquor will separate from the cocoa butter and the result will be a dull grainy finish instead of a nice shiny luster.

1 cup semi-sweet chocolate, chopped	¼ cup milk
	2 tablespoons granulated sugar
¼ cup half-and-half	2 tablespoons butter

Place the chocolate in the top of a double boiler over simmering, not boiling, water and stir until it melts. Remove from heat.

Combine the half-and-half, milk, sugar and butter in a saucepan and, whisking constantly, bring to a boil. Pour the mixture into the melted chocolate, stirring constantly, place the pan back on the heat and cook until it comes to a boil. Serve hot as a chocolate sauce or chill and whip as an icing.

Know Your Fire

Seafood

How to Buy Seafood

For successful fish buying you'll need a good nose or a reliable fishmonger. But, since noses vary and can be misled, the fishmonger is our salvation. The fish market should be spotless and smell of the sea; whole fish should be covered with chopped ice with only their heads peeking out. Fillets and steaks should never come in contact with ice, but rather be displayed on trays resting on ice in a refrigerated case.

Never buy the last piece of fish in the case. Who knows how long it's been there?

Whole fish should sparkle; the flesh should be firm and the skin taut. Lift up a gill and take a sniff; it should smell like the ocean. Scales should be tight and the gills cherry red. Look for clear, protruding eyes and generally inspect the fish for any marks of injury.

Fish steaks and fillets should be moist and have a translucent glow. The flesh should be dense. Any steak or fillet shining a rainbow opalescence on the surface should be avoided.

Shellfish has to be labeled as to date and place of harvest and, when you ask, the information should be readily available to you.

With the exception of scallops, shellfish should be tightly closed. If mussels and clams are slightly open, give them a firm rap. They should close immediately. If any do not close, discard them because they're probably dead. Also discard any that fail to open after cooking.

Ideally, a fishmonger will include a bag of ice along with the purchase to keep it cold until you get home. Seafood is particularly susceptible to bacterial spoilage and must be keep cold. Store whole fish and fillets wrapped in clean wax paper in the refrigerator and cook as soon as possible. Never store shellfish in a bowl of ice. Place them in a colander and cover lightly.

Mollusks and Crustaceans

There are three groups of mollusks: the gastropods such as abalone, which have a single shell and a single muscle; the bivalves such as clams, oysters and mussels which have two shells hinged together by a strong muscle; and cephalopods such as squid which have tentacles and ink sacs.

A crustacean has a long body and a crustlike shell such as lobster, crayfish, shrimp and crab. With the exception of shrimp, all crustaceans should be purchased alive and feisty.

How to Buy a Lobster

Ask the fishmonger to give you some seaweed or newspaper to wrap the live lobsters in for the ride home. Store it in the warmer part of the refrigerator, about 45°F. A colder temperature will cause lobsters to sleep and, consequently, die. Preferably you should cook the lobsters as soon as you arrive home. They can be stored no longer than 24 hours. Kill them quickly by placing them, head first, in a pot of boiling water or split them with a sharp knife through the eyes while they are on their backs.

If you're buying a lobster that was already cooked at the market, make sure you buy one that has a curled tail. This is the best indication that the lobster was alive when it was cooked (or killed immediately before). If the lobster was dead before it was cooked, the lobster meat will pull apart and disintegrate. Buying a cooked lobster is a good barometer to use when checking out a potential fishmonger. If he's selling lobsters that died before they were cooked, the fish market reliability is questionable.

Bay, Sea and Calico Scallops

Anyone who has ever bought a gallon of Shell gasoline and looked up at their logo knows what a scallop shell looks like, but few have ever seen a real one. Most scallops have already been shucked before they come to market and the scallop, which is the adductor muscle that holds the shells together, is the only part that is eaten in this country.

Inside the shell are 50 tiny "eyes," gills, a complete digestive system, red female ovaries or male reproductive glands. In the case of sea scallops, the adductor muscle is harvested and all the rest is thrown overboard while the boat is still at sea.

Sea scallops are the largest in size—about 1 inch high and ¾ to 1½ inches across. Bay scallops run ¾ to 1 inch high and ½ inch across. Calico scallops are about the size of miniature marshmallows and lack flavor.

Scallops should be cream colored or slightly pink, have a shiny finish and smell of the sea. Avoid those that are pure white because they have been soaked in water.

Try to buy scallops on the day you plan to cook them. If they must be stored, place them in a bowl, cover loosely with a wet towel, and refrigerate. Never store them in water because they will absorb liquid and when cooked, the liquid will run out and steam the scallops.

Scallops cook very quickly and become tough when overcooked. Begin testing for doneness after 1 minute.

Occasionally, round plugs of skate or shark flesh are sold as scallops, but they are easy to detect because they look like cookie cutter scallops: they're all exactly the same size.

Oysters, Anyone?

Jonathan Swift wrote, "He was a bold man who first ate an oyster." Yet, during the same century, Casanova devoured four dozen oysters a day because he believed, clinical research notwithstanding, they were "a spur to love."

Oysters were so plentiful at one time that poor people ate them instead of meat. Some roads in Baltimore are still paved with crushed oyster shells. Although they were cultivated over 2,000 years ago by the Chinese and the Romans, oysters have fallen victim to overharvesting, industrial pollution and oil spills. Eating oysters today is a luxury except in New Orleans, where an oyster bar can be spotted on every street and they are a common indulgence.

Oysters found in North America are divided into four classes or species: Atlantic or Eastern oysters gathered from the Canadian maritime provinces to the Mexican border of the United States; Pacific oysters from the Pacific coast waters; Olympia oysters from Washington State's Puget Sound; and belon oysters, which originated in France but are now cultivated in this country. Oysters are also found in England and Ireland but rarely exported.

Oysters are usually named for the area where they're harvested so you'll see names like Blue Point (Long Island), Wellfleet (Cape Cod), Apalachicola (Florida), Malpeque (Prince Edward Island), Willapa Bay (Washington) and Golden Mantle (British Columbia).

Oysters should be plump and moist, their color ranging from ivory to pale tan with flavors described as briny, mild, metallic and sweet. Their liquid must be clear and never cloudy.

Until recently, anyone avoiding foods with high cholesterol shunned oysters. However, nutritionists now believe that it's the saturated fat in other food that does the most harm to arteries. Oysters are low in fat and very low in saturated fat while they're high in niacin, iron, phosphorus and potassium and contain less cholesterol than egg yolks.

How to Shuck an Oyster

Scrub the oysters with a stiff brush under running water to get rid of any mud or grit. Beginning with the rounded side down to retain the oyster liquid, hold the oyster in a towel in your hand (the shell can be sharp) and insert an oyster knife or can opener (church key) into the hinge. Push down or twist the knife handle until the top shell begins to loosen. Slide the knife in, detach the muscle and remove the top shell. Run the knife around the inside of the bottom shell cutting through the adductor muscle to release the oyster. Remove any stray pieces of broken shell.

You can also open oysters in the microwave if you watch them carefully. Place the oysters in the freezer for 1 hour. Arrange no more than 6 oysters in a circle in a glass pie pan with their hinges toward the outside. Microwave on high for 2½ minutes rotating the dish after 1½ minutes. As soon as you see an oyster shell beginning to open, remove the oyster at once and place immediately on a bed of ice to stop it from cooking. Remove top shell. Set the timer for 30 seconds longer for the oysters that haven't opened and keep a close look.

Shrimp

Fish markets sell shrimp according to size: colossal, large, medium, etc., but a more accurate way to judge the size of shrimp is to buy them by counting them: colossal, less than 10 to the pound; jumbo, 11 to 15 to the pound; extra large, 16 to 20 to the pound; large, 21 to 30 to the pound; medium, 31 to 35 to the pound; small, 36 to 45 to the pound, and miniature, 60 to 100 to the pound.

Shrimp cooked in the shell has more flavor, but it's messy for those who have to peel it at the table.

To peel shrimp using your fingers, begin at the large end and peel away. Removing the tail fin is optional. It's handy to leave on if the shrimp is going to be eaten with the hands as in shrimp cocktail. Most people find the black vein running along the back of the fish offensive so if you're going to peel the shrimp, you may as well get rid of this too. Using a sharp paring knife, cut a shallow slit down the middle of the outside curve, pull out the dark vein and rinse the shrimp under cool water.

If you're a gadget person, there's one called a "shrimper," which shells and deveins shrimp in one fell swoop.

How to Fillet a Fresh Fish

There are two ways to fillet a fish, depending on whether the fish is a round fish such as a bass, or a flatfish such as flounder.

To fillet a round fish, it's easier to cut off the fillets without cleaning out the interior. Lay the fish on its side and with a sharp fillet knife, cut diagonally along the base of the head down to the bones. With the head facing away from you, slide the knife along the upper side of the backbone and cut into the flesh. Fold back the fillet with one hand while cutting the flesh away from the ribs with the other. Detach the fillet. Turn the fish over and repeat the procedure with the other side starting at the tail. To remove the skin, place the fillet, skin side down, on a flat surface with the tail toward you. Hold the tail and, with a sharp flexible knife, make a cut into the flesh about one inch from your hand. Holding onto this portion, run the knife between the skin and flesh, moving it from side to side as you push it away from you.

To fillet a whole flatfish, cut off all the fins with a scissors and cut out the gills. Cut along the base of the head down to the backbone with a sharp knife. Make ¼-inch cuts all around the whole fish. With the fish's head facing you, top or dark side up, cut down to the backbone through the lateral line, the line that separates the two fillets. Slide the knife under the fillet from head to tail and remove the fillet. Turn the fish around and remove the other fillet. Turn the fish over and remove the fillets from the other side in the same manner. Place the fillets, skin side down, and cut between the skin and the flesh with a sharp flexible knife, moving the skin back and forth while pulling away from you.

Cooking Fish and Shellfish

Fish is delicate and, unlike red meat, does not contain tough muscle, so it cooks very quickly. Whole baked fish needs little more than a squirt of lemon juice and a drizzle of olive oil. The rule of thumb is to buy what is in season and keep it simple.

The type of fish very often determines how it's cooked. Thin flounder or sole fillets are too delicate to grill and fare better when quickly sautéed, whereas oily fish such as bluefish and mackerel are perfect candidates for grilling.

Mussels and clams cook in 5 to 7 minutes in a pot or on the grill. They should be well scrubbed before cooking. When eating raw shellfish, always buy them from a reputable outlet. If you harvest them yourself, make sure they're from certified waters.

How to Tell if Fish Is Cooked

When fish is cooked, it turns opaque and its juices are milky white. Cooking should halt just as soon as the fish begins to flake. Once it falls apart easily, it's overdone. Sometimes it's necessary to cut a small slit in the thickest portion to check for doneness. An instant-read thermometer should register between 135°F and 140°F. As a rule of thumb, use the "Canadian Method" developed by the Canadian Department of Fisheries and Oceans, which recommends 10 minutes cooking time for each inch of thickness.

Broiling, Frying, Steaming, Poaching and Baking Techniques

Broiling/grilling: Choose steaks or fillets ¾ to 1 inch thick. Thinner slices will dry out and thicker ones may overcook on the outside while remaining raw on the inside. Leave the skin on; it holds the steaks and fillets together. Turn the fish only once using one or two wide spatulas. The grill must be very clean and lightly oiled to prevent the fish from sticking. When broiling, position the fish about 6 inches under the heat source.

Frying: Always dry off any pieces of fish before frying. Use oil or a mixture of butter and oil for a higher smoke point. Coat fish with flour, cornmeal or bread crumbs and refrigerate for 30 minutes so that the coating adheres better. However, refrigerating the fish too long will tend to make the coating soggy. If preparing the fish in a batter, dip it just before frying. Make sure the temperature is correct. Use an electric fry pan or a frying thermometer. Always drain the fish on a paper towel and blot the top to remove excess grease. To keep fish warm while the rest is cooking, lay the pieces on paper towel-lined pans and place in a 150°F oven.

Poaching: Set a fish poacher over two burners on your stove. When the cooking liquid comes to a boil, add the fish and, when the liquid has returned to a boil, begin timing the cooking. To keep fish white, add a few tablespoons of acid such as lemon juice or white wine. It's easier to remove a whole fish from a poacher if the fish has been wrapped in cheesecloth or placed on a screen or rack that can be lifted easily out of the poaching liquid. Make sure your pan is large enough to accommodate the fish and that the liquid covers the fish. Save the poaching liquid to use in soup or as the base for a sauce. If the fish is to be eaten cold, let the fish cool in the cooking liquid and remove the pan from the stove so that it doesn't continue to cook from the radiant heat.

To poach shrimp or scallops, place them in a saucepan and cover with water. Add a small amount of white wine or lemon juice, bring to a boil, lower heat to a simmer, and cook until opaque, about 2 to 3 minutes.

Baking: An oven temperature of 400° to 450°F seals in the juices and leaves fish moist and tender. Cover the fish with wax paper, bread crumbs, finely chopped vegetables or butter. Or fish can be wrapped in pastry, parchment paper or aluminum foil.

How to Deal with Frozen Fish

When buying frozen fish, the box itself is the best indicator of how the fish was stored. If the box is clean with no water stains, it's probably safe to say the fish has not defrosted and refrozen. Once the wrappings have been removed, examine the fish for dry spots that are the telltale signs of freezer burn.

Some fish is best cooked in its frozen state because it often loses natural moisture when defrosted. Frozen fillets need only be partially defrosted before cooking; add a minute or two to the cooking time to compensate for their frozen state.

Try soaking partially frozen fish in milk to restore a "fresh" flavor.

To defrost fish, place in the refrigerator and allow 1 day for each pound of fish. To hasten thawing, place the frozen fish in a plastic bag and place in cold water, changing the water every hour or so.

Frozen fish can be defrosted in the microwave oven, but it's chancy because the corners may begin to cook before the center is defrosted. Place the fish in a covered dish and microwave on 30 percent power for 6 minutes for 1 pound of fish. After 4 minutes, separate the pieces. Add 10 minutes of resting time. Pat the fish dry before proceeding with recipe instructions.

Once fish has thawed, it should never be refrozen.

Stuffed and Rolled Flounder

If you're used to stuffed flounder with stuffing heavy on bread, try this alternative. The brandy adds a little zip but you can substitute chicken or fish broth.

4 tablespoons butter

1 tablespoon olive oil

¼ onion, chopped

¼ cup chopped celery

¼ cup brandy

1 teaspoon dried thyme

¼ cup mayonnaise

½ cup fresh bread crumbs

4 ounces bay scallops, poached and chopped (pages 139 and 143)

4 ounces shrimp, peeled, deveined, poached, and chopped (pages 141 and 143)

8 pieces flounder fillet, about 2 pounds

Preheat the oven to 375°F.

Use 2 tablespoons of the butter to grease a medium casserole or oven-proof pan.

Heat the olive oil in a sauté pan. Add the onion and celery and cook 3 to 4 minutes over medium-high heat. Add the brandy and thyme, stir well, remove the pan the from heat and cool the vegetables. Add the mayonnaise, bread crumbs, scallops and shrimp to the vegetables, and mix well.

Lay the flounder fillets on a flat surface. Place an equal amount of filling at the middle of each fillet and fold the bottom and top ends over stuffing, over-lapping them slightly. Place the fish, seam side down, into the prepared pan leaving a small space between them. Melt the remaining 2 tablespoons butter and brush the fish. Bake for 10 to 12 minutes, or until the fish becomes milky white and begins to flake.

Monkfish in Oyster Sauce

Monkfish is another name for angler fish or lotte. It's a large flatfish but it's rather ugly because of its large mouth. Actually, only the tail is eaten. However, the flesh is mild and the flavor faintly resembles lobster. Oyster sauce is a thick brown Chinese condiment made from oysters, salt and soy sauce. It's used in stir-fries, as it is here, and as a table sauce. Oyster sauce and hoisin sauce are sold in most supermarkets.

1 tablespoon peanut or vegetable
  oil
2 pounds monkfish, skinned and cut
  into 3-inch pieces
¼ cup all-purpose flour for
  dredging
2 carrots, cut into 2-inch strips
6 scallions, cut into 1-inch pieces

6 cloves Caramelized Garlic
  (page 186)
1 tablespoon chopped fresh ginger
1 tablespoon sesame seeds
1 tablespoon soy sauce
1 teaspoon sesame oil
½ teaspoon chili oil or Tabasco
¼ cup oyster or hoisin sauce

Heat a wok or large skillet and heat the oil. Dredge the monkfish in the flour and quickly sear on both sides over high heat. Remove and set aside.

Add the carrots, scallions, garlic and ginger and cook 2 to 3 minutes, stirring constantly. Add the sesame seeds, soy sauce, sesame oil and chili oil. Lower heat, return the monkfish to the pan and cook 2 minutes longer. Stir in the oyster sauce and serve. Don't overcook the monkfish.

Halibut with Mustard Pepper Crust

Here's another quickly prepared fish dish made from ingredients you probably have in your home. Cod can be substituted for the halibut.

½ cup bread crumbs

¼ cup mayonnaise

2 tablespoons prepared mustard

1 tablespoon crushed peppercorns

1 tablespoon chopped fresh parsley

1 teaspoon Tabasco

4 tablespoons butter

2 (1-inch thick) halibut fillets, (about 2 pounds), skinned and any bones removed

Preheat the oven to 425°F.

Combine the bread crumbs, mayonnaise, mustard, peppercorns, parsley and Tabasco in a small bowl.

Grease an ovenproof casserole with 2 tablespoons of the butter and place the halibut in the dish. Melt the 2 remaining tablespoons butter and brush the fish with it. Pat the crumb mixture onto the top of the fish and bake approximately 10 minutes. Using a small knife, make a slit in the thickest portion of the fish. If the flesh is pure white and beginning to flake, remove it at once. If it is still translucent, cook it for 2 minutes longer.

Seafood

Bouillabaisse

The quintessential fish stew from Marseilles in the south of France is traditionally flavored with saffron, the world's most expensive spice. If saffron isn't in your budget, use turmeric for color. Originally, bouillabaisse was a fast fish stew that fishermen made from whatever seafood they couldn't sell. Some Frenchmen still feel it must contain "rascasse," also called scorpion or rockfish, a fish that is unmarketable and is never eaten any other way. Be that as it may, this American version is tops on my list.

2 cups dry white wine

2 cups fish, vegetable or chicken stock

4 plum tomatoes, peeled, seeded, and chopped

½ onion, sliced

½ bulb fennel, plus some of the stems, chopped

½ head Caramelized Garlic (page 186)

2 bay leaves

1 teaspoon saffron threads or ground turmeric

2 dozen Little Neck clams

2 to 3 pounds firm fish such as swordfish or monkfish

3 pounds mussels, scrubbed and debearded

3 pounds soft fish such as red snapper, sea bass or cod

4 (4 to 6 ounces each) lobster tails, split in half

1 pound medium shrimp, peeled and deveined

½ pound bay scallops

1 pound squid, cleaned and sliced

Chopped fresh parsley, lemon slices and Garlic Bread (page 187) for serving

Combine the wine, stock, tomatoes, onion, fennel, garlic, bay leaves and saffron in a very large soup kettle or Dutch oven and bring to a boil. Add the clams, the firm fish and mussels, cover, lower heat, and gently simmer 2 to 3 minutes.

Add the soft fish, lobster, shrimp, scallops and squid and simmer covered 6 to 8 minutes longer or until shellfish has opened and fin fish begins to flake. Discard the bay leaves.

Serve in large bowls topped with fresh parsley and lemon slices. Make sure there's lots of crusty garlic bread on the side for dipping.

Honey and Onion Shrimp

This is a really fast and easy way to cook shrimp. To speed up the works even further, buy shelled shrimp from your fishmonger. It's a little more expensive but when time is a factor, it's worth the price. The honey and vinegar give it a sweet-and-sour flavor.

1 pound shrimp, peeled and deveined	2 scallions, chopped
½ cup olive oil	2 tablespoons red wine vinegar
¼ cup honey	1 teaspoon Tabasco
1 red onion, chopped	2 tablespoons butter

Preheat the oven to 400°F.

Place the shrimp in a single layer in an ovenproof casserole or a sauté pan with an ovenproof handle. Mix together the olive oil, honey, red onion, scallions, red wine vinegar and Tabasco and pour over the shrimp. Bake until the shrimp turn white and the juices are bubbly, about 5 to 6 minutes. Add the butter and stir until the juices become creamy. Serve with Garlic Bread (page 187).

Seafood

Lobster Boil

To make clarified or drawn butter, slowly melt unsalted butter over low heat until the white milk solids sink to the bottom, leaving the golden liquid on top. Skim off any foam from the surface and pour off the clear liquid butter, which is called clarified or drawn butter. Clarified butter can also be made in the microwave by heating butter for 30 seconds on high.

Boil a 1-pound lobster for 7 minutes. For each additional 4 ounces, add 1 minute. A 1½-pound lobster should cook in 9 minutes. Two or more lobsters will cook in the same time providing the pot is large enough. When in doubt, use two pots or cook them separately. If the lobsters are overcrowded, it takes too long for the water to return to a boil.

4 (1½ pounds each) lobsters	¼ pound clarified or drawn butter
1 (12 ounce) can beer	(see note above)
¼ cup **Crab Boil** seasoning (available commercially)	2 lemons, cut into wedges
1 lemon, cut into slices	Oyster crackers

Leave the bands on the lobster claws.

Fill a very large pot with enough water to cover the lobsters and bring to a rolling boil. Add the beer, crab boil seasoning and lemon slices to the pot and bring the water back to a boil. Drop in the live lobsters, head first, and when the water boils, cover the pot and begin timing the cooking (see note above). Lobsters turn bright red when cooked. Remove at once with tongs.

Serve the lobsters with the clarified butter, lemon wedges and oyster crackers. Don't forget the seafood forks, lobster picks and plenty of napkins.

Grilled Lobster

Make sure your lobsters are alive when you buy them. A dead lobster is a field day for bacteria. There's an easy test you can do: pick up a lobster and if the tail curls, it's alive.

4 (1½ pound) lobsters, split

2 tablespoons olive oil

2 tablespoons **Crab Boil seasoning**
    (available commercially)

6 cloves **Caramelized Garlic**
    (page 186)

¼ **pound clarified or drawn butter**
    (page 150)

3 lemons, cut into wedges

To split a lobster, place it on its back on a cutting board. With a firm thrust of a sharp French knife, pierce the head. Bring the knife down firmly through the center of the lobster and split in half vertically. Using your hands, crack the shell and spread the lobster apart. Pull out the soft, beige intestinal vein from the tail and discard the papery stomach sac located just behind the eyes. Depending on your preference, you can lift out the coral and the gray-green tomalley and use them in a sauce or you can leave them in. Crack the claws with a nutcracker.

Preheat the grill.

In a small bowl, combine the olive oil, crab boil seasoning and garlic. Place the lobster on its back and brush with some of the oil mixture. Place the lobster on the grill, split side down, for 3 minutes. Brush with oil, turn, and cook until done, 5 to 6 minutes longer. A 1½-pound lobster should cook in 9 minutes: 7 minutes for the first pound and 1 minute for each additional 4 ounces.

Serve with the clarified butter and lemon wedges.

Lobster coral and tomalley Coral is another name for lobster roe or eggs, and it's only found in female lobsters. Once it has been cooked, the roe turns bright coral in color. Coral can be eaten as is, added to a sauce or blended with sweet butter and used as a spread.

Tomalley, which is green, is the lobster's liver. It has a very delicate flavor and can be eaten as is or added to sauces.

Seafood

Baked Stuffed Lobster

A true lobster is found only off the coast of northeastern United States and Canada and it's called a Maine lobster. They're mostly caught in lobster traps set out in rocky areas where lobsters like to dwell. A baked stuffed lobster is about as good as you can get.

4 (1½ pound) lobsters	**2 tablespoons brandy**
2 tablespoons butter	**1 bay leaf**
½ onion, chopped	**½ cup bread crumbs**
¼ cup finely chopped carrot	**¼ cup crumbled blue cheese**
3 cloves Caramelized Garlic	**2 tablespoons prepared mustard**
(page 186)	**½ pound medium or large shrimp,**
2 tablespoons all-purpose flour	**peeled, deveined and split in**
2 cups fish or chicken stock	**half**

Preheat oven to 375°F.

To split a lobster, place it on its back on a cutting board. With a firm thrust of a sharp French knife, pierce the head. This kills the lobster. Bring the knife down firmly through the center of the lobster and split in half vertically. Using your hands, crack the shell and spread the lobster apart. Pull out the soft, beige intestinal vein from the tail and discard the papery stomach sac located just behind the eyes. Depending on your preference, you can lift out the coral and the gray-green tomalley and use them in a sauce or you can leave them in. Crack the claws with a nutcracker.

Heat a saucepan and melt the butter. Add the onion, carrot and garlic and cook 2 to 3 minutes. Add the flour and cook 2 to 3 minutes, stirring constantly. Add the stock, brandy and bay leaf, bring to a boil, lower heat and simmer for 5 minutes. Stir in the bread crumbs, blue cheese and mustard and simmer for 2 to 3 minutes. Remove bay leaf and cool the sauce.

Add the shrimp to the sauce. Place the lobsters on an ovenproof platter or cookie sheet. Fill the lobster cavities with the sauce and bake for 10 to 12 minutes.

Clams with Garlic and Wine

Little Neck clams are hard-shell clams with a diameter of less than 2 inches. This recipe is for garlic lovers. Perhaps its name should be Garlic with Clams and Wine. Enjoy with crusty Italian bread and have plenty of paper napkins handy.

4 dozen Little Neck clams, well
    scrubbed

1 cup dry white wine

2 heads Caramelized Garlic
    (page 186)

1 tablespoon chopped fresh parsley

4 large basil leaves, chopped

1 teaspoon dried oregano

1 teaspoon red pepper flakes

4 tablespoons butter, softened and
    cut into small pieces

Place the clams into a very large soup kettle or Dutch oven. Add the wine, garlic, parsley, basil, oregano and red pepper flakes. Quickly bring to a boil, cover and cook, shaking pot occasionally, until clams open, about 5 to 8 minutes.

Remove clams and set aside. Pour liquid into a small saucepan and bring to a boil. Stirring constantly, add butter a piece at a time and cook until the sauce thickens slightly. Serve broth along with the clams.

Seafood

Chilled Mussels in Pesto Mayonnaise

There are uses for pesto besides adding it to linguine. Placing the mussels back into their half shells makes a nice presentation.

4 pounds mussels, well scrubbed and debearded	1 head Caramelized Garlic (page 186)
	1 teaspoon hot red pepper flakes
1 cup white wine	¼ cup pesto (page 133)
2 tablespoons butter	¼ cup mayonnaise

Combine the mussels, wine, butter, garlic and pepper flakes in a very large pot. Bring to a boil, cover and cook 5 to 7 minutes, shaking the pot several times during cooking. The mussels are fully cooked when they open. Discard any that do not open.

Remove the mussels from the shells and chill. Discard half the shells and keep the other half for serving.

Boil the cooking liquid until it reduces by half. Strain the broth through cheesecloth or fine strainer and chill.

Combine the pesto, mayonnaise and ¼ cup of the mussel broth. Marinate the mussels in the pesto sauce for 1 hour and serve on the mussel shells.

Crayfish Omelet

Crayfish look like miniature lobsters. In this country they can be found in Louisiana around the Mississippi delta. Like lobster, they turn red when cooked. You can find them in food specialty stores. If they cannot be found, you can substitute shrimp.

Adding a small amount of water to the eggs makes a tender omelet; using milk or cream toughens it. An omelet pan has a wide, flat bottom, shallow, sloping sides and a long handle. When buying one, make sure it has a nonstick finish.

FOR THE FILLING

2 tablespoons olive oil

1 green bell pepper, seeded and
   chopped

1 plum tomato, seeded and chopped

1 scallion, chopped

½ teaspoon dried thyme

½ teaspoon Tabasco

8 ounces shelled crayfish tail meat
   or peeled and deveined shrimp

¼ cup heavy cream

FOR THE EGGS

6 large eggs

1 teaspoon cold water

½ teaspoon Tabasco

Freshly ground black pepper to taste

1 tablespoon olive oil

To make the filling, heat a sauté pan and heat the olive oil. Add the green pepper, tomato, scallion, thyme, and Tabasco and sauté 1 minute. Add the crayfish and cook 2 minutes, stirring constantly. Stir in the heavy cream, bring to a boil, lower heat, and cook until the crayfish are tender, 3 to 4 minutes. Set aside and keep warm.

Break the eggs into a medium bowl and beat until frothy. Add the water and Tabasco and beat until they're well mixed.

Heat 1 tablespoon olive oil in a nonstick 8-inch omelette pan or sauté pan over high heat. Pour in the egg mixture and cook without stirring until the eggs begin to bubble around the edges. Begin to gather the mixture toward the center, while tipping the pan and allowing the uncooked egg to come to the edges. This should be done quickly without breaking up the omelet into pieces.

Place the hot filling in the center of the omelet and, using a spatula, fold the omelet in half and slide onto a plate. Serve immediately.

Seafood

**MAKES 4
SERVINGS**

Eggs and Oysters

This impressive brunch dish is so rich it should be called Eggs Rocke-feller. The old adage "Don't eat oysters in months without an 'R'" makes sense when you realize that oysters spawn during the summer months so they're soft and fatty.

FOR THE OYSTERS

2 tablespoons all-purpose flour

¼ teaspoon cayenne pepper

¼ teaspoon freshly ground black
   pepper

¼ teaspoon ground nutmeg

2 cups shucked large oysters, about
   2 dozen

2 tablespoons olive oil

FOR THE EGGS

12 eggs

2 tablespoons milk or cream

1 teaspoon chopped fresh parsley

½ teaspoon Tabasco

Freshly ground black pepper to
   taste

2 scallions, chopped

2 tablespoons butter

¼ cup seeded and chopped plum
   tomatoes

Combine the flour, cayenne pepper, black pepper and nutmeg in a shallow dish and mix well. Dredge the oysters in the flour mixture and shake off any excess. Heat a sauté pan and heat 2 tablespoons olive oil. Quickly sear the oysters on both sides, remove to a plate and keep warm.

Combine the eggs, cream, parsley, Tabasco and black pepper in a medium bowl and mix well. Heat a sauté pan and melt the butter. Add the egg mixture and quickly stir with a wooden spatula while shaking the pan. Remove the eggs as soon as they set and spread on a serving dish. Arrange the oysters on the eggs and top with the chopped tomatoes. Serve immediately.

Know Your Fire

Soups

Soup is the simplest of foods. There are no restricting rules, no watching the pot. All you need are a bowl for serving and a spoon for eating.

Cream Soups

Cream gives soup a rich flavor and silky texture. If you want to cut down on fat, substitute a puréed potato for the cream. Yogurt can be substituted, but you have to like the tang, and its flavor doesn't always complement the other ingredients. Reduced-fat sour cream is another choice, but it has to be added at the end. If the soup boils after sour cream is added to the pot, the soup may curdle.

When using a blender for puréeing soup, never fill it more than half full.

Some cream soups are thickened with cornstarch or flour. A roux, which is equal parts of flour and butter creamed together, can be whisked in at the end, but don't be overzealous because too much flour can make the soup gluey. (See thickeners, page 127.)

Stocks

Creating a soup using stock as the base instead of water adds a lot of flavor. Of course, the best stocks are homemade, but in a pinch you can resort to canned ones. Adding a carrot, a small onion, a rib of celery, and a few sprigs of parsley to canned stock and simmering it for 15 minutes greatly improves its flavor. Check the label on the can and be aware of whether you have to dilute it with water. Don't add salt until the very end of the cooking process because most canned stocks are salty to begin with. When you buy canned stock, you might want to look for the low-sodium varieties.

Chicken stock and beef stock are the most common stocks used, but vegetable stock is making strong inroads. It's easy to make: save your vegetable peelings and cook them in water for 1 hour. Strain and season with herbs, if desired.

Hearty Soups

A hearty one-dish soup is a meal in itself. It's the ultimate convenience food because it can be made in advance. If more people show up than you expect, just add another potato or two or some pasta. Try to make the soup the day before so that the flavors meld overnight.

Easier Soup Versus Tastier Soup

The easiest way to make a soup is to throw all the ingredients into a pot, turn on the heat and wait an hour. The tastiest way to make a soup is to grill or sauté the vegetables first in butter or olive oil to seal in their flavor rather than have it dissipate into the broth. This is especially true when making any type of vegetable soup.

What Does It Mean to "Sweat" Vegetables?

You won't find the technique of sweating vegetables in many cookbooks. It's a timely process that calls for cooking small pieces of vegetables in butter or oil over low heat. You can actually see the tiny droplets of moisture on the vegetables as they "sweat" and soften yet retain their natural moisture. The vegetables become translucent and keep their color, but should not brown.

How to Clarify Soup

A broth or stock can become cloudy after it's been cooking for several hours and you may want to "clean" it up, especially if you're serving it as a clear broth. To clarify a broth, add 2 or 3 eggshells or beaten egg whites to the pot and simmer the broth for 10 minutes. Skim the top of the broth or soup with a spoon. Allow the broth to come to room temperature and then run it through a cloth-lined strainer or a fine sieve to remove the residue before adding any other ingredients.

How to Make Soup from Leftovers

Some soups were invented to use up leftovers. In the south, the ham bone from Sunday's dinner, and any shreds of meat from the bone, go into Monday's bean soup. Thanksgiving's turkey carcass is the basis for cream of turkey soup. Saturday night's mashed potatoes can be transformed into a hot or cold potato soup.

Start with a pot of chicken broth and add any leftover vegetables, a can of beans and leftover cold pasta or rice from Chinese takeout and you have an instant meal.

How to Rescue Oversalted Soup

If soup is oversalted, add a peeled, sliced potato and simmer for about 15 minutes. Discard the potato before serving. The soup can be diluted by adding milk, tomato juice or salt-free stock. Always pour salt into a spoon or your hand rather than pour it into the pot straight from the box.

Some Soup Garnishes

The only garnish a vegetable soup needs is a dollop of pesto, but monotone cream soups benefit from a sprinkling of chopped fresh herbs such as chives, tarragon, basil or parsley. Garnish a cream soup with its chief vegetable, an asparagus tip, for instance, or some grated carrot. Add crunch to any soup with croutons, a few sliced almonds or popcorn, and add zip with a grating of Romano pecorino cheese. A drizzle of olive oil on a thick soup will give it an extra dimension of taste and texture.

How to Freeze Soup

Here are two ways to freeze soup: Place the soup in a rigid plastic container with straight sides, leaving ½-inch headroom, or pour the soup into freezer-weight plastic bags, seal, and lay flat (it will thaw faster).

If you're concerned about whether or not the soup will freeze well, freeze a cup of it overnight and defrost it the next day. Reheat the soup and, if you're not happy with the results, invite friends over for a soup party.

Lobster Broth

I wouldn't go out to buy lobsters to make a broth (shrimp shells work just as well) but if you're having a lobster bake or boiling a mess of lobsters, it's a good way to get some extra mileage out of the lobsters.

4 (1¼ pound) lobsters

2 tablespoons olive oil (for grilling)

2 tablespoons butter or margarine

I onion, thinly sliced

I leek, white part only, cleaned and
    chopped

I carrot, chopped

I rib celery, chopped

2 tablespoons tomato purée

I teaspoon sweet paprika

I teaspoon dried thyme

¼ cup dry white wine

8 cups fish stock (see page 189)

2 bay leaves

I cup spinach leaves, washed and
    cut into fine strips

Oyster crackers

Preheat the oven to 350°F or heat the grill to medium.

Split the lobsters (see page 151). If roasting, place them in a roasting pan, cut side up, and place them in the oven for 7 minutes. If grilling, place the lobsters cut side down on the grill for 2 minutes. Turn them over and cook 5 minutes longer, basting with the olive oil. Cool, remove the meat from the tail and claws and dice. Return the lobster shells to the oven or grill and brown them well, taking care that they don't burn.

Heat a large soup kettle, melt the butter and sweat the onion, leek, carrot and celery over low heat The vegetables should not color. When the vegetables are translucent, add the tomato purée, thyme and Tabasco and blend well. Add the roasted lobster shells and white wine and cook 2 to 3 minutes. Add the fish stock and bay leaves and bring to a boil. Lower heat and simmer the broth for 25 minutes. Pour the mixture through a fine strainer or through 2 layers of cheesecloth until the broth is perfectly clear.

Just before serving, reheat the broth. Divide the lobster meat and spinach among 6 bowls and ladle in the hot broth. Serve with oyster crackers.

Brandy and Cheese Soup

The brandy adds a certain something special to this soup made with (yep, count 'em) four different cheeses. This soup is so rich, it's almost a meal by itself and requires only a mesclun salad and a fruit dessert.

3 tablespoons butter or margarine

1 onion, diced

¼ cup diced celery

1 leek, white part only, cleaned and chopped

4 cloves Caramelized Garlic (page 186)

3 tablespoons all-purpose flour

8 cups hot chicken or vegetable stock

2 bay leaves

¼ teaspoon Tabasco

Pinch ground nutmeg

Pinch of freshly ground black pepper

¼ cup shredded sharp white Cheddar cheese

¼ cup Swiss or fontina cheese

2 tablespoons grated Parmesan cheese

¼ cup brandy

8 ounces ripe Brie

Heat a large soup kettle and melt the butter. Add the onion, celery, leeks and garlic. Sweat the vegetables over low heat until they become translucent. Stir occasionally. Do not brown the vegetables.

Stir in the flour and continue to cook, stirring constantly, for 2 to 3 minutes without browning the flour. Slowly add the hot stock, stirring constantly to break up any lumps. Bring the soup to a boil, add the bay leaves, Tabasco, nutmeg and black pepper. Reduce the heat and simmer 20 to 25 minutes.

Just before serving, whisk in the Cheddar, Swiss cheese, Parmesan cheese and brandy. Cut off the white rind from the Brie and cut into small pieces. Add a few pieces at a time to the soup and stir until they melt. Remove the bay leaves and serve.

Steak and Bean Soup

Not much is heard about skirt steak. It's cut from the beef flank and, although it can be tough, when cooked properly it's tender and delicious with a lot of beefy flavor. Two cans of red kidney beans, rinsed in cold water and drained, can be substituted for the dried kidney beans. Add them after the soup has cooked for 1 hour.

2 cups dried kidney beans	1 head Caramelized Garlic (page 186)
4 slices bacon, chopped	½ cup tomato purée
1 pound skirt steak, cut into 3 to 4 pieces	6 cups chicken or beef stock
	2 tablespoons balsamic vinegar
1 onion, chopped	2 bay leaves
½ cup chopped celery	¼ teaspoon Tabasco
½ cup diced carrots	

Rinse the beans in cool water, discarding any broken ones or twigs. Place the beans in a large bowl, cover with water and set aside for 8 to 12 hours.

Heat a large soup kettle over medium heat, add the bacon and cook until it renders its fat. Remove the bacon and drain on paper towels.

Raise the temperature to high, add the pieces of skirt steak and cook them until they're well browned on all sides. Remove the steaks from the pot, cut across the grain into thin slices, chop coarsely and set aside. Lower the heat, add the onion, celery, carrots and garlic and sweat the vegetables over low heat until they become translucent. Stir in the tomato purée, cook 2 minutes and return the chopped skirt steak to the pot. Add the stock, vinegar, bay leaves and Tabasco and stir well.

Drain the beans, add them to the soup and cook until the beans are tender, about 1 hour. Add additional stock if the soup becomes too thick. Discard the bay leaves. Serve the soup in bowls and sprinkle with the cooked bacon.

Corn Tortilla Soup

You won't find many soup recipes that require grilling, but taking the extra time to grill the vegetables adds a totally different flavor dimension to the soup.

Tortillas are the bread of Mexico. These thin pancakes are made from corn or wheat flour and are always baked on a griddle. Toasting the tortillas gives them a nice smoky flavor and the grilled strips, which wind up looking like macaroni, thicken the soup.

1 pound boneless chicken thighs	1 head **Caramelized Garlic,**
2 chorizos or spicy smoked sausages	(page 186), puréed
Olive oil	3 scallions, chopped
2 ears of corn or 1 cup canned corn	1 tablespoon ground cumin
kernels	6 cups hot chicken stock
1 onion, thickly sliced	1 tablespoon chopped fresh cilantro
1 red bell pepper, halved and seeded	2 bay leaves
1 green or yellow bell pepper,	1 teaspoon Tabasco
halved and seeded	3 (8-inch) flour tortillas
2 jalapeño peppers	Freshly ground black pepper to taste
3 to 4 plum tomatoes, halved	1 cup shredded Monterey Jack
2 tablespoons olive oil	cheese

Preheat the grill to medium and light the side burner.

Brush the chicken thighs and chorizos with olive oil, grill 7 to 8 minutes on each side and chop into bite-size pieces.

Grill the corn (see page 165).

Brush the onions, peppers, jalapeños and tomatoes with olive oil. Grill the onions 3 to 4 minutes on each side. Grill the bell peppers, jalapeños and tomatoes 2 to 3 minutes on each side. Chop the onions, peppers and tomatoes and cut the corn kernels from the cob.

Heat the 2 tablespoons olive oil in a large soup kettle or Dutch oven. Add the chicken, sausage, onion and garlic and sauté for 2 to 3 minutes. Add the peppers, scallions and cumin and cook 4 to 5 minutes. Add the tomatoes and corn and cook 2 minutes longer. Add the hot stock, cilantro, bay leaves and Tabasco. Bring to a boil, lower the heat and simmer for 30 minutes.

Meanwhile, reduce the grill heat to low. Place the tortillas on the grill and toast lightly on both sides. Cut the tortillas into strips 1 inch long and ¼ inch wide. Add the strips to the soup for the last 15 minutes. Remove the bay leaves and season with black pepper. Just before serving, slowly add the cheese and stir until it melts.

Grilling corn Pull back the husks, but do not remove. Remove and discard the corn silk. Brush the corn with melted butter and season with pepper. Reposition the corn husks over the kernels and wrap each ear in aluminum foil. Grill for 20 minutes, turning frequently.

Onion and Beer Soup

This soup blends the sweetness of the onion with the character of the beer, but by using different brands of beer, you can change the flavor of the soup. If heavy cream isn't in your diet, substitute milk or half-and-half. Use only sweet onions like Vidalia, Texas, Maui or Walla Walla, which have to be cooked very slowly so the onions will become brown and caramelized.

2 tablespoons butter

4 cups thinly sliced onion cut into
 1-inch pieces

2 tablespoons all-purpose flour

6 cloves Caramelized Garlic
 (page 186)

1 (12-ounce) can of beer

6 cups chicken stock

1 cup chopped canned or fresh
 tomatoes

2 tablespoons prepared mustard

1 teaspoon dried thyme

2 bay leaves

½ teaspoon Tabasco

1 cup heavy cream

Heat a large soup kettle and melt the butter over low-medium heat. Add the onions and let them cook until they are completely brown, stirring only once or twice. This may take as long as 20 minutes. Stir in the flour and the garlic and cook 2 minutes over medium-high heat. Stir in the beer and cook 1 minute. Add the stock, tomatoes, mustard, thyme, bay leaves and Tabasco and blend well. Bring to a boil, lower the heat and simmer for 30 minutes. Add the cream and heat, but do not boil. Remove the bay leaves and serve immediately.

Vegetables

The Legend of Alice Waters

America's love affair with vegetables began in California when New Jersey–born Alice Waters, the chef/owner of Chez Panisse, opened her restaurant in Berkeley in 1971. It was she who insisted on the very freshest and the very best seasonal ingredients. "So much commercial produce is grown for its looks and keeping properties, not for flavor," she wrote in *Chez Panisse Pasta, Pizza & Calzone*. It was Alice's mission to go to local growers and encourage them to nurture produce—not to throw seeds in the ground, fertilize like mad and pick them before they were perfectly vine-ripened because the produce had to travel across the country to market. The results were vegetables that tasted like vegetables, and her vision brought diners from all over the country to her California restaurant to see what was going on.

Until then, vegetables existed in restaurants because there was a space on the plate that had to be filled next to the roast beef and mashed potatoes.

Alice Waters inspired many chefs and raised their culinary awareness of vegetables. A new era had begun.

Vegetables Dos and Don'ts

Choose fresh vegetables with a firm texture, plump or crisp with good color, and buy as few as possible. If you can't resist a good buy or the garden is overflowing, blanch and then freeze them in meal-size portions

Cooking can either greatly enhance or ruin the appeal of vegetables. Not only do vegetables change in color, flavor, and texture the longer they cook, their valuable vitamins and minerals are reduced. Cook vegetables until just tender. Like pasta, vegetables should be cooked al dente. Rather than crowd them in a pot, cook them in several batches. Whenever possible, leave the skins on to preserve the vitamins and minerals, but scrub them well before cooking.

Dieters, especially, like to steam vegetables because it requires no fat, and most of the vitamins and minerals as well as the color and crunch are preserved. Many stockpots come with steamer baskets, or you can buy an inexpensive folding steamer insert that will fit any pot up to 10 inches in diameter.

The water level should always be below the vegetables. On the down side, steaming takes about one-and-a-half times as long to cook vegetables as boiling.

Vegetables should be stored in a cool, dry place. The drawer at the bottom of most refrigerators is perfect because the temperature is slightly warmer than that required by other perishables such as meat and dairy products.

Potatoes, onion, garlic and cabbage should not be refrigerated. Store in a dark, dry place at between 50° and 65°.

Let the natural flavoring of vegetables shine through by not masking them with too much butter or seasoning.

Cooking can improve the color of some green vegetables, if done right. For example, string beans and broccoli should be added to rapidly boiling water in an uncovered pot and cooked until just tender. Since vegetables will continue to cook as long as they're hot, drain immediately, dress and serve them or rinse in cold water to stop the cooking process if they are to be served later. Never use baking soda to keep the green color in vegetables because it destroys vitamin C and turns the vegetables mushy.

A red pigment called anthocyanin is found in vegetables such as red cabbage and beets. Since red pigments bleed in water, the basic cooking rule is to add some acid to enhance the color. Add orange juice to beets and vinegar to red cabbage and either steam them or cook them in as little water as possible.

Corn, carrots, winter squash, yams, sweet potatoes and rutabaga contain an orange or yellow pigment called carotenoid. These are the most hearty of all vegetables, and their flavor, texture, color and nutrients are stable and not affected by overcooking.

The white pigment found in potatoes, cabbages, onions and cauliflower is called flavone, and the color and nutrients of these vegetables are not affected by overcooking either. Yet the basic rule applies here too: cook in as little water as possible for the shortest possible time.

The Often Forgotten Parsnip, Rutabaga and Turnip

If a majority of people were asked to list the vegetables they liked the least, parsnip, rutabaga and turnip would probably be up close to the top.

The white-fleshed parsnip is the same shape as a carrot and just as sweet, especially when it's been exposed to near-freezing temperatures that convert its starch to sugar. Try it french fried, baked along with a roast or added to the vegetables in a stew.

The rutabaga, sometimes called yellow turnip, is often found covered in wax to prolong its shelf life. That's too bad because the young rutabaga has a wonderful earthy flavor. The yellow color indicates high levels of beta carotene. Try it puréed with butter and a dash of brown sugar or mashed with an equal portion of white potatoes.

The turnip is grown for the white root as well as the greens that can be cooked like spinach. Cook turnips and mash with butter and a dash of nutmeg, or purée with carrots or white potatoes. Turnips are traditional with duck and goose but if you add them to soup, add them at the end and only to the portion to be eaten immediately as the flavor will dominate the dish.

Carrots

Carrots with their tops still attached are best when purchased from a farm stand or a produce market. They should be purchased and consumed as close to harvesting as possible because leaving on the tops robs a carrot of nutrients, moisture and sweetness. Cello pack carrots are a good buy but be sure to inspect the bag for any that have developed cracks or long white hairs. These are telltale signs that the carrots have been in storage too long and will be limp, dry and tasteless.

Onions

True Vidalia onions are grown only in Vidalia county, Georgia. The soil produces an onion that is so sweet it can be eaten out-of-hand like an apple. Sometimes Vidalia onion seeds are planted in other areas and they can be sweet, but they're not quite the same. Legally, to be called a Vidalia onion, the onion has to be grown within 30 air miles of Vidalia, Georgia.

Maui onions, grown in Hawaii, are sweet onions similar to Vidalia as are Walla Walla onions, grown in the state of Washington.

Bermuda onions are very white in color and oval in shape with a green or grayish stripe from root to stem end. The early crop is always the sweetest, but they get "hot" the longer they're stored. They can quickly get moldy because of their high sulfur content.

Yellow onions are the most popular multipurpose onion used today. They're round, medium in size and have hard bright yellow skins. They have an intense onion flavor and store well.

Spanish onions are large round yellow onions that are sweet enough in flavor to be eaten raw on hamburgers or on liverwurst sandwiches. In cooked dishes, their flavor is mild.

Red onions come in a variety of sizes (small to large), shapes (round, elongated or flattened) and names (Italian onions, California reds). The smaller ones are used raw in salads. When cooked with other foods, they tend to bleed. If you find any that have been peeled down so that they no longer have their paper covering, it means they've been in storage too long. You can occasionally find braids of red onions imported from Italy.

The Ideal Knife: A Chef's Best Kitchen Companion

The most important thing to consider when buying a knife is whether you like the feel. The shape of the handle should be comfortable, and the knife should be well balanced. Pick up a few without looking at the price tags and see what feels good. Buy the best you can afford; it will last a long time.

The metal part of the knife should extend the length of the handle and be secured with at least three rivets. The handle can be wood or other material but there should be no gaps between the blade and handle material in which food could accumulate.

The best material for a knife blade is high-carbon stainless steel. It keeps a sharp edge and can be easily sharpened.

Make a lifetime investment by buying a good quality 6- or 8-inch utility or chef's knife. It's the most basic knife used for cutting, carving and chopping. The most frequently used knife is a paring knife used to peel and trim fruit and vegetables and cut small pieces of food. Another essential knife is a bread knife, which, in addition to slicing bread, can be used for carving meat, slicing tomatoes, cabbage, etc.

The one knife I find irresistible is an offset knife with a serrated edge. The handle and the blade are not in a straight line and this design allows me to do a multitude of cutting while holding the knife with a strong grip without banging my knuckles on the cutting board.

Another knife I'm particularly fond of is a scalloped carver, which has scallops ground into the side of the blade and is great for slicing meat, bread and tomatoes.

Additionally, you will want knives that fit your type of cooking: a cleaver for Chinese dishes, a carving knife for roasts, a cheese knife, a tomato knife, a boning knife, a fillet knife.

Knives are expensive, so take good care of them. Do not put them into the dishwasher. Store them in a knife block or on a magnetic bar instead of throwing them in a drawer.

Contact my web site at www.chefghirsch.com for more information on knives.

Preparing Vegetables: Dice, Cube, Cut on the Slant

How you cut vegetables has a lot to do with the way they will cook. To dice means to cut into tiny pieces less than ¼-inch square. To cube means to cut into ½-inch pieces. The smaller the size, the quicker the food will cook.

Most Americans cut vegetables such as asparagus, carrots and green beans into pieces with straight sides. Oriental-cut vegetables are sliced on the diagonal so that there is more cut surface to absorb seasoning. Because the pieces are tapered, they take less time to cook than pieces cut straight across.

Asparagus Many Ways

Asparagus seem to be in the market year round, but they're best in the spring when they come from local farms. Although most cooks boil them in a large stockpot, they can be cooked in a skillet and, if you're an ardent asparagus lover, you might want to invest in an asparagus steamer, a tall slender pot that allows the asparagus to be cooked vertically. You can get the same effect using a stovetop coffeepot.

Asparagus can also be grilled (brush with olive oil and grill over medium heat until tender, about 5 minutes) or roasted (brush with olive oil and place in a 450°F oven for 10 minutes). To store, remove the rubber bands that tie the bundles together then wrap with a few sheets of paper towel to absorb the moisture. Place in a plastic bag before refrigerating. If the bands are left on, asparagus wilt twice as fast.

1 bunch asparagus

Snap off the lower ends of the asparagus by gently bending each stalk. Beginning at the bottom, peel the stalks to within 1 inch of the tip. Rinse in cool water to remove any sand. (Thin asparagus, about the diameter of a pencil, does not have to be peeled.)

Bring a large pot of water to a boil. Add the asparagus and cook until tender, anywhere from 3 to 12 minutes, depending on their thickness. Remove the asparagus from the pan and immediately immerse in cold water to stop the cooking. Serve the asparagus with melted butter, a squeeze of lemon juice, in pasta or rice dishes, in omelettes or in one of the following ways:

Italian: with olive oil, garlic, white wine, basil, lemon juice and grated Parmesan cheese

Greek: with olive oil, lemon juice, oregano, crumbled feta cheese

Asian: with sesame oil, soy sauce, chopped water chestnuts

Southern: with sautéd bacon or ham and chopped scallions

Southwestern: with chopped jalapeño peppers, lime juice and cilantro

Beets in Orange Sauce

Beets are a bonus vegetable; you can eat both the root and the greens.
Cook the beets and serve warm as a vegetable or slice and add to a
salad. Cook the tops as you would spinach or cut them up and add to a
green salad.

1 bunch beets	Juice and zest of 1 orange
2 tablespoons butter	1 cup orange juice
½ onion, chopped	1 teaspoon dried parsley

Remove the beet tops (leaving about 1 inch of the stem), place the beets
in a pot of boiling water and simmer until fork tender, about 30 minutes for 1½-
inch beets. Larger ones will take longer. Remove the beets, cool and remove the
skins and stem and root ends. Slice the beets ¼ inch thick.

Melt the butter in a saucepan. Add the onion and the juice and zest from
the fresh orange and simmer 2 minutes. Add the cup of orange juice, parsley
and sliced beets and heat until very hot.

Vegetables

Couscous with Broccoli Rabe

Broccoli rabe has been a favorite dish of Italians for many years, but Americans have only lately discovered this pungent, bitter green of the cabbage and turnip family. The bright green stalks are about 7 to 8 inches long with clusters of tiny green broccoli-like buds. (When the buds blossom into yellow flowers, it's over the hill.) Broccoli rabe can be stir-fried or steamed with garlic and hot pepper or combined with pasta and sausage. It contains protein, calcium, vitamins A and C and dietary fiber. One of the nice things about couscous is that it doesn't need any cooking. Merely add hot water and wait 5 minutes. Avoid buying the expensive varieties of couscous in a box with a packet of seasonings. Pick some up at a Middle Eastern food store or at any health food store.

I bunch broccoli rabe	2½ cups chicken stock
I tablespoon olive oil	I teaspoon hot pepper flakes
½ onion, chopped	I cup couscous
I carrot, diced	I tablespoon chopped fresh basil
6 cloves Caramelized Garlic (page 186)	Grated Parmesan cheese

Fill a pot with 3 quarts of water and bring to a boil.

Trim off and discard the ends of the broccoli rabe. Rinse the broccoli rabe in cool water and cut into 1-inch pieces. Cook the broccoli rabe in the boiling water for 4 to 5 minutes or until almost tender. Drain well.

Heat the olive oil over medium high heat in a large sauté pan. Add the onion, garlic and carrot and cook 3 to 4 minutes or until the vegetables are almost tender. Stir in the stock and hot pepper flakes and bring to a boil. Stir in the couscous and basil and mix well. Place the broccoli rabe on top, cover the pan, remove from the heat and set aside for 5 minutes to allow the couscous to swell and absorb the stock. Remove cover and serve with grated Parmesan cheese.

Brussels Sprouts and Walnuts

If brussels sprouts are not on the top of your list of favorite vegetables, this version might change your mind. The best time for sprouts is in the autumn when you can buy them on the stalk from your local farm market.

1 pint brussels sprouts	1 teaspoon caraway seeds
1 cup small white onions, peeled	Juice of 1 lemon
2 tablespoons butter or margarine	½ teaspoon Tabasco
¼ cup finely diced carrots	Pinch of ground nutmeg
1 parsnip, peeled and diced	Pinch of finely ground black
¼ cup walnut halves, toasted	pepper

Remove any dark outer leaves from the brussels sprouts, trim off the stem end and cut an X in it with a sharp knife. Boil in a large pot of water, until almost tender, 6 to 7 minutes. Drain and set aside, reserving ¼ cup of the blanching water.

Boil the onions in a small pot until almost tender, 4 to 5 minutes. Drain and set aside.

Heat a sauté pan and melt the butter. Just before the butter begins to brown, add the carrots and parsnip and cook until they begin to brown, about 4 to 5 minutes, stirring constantly. Add the onions, walnuts and caraway seeds and cook until the onions begin to glaze, 1 to 2 minutes. Add the sprouts, lemon juice, Tabasco, nutmeg, black pepper, the reserved ¼ cup of the blanching water and cook until the sprouts are tender, 2 to 3 minutes longer.

Vegetables

Chinese Cabbage

Chinese cabbage is a catch-all name for a staple Asian vegetable known by at least a dozen aliases. Its wide pearly white ribs are edged with light green crinkly leaves. When cooked, it becomes tender, but never mushy. Chinese cabbage is found in many stir-fried dishes.

1 head Chinese cabbage, coarsely chopped

1 head Caramelized Garlic (page 186)

2 tablespoons peeled and sliced fresh ginger

4 to 5 scallions, cut into 1-inch pieces

1 tablespoon lite soy sauce

1 tablespoon sesame oil

Place the Chinese cabbage, garlic, ginger and scallions in a steamer basket or strainer over 2 inches of boiling water, cover and steam until just tender, about 15 to 20 minutes. Remove and drizzle with the soy sauce and sesame oil.

Cauliflower Blanc

In the fall, when local Long Island cauliflower makes its annual appearance, I like to cook it up several ways. Here's one of my favorites—simple, easy and delicious. This cooking method keeps the cauliflower pure white.

2 cups cold water

½ cup milk

1 tablespoon butter

1 tablespoon all-purpose flour

½ teaspoon Tabasco

1 head cauliflower, cut into florets

4 tablespoons clarified butter (page 150)

Juice of 1 lemon

1 tablespoon chopped fresh parsley

Combine the water, milk, 1 tablespoon butter, flour and Tabasco in a saucepan and bring to a boil. Add the cauliflower florets and cook until tender, about 15 to 20 minutes. Drain well. Place the cauliflower in a serving dish, add the clarified butter, lemon and parsley and toss lightly.

Know Your Fire

Cauliflower with Fontina Sauce

Fontina is one of Italy's great cheeses. It has a mild, nutty flavor and melts even better than mozzarella. It's an ideal complement to cauliflower's own subtle flavor.

1 head cauliflower	½ teaspoon dry mustard
2 tablespoons butter	½ teaspoon Tabasco
½ onion, chopped	½ cup shredded fontina cheese
2 tablespoons all-purpose flour	Pinch of ground nutmeg
2 cups half-and-half	

Trim off and discard any black spots from the cauliflower, remove the leaves and cut out the core with a sharp knife. Cut cauliflower into florets and place in a large pot of boiling water and cook until tender, about 15–20 minutes. Drain well and keep warm.

Heat a saucepan and melt the butter. Add the onion and sweat over low heat until it's translucent but not brown. Add the flour and cook 1 to 2 minutes, stirring constantly. Slowly whisk in the half-and-half. Add the dry mustard and Tabasco and simmer 15 to 20 minutes. Remove the pan from the heat, add the fontina cheese and the nutmeg and stir until the cheese melts. If the sauce is too thick, add another tablespoon or two of half-and-half. Pour the sauce over the cauliflower and serve immediately.

Vegetables

177

Chayote Stuffed with Chorizo

Chayote (chi-OH-tay) is a member of the winter squash family. A native of Mexico, it is known by many different names. Because of its pear shape and thin, light green skin it is often called a vegetable pear. Because it has one large seed in the center, it is also called a one-seeded cucumber. It is also known as mirliton squash. The skin is usually not eaten.

If chayote is not available, you can substitute 2 medium zucchini.

2 (8 ounce) chayotes

2 tablespoons olive oil

8 ounces chorizo, chopped

½ onion, chopped

1 red bell pepper, seeded and
   chopped

4 to 5 cloves Caramelized Garlic
   (page 186)

2 jalapeño peppers, seeded and
   chopped

2 tablespoons bread crumbs

Juice of 1 lime

1 tablespoon chopped fresh
   cilantro

Preheat the oven to 350°F.

Cut the chayotes in half, scrape out the pulp with a spoon and chop coarsely. Reserve the skins.

Heat a sauté pan over medium heat until very hot and heat the olive oil. Add the chorizo, onion, red pepper, garlic, jalapeños, bread crumbs and chayote pulp and cook 3 to 4 minutes, stirring frequently. Stir in the lime juice and the cilantro and stuff the chayote halves with the mixture. Place them in an oven-proof pan and bake 35 to 40 minutes.

Hot and Sour Collards

If you're compiling a list of soul food dishes, certainly collards or collard greens must be high on the list. In the South collards are boiled with a ham hock and cooked for a long time and everyone wants the "pot likker" or the intensely flavored liquid in the bottom of the pot. Collard greens are a member of the cabbage family and contain good amounts of vitamins A and C, as well as calcium and iron.

1 bunch collards	4 serrano chilies, seeded and
2 tablespoons olive oil	chopped
1 onion, chopped	2 tablespoons cider vinegar
1 head Caramelized Garlic	
(page 186)	

Wash the collards in cool water to remove grit. Discard any tough stems and cut the leaves into bite-size pieces. Place the collards into boiling water and cook until tender, anywhere from 10 to 20 minutes, depending on how young the leaves are. Drain well.

Heat a large sauté pan and heat the olive oil. Add the onion, garlic and serrano chilies and sauté 2 minutes. Add the collards and vinegar and cook 4 to 5 minutes longer.

Vegetables

Stuffed Portobello Mushrooms

Portobello mushrooms are the largest mushrooms grown. These monsters grow to about 6 inches in diameter and are rather flat, which makes them perfect for stuffing. They have a meaty texture that some mushroomophiles swear can pass for a tender beef steak. Serve them as an appetizer or a side dish with steak.

4 Portobello mushrooms	8 cloves Caramelized Garlic
2 tablespoons olive oil	(page 186)
2 tablespoons butter	1 teaspoon dried rosemary, crushed
6 slices very thinly sliced pancetta	1 teaspoon dried thyme
or bacon	¼ cup dry white wine
1 red bell pepper, seeded and	1 cup fresh bread crumbs
chopped	4 slices mozzarella cheese
½ onion, chopped	

Preheat the grill to medium or an oven to 350°F.

Rinse the mushrooms quickly under cool water. Remove the stems. Chop the stems and set aside. Brush the caps with the olive oil.

Heat a medium skillet and add the butter. When the butter has melted, cook the pancetta until it's crisp. Remove the pancetta from the pan, leaving the drippings behind. Add the chopped mushroom stems, bell pepper, onion, garlic, rosemary, and thyme to the skillet and cook until the vegetables are tender, about 7 minutes. Add the wine and cook 1 minute. Chop 2 slices of the cooked pancetta and add it and the bread crumbs to the vegetable mixture and mix well.

Place the mushrooms, gill side down, on the grill and cook 2 minutes or put in a shallow casserole in a single layer and place in the oven for 3 minutes. Remove, turn the mushrooms over, fill with the vegetable mixture and top each with a slice of the cooked pancetta. Return to the grill or place in the oven to cook for 4 to 5 minutes. Top with the mozzarella cheese and cook until the cheese is melted, about 2 minutes.

Pumpkin and Acorn Squash

Don't wait for Thanksgiving to make this. Jack-o-lantern pumpkins are especially developed to be thin walled and oversized with a relatively small amount of flesh. A sugar or cheese pumpkin is ideal for this dish.

I pumpkin, about 12 to 14 inches in
    diameter
I acorn squash
2 tablespoons butter or margarine
2 Granny Smith apples, peeled,
    cored and sliced

I onion, chopped
½ cup vegetable or chicken stock
¼ teaspoon ground cinnamon
¼ teaspoon ground nutmeg
2 tablespoons hulled, toasted
    pumpkin seeds

Cut the pumpkin and the acorn squash in half, discard acorn squash seeds, and cut the flesh into 1-inch pieces.

Heat a large, wide saucepan and melt the butter. Add the pumpkin, squash, apples, onion, stock, cinnamon and nutmeg and cook until the vegetables are tender, about 30 minutes. The consistency should be souplike, so if it becomes dry, add a little more stock. Top with the pumpkin seeds and serve.

Vegetables

**MAKES 4
SERVINGS**

Roasted Vidalia Onions

Roasting Vidalia onions enhances their already sweet flavor. The addition of the seasoned vegetable gravy makes for an unusual appetizer.

2 Vidalia onions, each about 4
    inches in diameter
I tablespoon olive oil
I carrot, finely chopped
I parsnip or small white turnip,
    finely chopped
I cup beer

¼ cup sliced shiitake mushrooms
I tablespoon fresh rosemary leaves
I teaspoon fresh thyme
½ teaspoon Tabasco
Freshly ground black pepper to
    taste

Preheat the oven to 350°F.

Peel the onions and rub them with the olive oil. Place them in a small roasting pan or sauté pan with an ovenproof handle. Scatter the carrot and parsnip around the onions and roast, uncovered, until the onions begin to brown, about 15 to 20 minutes.

Add the beer, shiitake mushrooms, rosemary, thyme, Tabasco and black pepper to the pan and return it to the oven for 5 minutes or until the onions are tender. Remove the vegetables with a slotted spoon and place in a serving dish. Divide the onions onto 4 small plates. Heat the juices on the stovetop until reduced by one half and pour over onions.

Spinach and Pancetta

There are two major varieties of spinach sold in the market: the crinkly dark green Savoy and a flat leaf New Zealand spinach that tolerates hot weather, something that proper spinach does not. Pancetta is an Italian bacon cured with salt and spices but, unlike American bacon, it isn't smoked. It comes in a roll and you cut off as many slices as you need. If you can't locate it in an Italian deli, substitute bacon that has been blanched in boiling water for 2 minutes.

6 pints spinach leaves, about
    2 pounds

8 thin slices pancetta or 6 slices
    bacon

1 to 2 tablespoons olive oil

1 head Caramelized Garlic
    (page 186)

1 teaspoon fennel seeds

½ cup peeled, seeded and chopped
    plum tomatoes

Juice of 1 lemon

½ teaspoon hot pepper flakes

¼ cup dry white wine

Freshly ground black pepper to
    taste

Wash the spinach (see salad greens, page 119) discard the stems and leave on any water clinging to the leaves.

Heat a very large sauté pan and slowly cook the pancetta over medium heat until it gives up its fat and browns lightly. Remove the pancetta, chop it and set aside. Depending on how much fat is in the pan, add 1 to 2 tablespoons olive oil and sauté the garlic and fennel seeds 1 minute. Add the tomatoes, lemon juice and hot pepper flakes and sauté 1 minute. Add the spinach leaves and stir until they begin to wilt. As soon as they cook down enough to allow you to cover the pan, add the wine, cover and cook 2 minutes. Remove the cover, season with black pepper and top with the reserved pancetta. Serve at once.

Sweet Potatoes Stuffed with Peaches

Although sweet potatoes and yams look the same, taste the same and are interchangeable in recipes, they are two very different vegetables. A sweet potato is a member of the morning glory family and indigenous to the American tropics. The pale sweet potato has a thin, yellow skin and pale yellow flesh. The flavor is not too sweet and the texture is dry and crumbly. The darker sweet potato has a thicker, darker orange skin and the sweet, moist flesh is a vibrant orange. The yam, on the other hand, is grown in South and Central America, the West Indies and parts of Asia and Africa and seldom found in this country unless you shop at Latin American markets. On the outside yams range in color from off-white to dark brown. Inside the flesh can be off-white, yellow, purple or pink and the texture moist and tender to dry, coarse and mealy.

Sweet potatoes are no strangers to companion flavorings, but this version becomes so creamy, it's like eating a custard dessert. Serve with duck, lamb or pork.

6 sweet potatoes, preferably all the same size and shape

3 peaches, pitted and poached, or 6 canned peach halves, coarsely chopped

2 tablespoons melted butter

2 tablespoons brown sugar

¼ teaspoon ground allspice

1 tablespoon honey

2 tablespoons bread crumbs

Preheat the oven to 400°F.

Scrub the sweet potatoes and pat dry. Poke the potatoes on all sides with a fork and bake until soft, 45 to 60 minutes. Cool.

Reduce the oven temperature to 375°F.

Split open the top of each potato, scoop out about ¾ of the pulp and mash until smooth. Add the peaches, butter, brown sugar and allspice and blend well. Refill the sweet potato cavities with the mixture and drizzle the tops with honey and sprinkle with the bread crumbs. Bake the sweet potatoes for another 20 minutes and serve.

Know Your Fire

Basic Recipes

Basic recipes are to cooking what the A, B, Cs are to spelling. You can't do without them. Recipes such as Caramelized Garlic are the cornerstone of many of the recipes in this book. I use hundreds of heads of garlic during the filming of every television series. Whenever you're using the oven, add a few heads of garlic and let them cook along with the roast or casserole.

The stock recipes are the basis for good soup. Making stock may seem troublesome and a lot of extra work, but the benefits outweigh any extra effort. Once you've done the preparation, the stocks literally cook themselves. The stocks can be made in advance, and I've included freezing instructions.

Garlic bread is a favorite of mine, and I eat it with all kinds of dishes, not just Italian ones. You might even make the vegetarian or English versions and serve them as appetizers.

The pizza dough recipe is different from most because it requires a long rise in the refrigerator. I find this method develops a better flavor, and that's what cooking is all about.

Caramelized Garlic

Something wonderful happens to garlic when it's roasted. Its flavor mellows and it becomes so sweet that it can be used as a spread for bread. You'll find many recipes in the book calling for Caramelized Garlic, so it's good to make up a batch and refrigerate it so you'll be ready to cook at any time. Wrapped in foil, it will keep for up to 2 weeks.

6 heads fresh garlic   **¼ cup olive oil**

Lay each garlic head on its side and cut off ¼ inch from the bottom, or root end, exposing the garlic cloves. Remove as much of the papery covering as possible, leaving the head intact. Place the heads, exposed end down, in a single layer in an ovenproof dish and drizzle with the olive oil. Roast in a 375°F oven for 20 minutes, uncovered. Cover with aluminum foil and cook 10 to 15 minutes longer.

Caramelized Garlic can also be made on a grill. Remove ¼ inch from the bottom of each head, brush with oil and place on the cooler edges of the grill for 20 to 30 minutes. Cover the heads with a 12-inch square of aluminum foil and continue grilling until the cloves are soft, about 20 to 30 minutes.

To remove the garlic, regardless of method, separate the cloves and squeeze out the garlic.

Garlic Bread

There are hundreds of versions of garlic bread, but I'm giving you the basic one plus several variations that use different cooking methods to give you soft-and-moist or crisp-and-crunchy results, to use with different ethnic dishes.

4 tablespoons olive oil	1 teaspoon paprika
4 tablespoons butter	1 loaf French or Italian bread,
1 head Caramelized Garlic (page 186)	2 days old
1 teaspoon dried basil	1 tablespoon grated Parmesan cheese

Place the olive oil and butter into a small saucepan and heat until the butter melts. (This can also be done in the microwave oven.) Stir in the garlic, basil and paprika.

Split the bread lengthwise and brush with the garlic mixture. Sprinkle with the Parmesan cheese and the black pepper.

Heat the oven to 350°F.

For soft-and-moist garlic bread, put the two halves of the loaf back together, wrap in foil and bake in a 350°F oven for 10 to 12 minutes.

For crisp-and-crunchy garlic bread, place the halves on a baking sheet and bake 5 to 6 minutes. Watch carefully because the bread can go from crisp to burnt very quickly.

Variations

Italian: add a few slices of mozzarella and prosciutto on top, then bake until the cheese melts

Greek: crumble a few tablespoons of feta cheese and sprinkle with oregano before baking

Southwestern: after baking, top with 2 to 3 chopped jalapeño peppers and sprinkle with chopped fresh cilantro

Vegetarian: when it comes out of the oven, top with cooked and drained chopped spinach, grilled Portobello mushrooms and roasted peppers

English: sprinkle with shredded Cheddar cheese and cooked bacon, then bake until cheese melts

German: substitute pumpernickel bread for the Italian bread, omit the olive oil and use 8 tablespoons butter and add a few slices of Muenster cheese

Basic Recipes

187

Chicken Stock

A good stock is the basis for a good soup. Although it may be time-consuming, the results are worth it. Look for chicken backs and wings at your supermarket or save them from whole chickens you buy and freeze until you have enough.

4 pounds chicken parts (necks,
    backs, wings)

2 onions, quartered

2 carrots, cut into large chunks

2 ribs celery, cut into large chunks

I each: white turnip, leek, parsnip,
    cut into large chunks

4 cloves garlic, peeled

6 black peppercorns

2 bay leaves

3 stems fresh parsley

I whole clove

Pinch dried thyme

10 cups cold water

Wash the chicken parts and place into a large soup kettle or stockpot. Add the onions, carrots, celery, turnip, leek, parsnip, garlic, peppercorns, bay leaves, parsley, clove and thyme. Add the water, bring to a boil, lower heat, and simmer uncovered for 1½ hours. Skim off any scum from the surface with a ladle. Strain the stock and discard the solids. After the stock has chilled, remove any congealed fat, if desired. Refrigerate for 2 to 3 days or freeze up to 2 months.

Know Your Fire

Fish Stock

Fish stock should cook no longer than 20 to 25 minutes. Do not add any celery leaves or onion peelings for extra flavor because they will make the stock cloudy. Fishmongers used to give fish bones away, but today you may have to pay for them.

1 tablespoon olive oil

1 large leek, white part only, cleaned and chopped

1 onion, peeled and chopped

1 rib celery, chopped

1 parsnip, chopped

1 pound fish bones (flounder,

halibut, cod) or shellfish shells (lobster, shrimp)

1 cup white wine

2 bay leaves

4 stems fresh parsley

4 stems fresh thyme

5 cups water

Heat the olive oil in a 2-quart stockpot and add the leek, onion, celery and parsnip. Sauté the vegetables, but do not allow them to brown. Add the fish bones or shells, wine, bay leaves, parsley, thyme and water. Bring to a boil, lower heat and simmer 20 to 25 minutes. Strain and discard the solids. Cool the stock and refrigerate for up to 2 days or freeze up to 2 weeks.

Vegetable Stock

If the vegetables are caramelized before the liquid is added, the stock has more flavor. There are a number of ways to caramelize vegetables (see below). The darker the vegetables are caramelized, the darker the stock. Use vegetable stock for vegetarian soups, sauces and casseroles. You might want to add corn and sweet potatoes to this stock.

2 tablespoons olive oil	2 tomatoes, chopped fine
2 large onions, chopped fine	3 bay leaves
3 ribs celery, chopped fine	4 to 6 fresh parsley stems
3 carrots, chopped fine	½ teaspoon dried thyme
2 parsnips, chopped fine	4 cloves garlic, chopped
2 white turnips, chopped fine	7 cups water

Heat a large stockpot and heat the olive oil. Add the onion, celery, carrot, parsnips and turnips. Cook over high heat, stirring frequently, until the vegetables are light brown. Add the tomato, bay leaves, parsley, thyme, garlic and water. Bring to a boil, lower heat and simmer for 1½ to 2 hours. Strain and discard the vegetables. Cool the broth and refrigerate for up to 4 days or freeze for up to 2 months.

If using the grill, cut the onion, parsnip and turnip into thick slices. Cut the carrot and tomato in half lengthwise. Brush with the olive oil and grill over medium heat until they are brown. Remove vegetables from grill, chop fine, and follow directions for preparing stock.

Caramelizing vegetables When we think of caramelizing, we think of sugar. Vegetables contain natural sugars and when these sugars get hot and turn brown, the vegetables take on a sweet flavor. Onions, tomatoes, carrots and sweet potatoes have a lot of natural sugars and will brown more readily than green vegetables like broccoli and string beans. Vegetables can be caramelized in a pot on the stovetop, in the oven at 400°F or on a grill.

Beef or Veal Stock

A good beef or veal stock has always been the major foundation of many sauce and soup preparations. Today it's seldom made from scratch because it can take anywhere from 8 to 10 hours of cooking and it's hard to find bones because very little meat comes into butcher shops as major prime cuts. Also, the long cooking time necessary to produce a hearty stock promotes the buildup of excessive bacteria. But, rather than resort to canned beef stock or bouillon cubes, here's an updated version of beef stock.

4 pounds veal or beef bones, sliced 2 inches thick by the butcher

4 tablespoons tomato purée or tomato paste

1 onion, chopped

1 carrot, chopped

1 rib celery, chopped

½ white turnip, chopped

¼ cup dry white wine

4 quarts ice cold water

2 bay leaves

2 cloves garlic

3 sprigs fresh thyme

Preheat the oven to 375°F.

Place the bones in a large roasting pan and roast until they are well browned, 30 to 40 minutes. Stir in the tomato paste and return to the oven 10 minutes longer. Add the onion, carrot, celery and turnip and roast until the vegetables are browned, 20 to 30 minutes. Place the bones and vegetables into a large stockpot.

Pour the wine in the bottom of the roasting pan, scrape the bottom until all the food particles are loose and pour the mixture into the stockpot. Add the water, bay leaves and garlic and bring to a boil. Simmer the stock for 4 hours, skimming off any scum that accumulates on the top. Pour the stock through a fine strainer or cheesecloth and discard the bones and vegetables. Cool the stock as quickly as possible by pouring it into a clean bowl and placing it in a larger bowl containing ice cubes. Because the stock is high in protein and very susceptible to the growth of bacteria, refrigerate immediately. It will keep for up to 2 days. Freeze the stock for longer storage.

Basic Recipes

Potato Bread

Mashed potatoes give this basic white bread a wonderful chewy texture. If you use russet potatoes, which are the least moist, you'll use less flour than if you use mashed potatoes made from all-purpose potatoes. Also, if the weather is very humid, you'll need more flour. The bread stays fresh for several days and is delicious toasted.

The dough can be kneaded by hand, or with a heavy-duty mixer. If you use a mixer, knead it by hand for about a minute to smooth out the dough after you take it out of the mixer.

If you buy active dry yeast by the jar, use a scant tablespoon of yeast.

1 package active dry yeast	½ cup mashed potatoes, seasoned
½ cup warm water, approximately	or unseasoned
95° to 105°F	1 cup milk, warmed to 95°F
⅓ cup granulated sugar	1 teaspoon salt
4 egg yolks	6 to 7 cups bread or all-purpose flour

Combine the yeast, water and 1 tablespoon of the sugar in a small warm bowl and mix well until the yeast and sugar dissolve. Set aside for 10 minutes.

In the large bowl of an electric mixer, combine the egg yolks and mashed potatoes and mix well. Add the milk and stir until the mixture is smooth. Stir in the remaining sugar, salt and the yeast mixture. Add 6 cups flour and mix with the paddle until the ingredients form a dough. Change to the dough hook and knead for 6 to 7 minutes, adding additional flour a little at a time if the dough is sticky. Or, using the instructions on page 194, knead the dough on a lightly floured surface until smooth and elastic, about 10 minutes.

Place the dough in a greased bowl and turn it over so that it is thoroughly greased. Cover with plastic wrap and set aside in a warm area until the dough doubles in size, about 1 hour. The dough can also be placed in the refrigerator to rise, but this cold-rise method will take about 8 hours. You can tell if the dough has risen by poking a finger into it. If the dent remains, the dough has risen.

Remove the dough from the bowl, punch it down, knead for 30 seconds, and divide evenly into 2 portions. Shape each into a ball, place on a greased cookie sheet, cover with a damp cloth and set aside in a warm area until the balls double in size, about 30 minutes. About 15 minutes before the dough is ready, preheat the oven to 400°F.

Lightly brush the tops of the dough with water and dust with flour. Using a serrated knife or sharp, single-edge razor blade, make a ⅛-inch deep criss-cross on top.

Place the loaves in the oven for 10 minutes. Reduce the heat to 375°F and bake 30 to 35 minutes longer. To test the bread for doneness, turn it over and tap the bottom with your index finger. If it sounds hollow, it's done. It it's soft and unresponsive, return the bread to the oven for 5 or 10 minutes longer.

**MAKES ABOUT
I POUND**

Pizza Dough

There are many recipes for pizza dough. They all contain flour, yeast and water. This version is a little different because the dough is refrigerated for several hours to allow the flavors to develop, so you'll have to set aside extra time. Otherwise, you can buy pizza dough at most supermarkets or you might even buy a pound or two from your local pizzeria.

Pour some hot water into your mixer bowl and leave it there for about 5 minutes to heat the bowl before adding the yeast mixture. Instructions are given for kneading the dough with a dough hook and by hand.

I cup warm water, 95° to 105°	3½ cups all-purpose flour
I teaspoon active dry yeast	¼ teaspoon salt
I teaspoon granulated sugar	2 tablespoons olive oil

Combine ¼ cup of the water, yeast, and sugar in the bowl of a heavy-duty mixer and stir until the yeast is dissolved. Set aside for 5 minutes. Add the remaining ¾ cup of water and stir well. Add 3 cups of flour, the salt and 1 tablespoon olive oil and mix until well blended. Set the dough hook in place and knead until the dough is smooth and elastic, 7 to 9 minutes. Add the remaining ½ cup of flour a little at a time if the dough is sticky.

Or knead by hand. Kneading by hand is a rhythmic push, fold and turn. Place the dough on a lightly floured surface and lightly flour your hands. Push the heel of your hand down into the dough, moving it away from you. Fold the dough over again, give it a quarter turn and push down again. Repeat until the dough is smooth and elastic.

Regardless of which kneading method you use, press two fingers into the dough. If the indentation springs back, the dough has been kneaded enough.

Gather the dough into a ball and divide into 3 or 4 pieces. Roll each portion into a ball and place in a large greased bowl. Cover with a towel and set in a warm place (but not on the stove) and let rise until double in size, about 45 to 60 minutes. Brush the dough with the remaining tablespoon of olive oil, cover each ball with plastic wrap and refrigerate 2 to 4 hours.

Use the dough immediately or place it in freezer-quality plastic bags and freeze up to three months. To defrost, remove the dough from the freezer and thaw overnight in the refrigerator. When defrosted, brush with olive oil, cover and refrigerate 2 to 4 hours or until the dough doubles in volume.

Know Your Fire

Cooking Methods

How To Cook It

Introduction

Moist Versus Dry Heat Cooking

There are only two choices when it comes to cooking—moist heat or dry heat. Whenever food is cooked with a liquid, it's called moist-heat cooking. Braising and poaching are the two most common forms of this technique. Simmering and boiling are also forms of moist-heat cooking. When simmering, the water is a little hotter than poaching (you might see a few bubbles), and boiling calls for a temperature of 212°F and lots of bubbles.

Although poaching is often associated with eggs, other delicate foods like chicken breasts, fish, even fruit, benefit from poaching's gentle method, which keeps food moist and tender.

Roasting, frying, grilling and broiling are examples of dry-heat cooking. A vast majority of our foods are cooked using these methods. Most poultry, fish and vegetables can be roasted, fried, grilled and broiled but using these dry-heat methods at very high temperatures can toughen and shrink the protein in large pieces of meat and cause loss of moisture. If you want to prevent your roast from reducing to half its size, cook it at lower temperatures.

Two exceptions to cooking meat at high temperature are grilling and broiling. These methods are used for steaks, chops and other thinner cuts of meat that are cooked quickly. Usually meats with good marbling are grilled or broiled, and the fat acts as a self baster. Fat inside the muscle melts away leaving the meat tender.

Dry heat and moist heat will also affect the flavor of the food you're cooking. The example I like to use most often is the following: picture two thick, juicy, tender, expensive steaks. Imagine a hot sizzling grill and next to it a pot of boiling water on a stove. In your mind, place one of the steaks on the grill and the other in the pot of water. When cooked, the first will be caramelized and nicely browned on the outside with lots of beefy flavor. The second will be grayish in color and bland in flavor.

Your choice, simply put, is dry heat or moist heat.

Both dry heat and moist heat are ideal cooking methods when used properly. Sometimes they're used in combination. When braising a pot roast, for example, the meat is first browned (dry heat) and then cooked in a small amount of liquid (moist heat) until tender.

Sautéing and stir-frying can be classified as dry-heat cooking, but when a sauce is added toward the end, the moist-heat method is being used.

Braising

Braising is a combination of dry heat and moist heat, and the best thing that ever happened to a tough piece of meat. During boiling, simmering or poaching, the only additional flavor comes from the cooking liquid. But in braising, the food caramelizes as it is seared or browned on the outside and then is tenderized by cooking for a long time in a liquid.

Stovetop or Oven?

For years I have been demonstrating that the outdoor grill is an extension of the kitchen stove and, once you "Know Your Fire," you'll realize that heat can be adapted to any food surface. Once meat and vegetables have been browned, the pan can go into the oven where the meat will braise more consistently because the heat is even all around. On the stovetop, the heat comes only from the bottom. The next time you put a hamburger or a steak on the grill, remember you could have braised it.

How to Brown Meat and Poultry Before Braising

Coat the outside of the meat with a light dusting of flour. Heat a small amount of butter or oil in a large preheated saucepan or stockpot, add the meat and brown it on all sides over fairly high heat. This can take as long as 30 minutes and should not be rushed. The better it's browned, the better the flavor. The meat can also be browned on the grill or in the broiler. Add onions, garlic, carrots, celery, leeks and so forth and cook until they're a golden brown, stirring occasionally. By browning or caramelizing the vegetables, they will be sweeter in taste, and the sauce you make from them will be more flavorful with a darker, richer color.

A Pot with a Tight-Fitting Cover Is a Necessity

Once the meat and vegetables have browned, it's time to add some liquid such as wine, vinegar, beer, stock, or fruit juice. The liquid should come up one-half to two-thirds the height of the meat. If the meat is covered, it will be poached or stewed and not braised. Loosen any tiny food particles stuck to the bottom of the pan with a wooden spoon. These particles have the strongest concentration of taste and make the sauce full of flavor. Bring the liquid to a boil, reduce the temperature to a gentle simmer and cover the pot tightly.

How to Make a Less Expensive Cut of Meat Taste Like Something Special

Braising is especially effective for more economical cuts because when meat is cooked at a low temperature using moist heat for a long period of time, the connective tissues soften and the texture of a tough piece of meat changes so that it can be cut with a fork. The liquid should never boil because high temperatures will toughen a less tender cut of meat even more.

What Else Can Be Braised?

Braising is not done exclusively with meat. The flavor of seafood and vegetables can also benefit from this form of cooking. Once they have been browned, certain fish and high-moisture vegetables need very little additional liquid added. If the pan is tightly covered, the moisture contained in the food is usually sufficient to cook it fully. Vegetables, especially cabbage and carrots, that take a long time to become tender are tastier when braised in a flavorful cooking liquid. See the following recipes for more detailed instructions for braising fish and vegetables.

**MAKES 4
SERVINGS**

Grits and Grillades

Grits, coarsely ground dried corn, are a Southern classic that can turn up at almost any meal. Grillades means "broiled" meat in French. In Louisiana, this combination is referred to as one dish—Grits and Grillades. The grits can be cooked while the grillades are simmering.

TO MAKE THE GRITS

3 cups water

1 tablespoon butter

½ teaspoon Tabasco

½ cup regular grits, not instant

Bring the water to a boil in a heavy 3- or 4-quart saucepan and add the butter and Tabasco. Slowly pour in the grits, stirring constantly, and when the water returns to a boil, reduce the heat so that the grits simmer slowly. Stirring occasionally, cook the grits until they absorb all the water and the mixture is thick and smooth, about 15 to 20 minutes.

TO MAKE THE GRILLADES

1½ pounds bottom round beef or
   pork shoulder

4 tablespoons all-purpose flour

¼ cup vegetable oil

1 onion, chopped

1 rib celery, chopped

1 red or green bell pepper, chopped

8 cloves Caramelized Garlic
   (page 186)

8 plum tomatoes, chopped, or 2
   cups canned plum tomatoes

1 tablespoon fresh chopped parsley
   or 1 teaspoon dried

1 teaspoon dried thyme

½ teaspoon Tabasco

2 cups beef or chicken stock

1 tablespoon vinegar or juice of
   ½ lemon

Freshly ground black pepper to
   taste

Cut the meat into thin slices and pound them between two sheets of wax paper until they are ¼-inch thick. Lightly dredge the meat in 2 tablespoons of the flour and shake off any excess. Heat the oil in a large saucepan or deep skillet and quickly sauté the meat on both sides over high heat until brown. Do not crowd the pieces. Remove the meat and drain off all but 2 tablespoons of the oil from the pan.

Add the onion, celery, bell pepper and garlic to the pan and cook the vegetables over high heat until they begin to brown, about 5 to 7 minutes. Stir in

Know Your Fire

the tomatoes, parsley, thyme, Tabasco and 2 tablespoons of the reserved flour and cook 3 to 4 minutes. Stir in the stock and vinegar and mix well. Return the meat to the pan, cover with the sauce and simmer until the meat is tender, about 35 to 40 minutes.

To serve, spread the grits in the center of 4 dinner plates and top with the grillades.

Red Snapper with Black Bean Jambalaya

This is a wonderful Cajun/Creole dish that begins as so many of these dishes do with the holy trinity of this cuisine—onion, celery and bell pepper. Filé powder is a mainstay of southern Louisiana cuisine. It's made from the ground, dried leaves of the sassafras tree and used to thicken many one-pot dishes. Some feel its flavor is woodsy and faintly resembles root beer. Look for it in specialty food stores

Cook the dish in a stovetop casserole and bring it right to the table.

2 tablespoons olive oil

8 ounces andouille sausage or kiel-
    basa, cut into ½-inch slices

½ onion, chopped

I rib celery, chopped

I green bell pepper, seeded and
    chopped

2 scallions, chopped

I head Caramelized Garlic
    (page 186)

2 cups fish or chicken stock

I teaspoon dried thyme

I teaspoon dried rosemary

I teaspoon Tabasco

2 bay leaves

I cup long-grain rice

I (16 ounce) can black beans

I teaspoon filé powder

1½ pounds red snapper fillets, cut
    into chunks

Heat a large pan with a cover over medium high heat and heat the olive oil. Add the sausage and cook 1 minute. Add the onion, celery, green pepper, scallions and garlic and cook until the vegetables are light brown, about 4 to 5 minutes.

Add the stock, thyme, rosemary, Tabasco and bay leaves and blend well. Stir in the rice, bring mixture to a boil, cover, lower heat and simmer 15 minutes.

Rinse the beans in a colander under cool water and drain well. Add the beans and filé powder to the pot and place the snapper pieces on top. Replace the cover and cook until the fish begins to flake, about 8 to 10 minutes, being careful not to overcook the fish. Discard the bay leaves and serve immediately.

Swiss Steak

MAKES 4
SERVINGS

Swiss steak isn't Swiss at all. It originated in England where it was called smothered steak. You can enjoy the same taste and flavor of a pot roast with half the cooking time.

4 (8 ounce) beef round or chuck
    steaks, approximately ½-inch
    thick
2 tablespoons all-purpose flour
1 tablespoon olive oil
1 tablespoon butter
½ onion, chopped
6 cloves Caramelized Garlic
    (page 186)

¼ cup chopped carrots
¼ cup chopped celery
¼ cup tomato purée
¼ cup dry red wine
1 teaspoon dried thyme
2 bay leaves
2 cups beef or chicken stock

Lightly dredge the meat with the flour, tapping off any excess.

Heat a casserole-type pan or large skillet over medium-high heat. Add the oil and butter and when they're hot, brown the meat on all sides. Do not crowd the steaks. Remove the meat and set aside. Add the onion and garlic to the pot and cook until they're light brown, about 4 minutes. Add the carrots, celery and tomato purée and cook 2 to 3 minutes. Stir in the red wine, thyme and bay leaves, raise the heat and cook until the liquid is reduced by half. Stir in the stock, return the steaks to the pan and bring to a boil. Lower heat to a simmer, cover and cook until the meat is fork tender, about 1 hour. Remove bay leaves and serve.

Braising

Burgundy Pot Roast

Cooking a tender, tasty pot roast is based on two principles of braising, using both dry and moist heat which takes a bland, tough piece of meat and transforms it into a moist and flavorful dinner.

Serve with mashed potatoes or rice to lap up the gravy.

4 pound beef round or chuck roast

2 tablespoons all-purpose flour

1 tablespoon olive oil

1 tablespoon butter

½ onion, chopped

6 cloves Caramelized Garlic
  (page 186)

⅓ cup chopped carrots

⅓ cup chopped celery

¼ cup tomato purée

½ cup Burgundy

1 teaspoon dried thyme

2 bay leaves

2 cups beef or chicken stock

Lightly dredge the roast with the flour, tapping off any excess.

Heat a casserole-type pan or large deep saucepan with a cover. (The pan must be large enough to hold the roast when covered.) Add the oil and butter and, when they're hot, brown the meat on all sides. Remove the meat and set aside. Add the onion and garlic to the pot and cook until they're light brown, about 4 minutes. Add the carrots, celery and tomato purée and cook 2 to 3 minutes. Stir in the Burgundy, thyme and bay leaves, raise the heat and cook until the liquid is reduced by half. Stir in the stock, return the roast to the pan, and bring to a boil. Lower heat to a simmer, cover and cook until the meat is fork tender, about 2½ hours. Remove bay leaves. Let the roast rest 10 to 15 minutes before slicing.

Braised Cabbage

When we talk about braising as a cooking technique, it's usually associated with meats such as pot roast. Since braising is a combination of dry
heat and moist heat, the cabbage is cooked over high heat first and then
simmered in chicken stock. Cabbage is a tough vegetable, and braising
makes it soft and tender.

Researchers believe that eating cabbage, one of the cruciferous
vegetables, lessens the risks of cancer. Both white and red cabbage are
very hearty, widely available and will keep for weeks. Serve with roast
pork, duck or beef.

4 slices thinly sliced pancetta, chopped	**¼ cup thinly sliced onions**
2 tablespoons olive oil, if the pancetta is very lean	**2 tablespoons cider vinegar**
	1 cup chicken stock
1 small head red or white cabbage, cored and sliced thin	**1 teaspoon chopped fresh parsley**
	Freshly ground black pepper to taste

Heat a large, deep pan. Add the pancetta and cook over high heat until it
becomes crispy. Remove and set aside. If there isn't much fat in the bottom of
the pan, add the olive oil. Add the cabbage, onions and vinegar and cook on
high heat for 5 minutes. Add the chicken stock, bring to a boil, lower the heat,
cover and cook 20 minutes. Add the reserved pancetta, parsley and black pepper and mix well.

Braising

Frying

Frying is cooking food in fat over high heat and includes deep-fat frying, pan-frying, french frying, stir-frying and sautéing (see page 229).

Deep-Fat Frying

Deep-fat frying is an example of dry heat cooking using fat that requires the food to be totally submerged in hot oil. Foods low in moisture content are best suited for this method. Perfectly deep-fried food will be seared and have a crispy brown exterior.

Temperature is critical. If it's too hot, the food will burn. If it's not hot enough, the food will absorb the oil and become soggy. There is no one perfect deep-frying temperature, but temperatures generally range between 350° and 375°F. Use a deep-fat thermometer or an electric fryer to maintain the correct temperature, if possible.

Don't overload the oil. The temperature will go down when food is added, so if too much food is added at one time, it will become greasy by the time the temperature has recovered. There should be enough oil in the pan so that the food is completely covered and enough space for it to move around. I never add salt to food I'm deep-frying because it draws the moisture out of the food and can cause the oil to bubble up and spatter.

When deep-frying several batches, crumbs or food particles can gather on the surface and these should be skimmed off before they burn.

When using a skillet or saucepan for deep frying, make sure the pan is deep enough and no more than half filled with oil.

Always drain deep-fried foods on paper towels. The food can be kept warm in a low-temperature oven until the remainder of it is fried.

Frying oil can be reused. After it has cooled, strain it or put it through cheesecloth, then store it in a tightly sealed bottle and refrigerate. The oil can pick up some flavor from the food previously fried so, ideally, oil can be used for frying dessert, then potatoes, then chicken and then fish but *not* in the reverse order. Frying oil should be discarded when it gets dark or begins to smell rancid.

Always make sure that there are no small children or pets around when you're deep frying.

Pan Frying

Pan frying, another example of dry heat cooking using fat, is very similar to sautéing, which will be discussed on page 229. However, slightly more fat is used and the pieces, such as steaks and chops, are larger. The food is generally turned once and the temperature is slightly lower than sautéing, allowing the thicker pieces of food to cook on the inside before they burn on the outside.

Two-Step Frying, or French Frying

No one is exactly sure how french fries got their name. Some say it was because they were "frenched" or cut into lengthwise shapes, but it's generally believed that french fries originated in Belgium. Although Americans are famous for using ketchup on their french fries, the Brits sprinkle them with malt vinegar and the Belgians dip them into mayonnaise.

Peel the potatoes, or leave them unpeeled, and cut into ¼- to ½-inch fingers. Pat dry on paper towels. Heat oil in a deep-fat fryer to 350°F, add the potatoes and cook until they begin to get limp, about 5 minutes. They should not brown. Remove the potatoes and drain on paper towels. When the potatoes cool, heat the oil again to 390°F and cook the potatoes, a handful at a time, until they're golden brown, about 3 minutes. Keep them warm in a 250°F oven until each batch is cooked.

Stir-Frying

Stir-frying is an Oriental cooking technique usually done in a wok or large skillet. It requires all the ingredients to be ready before heating the pan because once you begin cooking, the process cannot be interrupted. Stir-frying uses a minimum of oil in a sizzling hot pan and the food is literally stirred constantly while it's being fried. The diced, shredded or thinly cut pieces of meat and vegetables are cooked very quickly until crisp tender, and a simple sauce is often added at the last minute.

What Are the Best Fats for Frying?

The smoking point, the temperature at which an oil is so hot that it begins to smoke, is highest for peanut, safflower and soybean oils, about 450°F, which makes them most desirable oils for any kind of frying. The smoking point for canola oil is 435°F and for both corn and olive oils it's 410°F .

Lard and hydrogenated fats are high in saturated fats and are not recommended for deep-fat frying for anyone concerned about nutrition.

Coating Foods for Frying

The secret to coating foods successfully with bread crumbs, flour, cornmeal or cornstarch before frying is to pat the food dry first and keep the coating light and unbroken. The coating keeps the food moist inside and gives a crisp exterior when cooked.

Flour gives a delicate coating and should be used for fragile fish, veal cutlets or chicken cutlets. Bread crumbs make a slightly thicker crust and are used for chunkier pieces of fish, chicken or meat. Use cornmeal when you want a firm coating for slices of green tomatoes, catfish or cod. Cornstarch is used in Oriental cooking for a very crisp finish.

After it's coated, the food is often refrigerated for 30 minutes. This gives the coating a chance to adhere to the food and prevents it from falling off during cooking.

Breading is another story: Here you need a dish of flour, an egg beaten with a teaspoon or two of water or milk and a dish of bread crumbs. The food must be patted dry, dipped in the flour, the egg and, lastly, the bread crumbs. Place the pieces on a rack for about 20 minutes to dry before frying. If refrigerated, the food will absorb fat during the frying process.

How to Fry Without Adding up Calories

Since fat has become a bad word these days, an alternative to frying would be to spray the food with cooking spray or brush it lightly with oil and cook it in a hot oven. Its texture will be fairly similar to fried food, but without the fat. Of course, this technique doesn't work with all fried foods, especially those that are normally deep-fried, but it works well with potatoes, fish and chicken.

Fried Grits and Mushrooms

Down South grits are usually served for breakfast with sunny-side up eggs or as a cereal. I've gussied up humble grits and made them into dinner fare. Serve with ham, pork or grilled meats.

FOR THE GRITS

1½ cups chicken stock

½ cup heavy cream

5 cloves Caramelized Garlic
   (page 186)

1 tablespoon butter

¼ teaspoon Tabasco

½ cup regular grits, not instant

¼ cup shredded Cheddar cheese

FOR THE MUSHROOM SAUCE

4 slices bacon, chopped

2 tablespoons olive oil

2 tablespoons butter

1 onion, thinly sliced

2 cups sliced shiitake mushrooms

½ cup heavy cream

2 tablespoons cane syrup, corn
   syrup or maple syrup

2 tablespoons chopped scallions

¼ teaspoon Tabasco

¼ teaspoon dried thyme

To make the grits, combine the chicken stock, cream, garlic, butter and Tabasco in a heavy saucepan and bring to a boil. Stirring constantly, slowly pour in the grits and bring the mixture back to a boil. Lower the heat to a simmer and cook 12 to 15 minutes, stirring occasionally. Remove the pan from the heat, add the Cheddar cheese and stir until it's melted. Pour the grits into a buttered 9-inch pie pan and chill until firm. Cut the chilled grits into 6 wedges.

To make the mushroom sauce, heat a heavy sauté pan, add the bacon and cook until it gives up its fat. Remove the bacon and set aside.

Add the olive oil to the bacon fat and increase the temperature to high. The olive oil raises the smoking point of the fat (page 208). Add the grit wedges to the pan and brown on both sides. Remove and keep warm.

Melt the butter in the pan, reduce the heat to low and caramelize the onion (page 238). Raise the temperature to high, add the mushrooms and sauté until light brown, 3 to 4 minutes. Add the cream, cane syrup, scallions, Tabasco and thyme. When the mixture boils, reduce heat and simmer 2 to 3 minutes.

To serve, top the grits with the mushroom sauce and sprinkle with the bacon pieces.

Clam or Oyster Fritters

Adding the clam juice to the fritter batter heightens its flavor. You can keep the first ones warm while frying the rest by placing them in a single layer on paper towel–lined tray in a 150°F oven. Serve as an appetizer with lemon wedges or tomato sauce.

3 eggs

⅓ cup sour cream

¼ cup clam or oyster juice

3 cups all-purpose flour

2 teaspoons baking powder

¼ teaspoon salt

6 cloves Caramelized Garlic
   (page 186)

2 scallions, chopped

I tablespoon chopped fresh parsley

½ teaspoon Tabasco

3 cups shucked and chopped clams
   or oysters

Vegetable oil for frying

Beat the eggs and slowly mix into the sour cream. Stir in the clam or oyster juice and mix until well blended.

In a medium bowl, combine the flour, baking powder, salt, garlic, scallions and parsley and toss gently to combine. Add egg mixture into the flour mixture and stir until smooth. Add the Tabasco and fold in the chopped clams or oysters.

Let the batter rest while heating the oil. Fill a deep-fat fryer with 2 to 3 inches of vegetable oil and heat to 370° to 375°F. Without crowding them, drop tablespoons of the fritter batter into the hot oil. When they rise to the surface, turn them over and cook until well browned on all sides, about 4 to 5 minutes. Drain the fritters on paper towels and serve hot.

Frying

MAKES 4 SERVINGS

Beer Batter Cod

The carbonation in the beer makes the batter exceptionally airy and produces a crispy coating. Malt vinegar is a British favorite on fish and chips.

1¼ cups all-purpose flour	1 teaspoon Tabasco
¼ cup granulated sugar	1 cup beer
2 teaspoons baking powder	vegetable oil for frying
Freshly ground black pepper to taste	2 pounds cod fillet, cut into serving pieces
2 eggs	Malt vinegar for serving

Combine 1 cup of the flour, sugar, baking powder and black pepper in a medium bowl. Stir in the eggs and Tabasco. Slowly pour in the beer, stirring constantly, until the foam subsides and the batter is smooth. Let the batter rest for 15 to 20 minutes.

Heat 2 to 3 inches of oil to 370°F in a deep-fat fryer.

Dredge the cod in the remaining ¼ cup flour, shaking off any excess, and dip into the batter.

Carefully slip the pieces into the hot fat and cook until brown on both sides, turning once. Drain on paper towels. Serve with french fries (page 209) and malt vinegar.

Know Your Fire

Stir-Fried Beef with Cashews

Stir-frying is traditionally done in a wok, but if you don't own one, use a large deep skillet. The food must be kept constantly in motion. Asian cooks use a special wok spatula with a rounded outside edge that fits the shape of the wok. Try using two wooden spatulas or a spatula and a serving spoon with long handles. Freezing the beef for 30 to 45 minutes makes it firm enough to cut into very thin slices. Like so much Asian stir-fry cooking, most of the work goes into the chopping and slicing, but once that's done, its a fast trip from the wok to the table. Serve this orange-flavored beef dish on a bed of brown rice. With the fast cooking time be sure to time the cooking of the rice so it will be ready at the same time as the stir-fry.

I pound top round steak	2 tablespoons peanut oil or
2 tablespoons lite soy sauce	vegetable oil
2 tablespoons steak sauce	I onion, sliced thin
4 cloves Caramelized Garlic	I red bell pepper, seeded and cut
(page 186)	into I-inch strips
I tablespoon chopped fresh ginger	¼ cup unsalted cashews
I teaspoon sesame oil	2 scallions, cut on a diagonal into
I teaspoon Tabasco	I-inch pieces
2 tablespoons cornstarch	I cup orange juice

Cut the steak into thin strips, 2- by 1- by ⅛-inch thick.

In a plastic bag combine the soy sauce, steak sauce, garlic, ginger, sesame oil and Tabasco and mix well. Add the beef strips and marinate for 30 minutes, turning the bag frequently.

Remove the beef from the marinade, drain well, and toss with the cornstarch in a medium bowl.

Heat a wok or large sauté pan until very hot and add 1 tablespoon peanut oil. When the oil is hot, add the beef and quickly stir-fry until light brown. Remove the meat and add the remaining tablespoon of peanut oil. When the oil is hot, add the onion, bell pepper, cashews and scallions to the wok and stir-fry 1 minute. Add the orange juice and bring to a boil. Return the beef to the pan and cook until sauce thickens, about 1 minute.

Frying

Sweet Potato Straws

Sweet potato straws are so delicious that you'll probably never go back to eating ordinary french fries again.

3 sweet potatoes, peeled	**2 russet potatoes, peeled**
2 onions, peeled	**Vegetable oil**

Cut the sweet potatoes, onions and russet potatoes into long thin pieces, roughly ⅓ by ⅓ by 3 inches.

Fill a deep fryer with several inches of vegetable oil and heat to 360°F. Add the sweet potatoes, onions and russet potatoes separately in several batches and cook until they're just beginning to color. Remove, drain on paper towel, and set aside until all are done.

Increase the temperature to 380°F, and cook the vegetables separately for a second time until they're golden brown.

Know Your Fire

Hush Puppies

Hush puppies were the scraps of cornbread dough that were deep-fried and tossed to dogs to "hush them up" when they sat up begging 'round the stove at mealtime. If you don't have any dogs, it works equally well with the kids. In the South, they are traditionally served with fried catfish.

1 cup cornmeal	½ cup milk
1 teaspoon baking powder	1 egg, lightly beaten
½ teaspoon salt	2 tablespoons melted butter
¼ teaspoon black pepper	Vegetable oil for frying

Combine the cornmeal, baking powder, salt and pepper in a medium bowl. Add the milk and egg and beat with a whisk or fork until the batter is smooth and no lumps remain. Stir in the butter and set the batter aside for 15 to 20 minutes.

Fill a deep saucepan or deep-fat fryer with 2 to 3 inches of vegetable oil and heat to 360°F. Scoop up a scant tablespoon of batter while rounding off the rough edges with another spoon. Push the batter off the spoon into the hot fat and, when the hush puppies rise to the top in about 1 minute, turn them over and cook until evenly brown, about 2 minutes total. Remove and drain on paper towels. Hush Puppies should always be served piping hot.

Frying

**MAKES 6 TO 8
SERVINGS**

Calas

In New Orleans this deep-fried breakfast "doughnut" is made from a rice-infused yeast dough. Early on Sunday mornings, vendors walk the streets of the French Quarter calling, "Belles calas tout chaud," which translates loosely as "Get 'em while they're hot."

Ever cook too much rice? If so, plan on frying calas for tomorrow's dessert. You'll continue to make extra rice from now on.

1 cup long-grain rice (to make 3 cups cooked rice)	½ cup granulated sugar
1 tablespoon active dry yeast	4 eggs
½ cup warm water, 90° to 100°F	1 tablespoon grated orange peel
1 teaspoon granulated sugar	2 teaspoons vanilla
¼ teaspoon salt	1 teaspoon ground cinnamon
1½ cups all-purpose flour	Vegetable oil for deep frying
	Confectioners' sugar

Cook the rice in 2¼ cups water until very tender, about 25 to 30 minutes.

Combine the yeast and water in a large mixing bowl and mix in the cooked rice, sugar and salt and mix until well blended. Cover the bowl and set aside for 2 hours at room temperature.

Combine the flour, sugar, eggs, orange peel, vanilla and cinnamon with the rice mixture and blend well.

Fill a deep-fat fryer with 2 to 3 inches of vegetable oil and heat to 375°F. Using an ice cream scoop or two tablespoons, form the rice mixture into 2-inch balls and drop into the hot fat. Cook the calas until golden brown, about 4 to 5 minutes. Remove, drain on paper towels and sprinkle with confectioners' sugar.

Know Your Fire

Fruit Fritters

These batter-dipped and deep-fried fruit fritters are really easy to make and a good introduction to using yeast. They taste best when eaten right away. If you run out of confectioners' sugar, place granulated sugar in a food processor and process for several minutes until it's as fine as confectioners' sugar.

About 6 cups assorted ripe but firm
    fruit such as bananas, apples,
    pears, peaches or pineapple
½ cup brandy or liqueur such as
    Grand Marnier, Triple Sec
    or rum
1½ teaspoons active dry yeast
8 ounces beer, at room temperature
½ cup milk, warmed to 85°F

2 egg yolks
2¼ cups all-purpose flour
Pinch salt
3 egg whites
½ cup granulated sugar
1 cup cornstarch or flour
Vegetable oil for deep frying
Confectioners' sugar or Fruit Sauce
    (page 135)

Peel, core and seed the fruit (as appropriate) and cut into bite-size pieces. Marinate in brandy or liqueur, stirring occasionally.

Dissolve the yeast in the beer in a small bowl and set aside for 10 minutes.

Combine the milk and the eggs yolks in a small bowl and beat well.

Combine the flour and the salt in a large bowl. Add the yeast mixture to the flour, and then slowly add the milk mixture, stirring constantly, until the batter is completely smooth. Cover the bowl and set aside at room temperature for 2 hours.

Beat the eggs whites, adding the sugar gradually, until stiff peaks form. Gently fold the meringue into the batter, about ¼ at a time.

Fill a deep-fat fryer with 2 to 3 inches of vegetable oil and heat to 370°F.

Remove the fruit from the marinade and dry slightly. Lightly dip the fruit with the cornstarch and tap off any excess. Dip each piece of fruit into the batter, covering it completely yet allowing any excess to drip off. Carefully drop the pieces into the hot fat taking care not to crowd them. When the fritters rise to the surface, turn them over. They should be done when they're light brown, about 4 to 5 minutes. Remove with a slotted spoon and place on paper towels to drain.

Dust with confectioners' sugar or serve with fruit sauce. These are best when eaten warm.

Frying

Poaching

Poaching is a moist-cooking technique in which the food is placed in water or a flavored liquid and cooked at a low temperature, somewhere between 160° and 180°F.

Poaching retains the intrinsic flavor of food such as eggs, fish, chicken, fruits and vegetables that might otherwise be overpowered by other cooking methods. The low temperature and calm cooking liquid keep delicate foods from falling apart. When it's necessary to cover the food, a tight-fitting lid is rarely used. Rather, the food is cooked without a cover or with the lid partially covering.

Poaching Fruit in a Sugar Syrup

Almost any fruit can be poached in a sugar syrup. To poach fruit, place it in boiling sugar syrup, lower the heat and poach until tender. Remove the fruit immediately lest it get mushy. Use a thin syrup (1 cup granulated sugar to 3 cups water) for apples, grapes and pineapple; a medium syrup (1 cup granulated sugar to 2 cups water) for apricots, cherries, pears and prunes; and a heavy syrup (1 cup granulated syrup to 1 cup water) for berries, figs, peaches and plums.

Poaching in a Court Bouillon

A court bouillon, which originally meant a "short sauce" or "small flavoring agent," is a flavored liquid used to poach fish, meat or vegetables. In addition to water and vinegar, and depending on what food is being cooked, the ingredients may include wine, seasoning, herbs and spices. After the food is cooked, the court bouillon can be strained and used as the liquid for making the sauce.

Poaching Poultry in Bouillon

When a chicken is poached in plain water, most of its flavor goes into the water. However, when a chicken is poached in a bouillon, the chicken absorbs the flavor from the cooking liquid. Boosting the flavor is especially important when you want to use the meat in a salad or pot pie.

Poaching Eggs in Champagne

There are few brunch dishes more decadent than eggs poached in champagne. (Or use an inexpensive sparkling wine since it can't be drunk afterward!) Serve the eggs on slices of toasted brioche and sprinkle with caviar. Wash them down with a really nice bottle of champagne.

Poaching

Poached Bass with Sweet Potato Straws

Bass is a large family with many species. Use sea bass, striped bass or grouper. Poaching the fish in the oven keeps it nice and moist.

2 pounds bass fillet

3 tablespoons butter

Zest and juice of 1 orange (about
　½ cup)

¼ cup dry white wine

1 leek, white part only, cleaned and
　chopped

1 tablespoon honey

¼ teaspoon ground allspice

¼ teaspoon Tabasco

Sweet Potato Straws (page 216)

Preheat the oven to 375°F.

Skin the bass, remove any bones and cut into 4 servings. Place the fish in a buttered casserole or ovenproof pan. Combine the orange juice and zest, wine, leek, honey, allspice and Tabasco in a small bowl and mix well. Pour the liquid over the fish and bake for approximately 10 to 12 minutes. The fish is done when it turns opaque and begins to flake. Remove the fish to a serving platter. Bring the pan juices to a boil on the stovetop and reduce until thick, about 5 minutes. Pour the sauce over the fish and serve with Sweet Potato Straws.

Turkey and Walnut Salad

This is the ultimate turkey salad. Roasting a boneless turkey breast or tenderloin often turns out dry and stringy but poaching the turkey keeps it moist and juicy. To toast the walnuts, place them in a pie pan and put it into a 350-degree oven for about 8 minutes. Check them after 5 minutes and shake the pan so that they toast evenly and don't burn.

2 cups chicken stock

1 (12 ounce) turkey tenderloin

½ cup toasted walnut halves

½ cup green seedless grapes, cut in half

¼ cup diced celery

1 small carrot, finely diced

¼ cup finely chopped red onion

¼ cup Herb Vinaigrette (page 76) or Thousand Island Dressing (page 79)

Lettuce leaves

Bring the stock to a boil in a medium saucepan. Add the turkey tenderloin and simmer until no longer pink in the center, about 20 minutes.

Allow the turkey to cool in the stock, remove and cut into ½-inch dice. In a medium bowl combine the turkey with the walnuts, grapes, celery, carrot, onion and dressing and toss lightly. Line a serving dish with the lettuce leaves and arrange the salad on top.

Poached Oysters on Spinach Salad

We hear more and more warnings about the dangers of consuming raw shellfish, especially oysters. Once the oysters are cooked properly, however, they are perfectly safe to eat. Try this dish when you seek a change from fried oysters.

I cup shucked oysters with their juices
4 thin slices pancetta or bacon, chopped
¼ cup chopped onion
½ cup dry white wine
I teaspoon dry mustard

½ teaspoon Tabasco
2 tablespoons brandy
2 tablespoons butter
3 cups fresh spinach leaves, washed and dried
Toasted French bread

Drain the oysters and set aside the juices. Heat a sauté pan and cook the pancetta until it's crisp. Remove the pancetta and set aside, leaving any fat in the pan. Add the onion and cook over low heat until transparent, about 5 minutes. Add the wine, dry mustard, Tabasco and the juice from the oysters. Bring the mixture to a simmer, add the oysters and poach until they plump up, about 5 minutes. Once the oysters shrink and curl up, they're overcooked. Add the brandy and butter and stir until the butter melts.

To serve, divide the spinach between two dishes, top with the oysters and hot juices and sprinkle with the pancetta. Serve with the toasted bread.

Poached Pear and Blue Cheese Salad

Pears can be poached in either white or red wine, but the red wine colors the outside a lovely shade of red. Any dry red wine such as a Côte du Rhône or a merlot can be used as the poaching liquid. The pears are cooked when the point of a paring knife can pierce them easily. The sweet mellow flavor of the poached pears contrasts nicely with the strong taste and aroma of the cheese.

I cup dry red wine

4 Bosc, Anjou or Bartlett pears, peeled, halved and cored

I cup Fruit Dressing (page 80)

4 tablespoons blue cheese (Roquefort, Danish blue or Gorgonzola), crumbled

2 cups mesclun

Heat the wine in a small saucepan and add the pear halves. Slowly cook the pears at a gentle simmer until they're tender, 15 to 20 minutes. Remove the pears from the wine and, when they come to room temperature, place in the refrigerator to chill.

To serve, divide the mesclun among 4 dessert dishes. Place two pear halves on each dish with 2 to 4 tablespoons of the fruit dressing and sprinkle with a tablespoon of blue cheese.

Poaching

Eggs Benedict

This dish was supposedly named for Mr. and Mrs. LeGrand Benedict, two regular customers of Delmonico's restaurant in Manhattan. When they complained that the menu was boring them, the maitre d' and Mrs. Benedict devised this now famous egg dish.

This is a classic rendition of one of the world's most popular brunch dishes. I suggest using a packaged mix to make the hollandaise because it's tricky to cook and, should it separate, you'll have eggs with ham on English muffins rather than eggs Benedict. When poaching, add vinegar to the water to help coagulate the egg white. Also, the fresher the egg, the less it will spread. Never poach eggs in a cast-iron pan as it may discolor them.

You can make the eggs in advance. Place the poached eggs in cold water and refrigerate until serving time. To reheat the eggs, place them in a bowl of hot water for a few minutes or simmer them in water for 1 minute.

4 slices Canadian bacon or smoked ham	1 tablespoon white distilled vinegar
4 slices white bread or English muffin halves	4 very fresh eggs at room temperature
½ cup hollandaise sauce, prepared from a packaged mix	½ teaspoon Tabasco
	Freshly ground black pepper to taste

Heat the Canadian bacon or smoked ham in a skillet.

Toast the bread or English muffins. Place a slice of Canadian bacon on top of each piece of toast.

Prepare the hollandaise sauce according to package directions.

Fill a 10-inch skillet with water to the depth of 1½ inches, bring to a boil and add the vinegar. Break the eggs, one at a time, into a small dish or custard cup. Stir the water into a whirlpool with a wooden spoon and slip the eggs in, one at a time. Simmer the eggs 3 to 5 minutes, depending on how cooked you like your eggs. Remove the eggs with a slotted spoon, shake off any excess water and trim off the wispy edges with scissors. Place each egg on top of a prepared muffin half, season with the Tabasco, salt and pepper and cover with 2 tablespoons of the hollandaise sauce. Serve immediately.

Eggs in a Wink

You can tell if an egg isn't fresh because the white portion will begin to break up as soon as the egg is placed in hot water. Adding a tablespoon of vinegar helps to coagulate the white, but the down side is that it will toughen the egg slightly and it won't be as shiny. If the white portion gets wispy around the edges, trim it with scissors for a neater look.

This is an easier. and less caloric, spinoff of Eggs Benedict and a favorite with children.

4 slices white bread	I teaspoon Tabasco
2 tablespoons butter	I teaspoon chopped fresh chives
4 eggs	Salt and pepper to taste
I tablespoon white distilled vinegar	

Toast the bread on both sides, spread with butter and cut a hole in the center of each slice with a 2-inch cookie cutter. Reserve the centers. Place each slice of toast on a serving dish.

Fill a medium skillet with water, bring to a boil and add the vinegar. Break the eggs, one at a time, into a small dish. While swirling the water in the pan with a spoon, slide the eggs, one at a time, into the water. Simmer the eggs 3 to 5 minutes depending on how cooked you like your eggs. Remove the eggs with a slotted spoon and drop each into the center of a piece of toast. Season with a drop of Tabasco, chives, salt and pepper. Top with the center of the toast and serve immediately.

Poaching

MAKES 4 SERVINGS

Poached Pear Dessert

Desserts can be more than a slice of cake, a wedge of pie or a dish of chocolate mousse. The next time the sweet tooth begins to ache, look toward the fruit bowl.

The pears are cooked in a simple syrup, a combination of sugar and water flavored with citrus. This syrup is to desserts what stock is to sauces and soups—it provides a depth of flavor. The syrup can be made in advance and stored in a clean jar in the refrigerator for several weeks. Use it for poaching fruit, fruit sauces and fillings.

2 cups granulated sugar	2 cinnamon sticks
I cup water	4 pears
I orange, sliced	½ cup Triple Sec
I lemon, sliced	Chocolate Sauce (page 136)

In a small, nonreactive saucepan, combine the sugar, water, orange, lemon and cinnamon sticks. Bring to a gentle boil over medium high heat for 10 minutes.

Peel the pears and cut out the cores from the bottom, leaving the pears whole. If they have stems, leave them on. Place the pears in a small saucepan and cover with the simple syrup. If the syrup does not cover them, the pears can be cut in half, but this doesn't make for as good a presentation. Add the Triple Sec and bring to a boil. Lower the heat and slowly poach the pears at about 160°F until they're tender (anywhere from 5 to 15 minutes depending on their ripeness), but not soft. When pierced with a knife, there should be a little drag. Remove the pan from the heat, and cool the pears in the syrup. Discard the simple syrup, and serve the pears with the chocolate sauce.

Know Your Fire

Sautéing

Sautéing is a fast, dry-heat method of cooking done in a skillet or sauté pan using a very small amount of fat to prevent the food from sticking. The literal translation of sauté is from the French word *sauter* meaning "to jump." The pan must be very hot and the pieces of food should not be too large or too thick.

How to Sauté

Because sautéing is such a speedy cooking method, be sure to have all your ingredients close at hand. There will be no time to stop and chop some garlic or slice an onion once you begin to cook. A good habit to get into is "mise en place," a French term that means having everything in place before you start.

Preheat the pan on the stove. Do not add the fat until the pan is hot. Always wait a few seconds for the fat to heat before adding the food so it does not simply absorb the fat.

Since sautéing requires very high heat, butter is not a good fat choice unless it's clarified (see page 150) or combined with olive or vegetable oil, which have a higher smoking point (the temperature at which fats begin to smoke and transfer an unpleasant flavor to food). Butter's smoking point is around 350°F, whereas vegetable oils such as peanut and safflower oil have a smoking point of around 450°F. The smoking point of olive oil is 410°. Do not use "lite" margarines that may contain water.

To prevent meat, fish or chicken from sticking, they should first be patted dry with paper towels and then very lightly dusted with flour in order to achieve a nicely browned surface.

Many foods such as fish fillets and chicken cutlets can be sautéed and served as is or enhanced with vegetables and a sauce. If you are preparing a sauce, onion, garlic or shallots can be added to the pan. At this point, the bottom of the pan will have a buildup of food particles that will begin to stick. Do not clean out the pan, as these small bits of food will intensify the flavor of the sauce. As you add the flavoring liquid—wine, vinegar, stock or prepared sauce—loosen these particles with a spoon. Remove the meat and vegetables to a warm dish. Raise the heat and reduce the liquid in the pan, thereby concentrating the flavor and thickening the sauce naturally.

Is a $100 Pot Worth the Price?

A kitchen doesn't need to be equipped with every pan ever invented. But it does need a few basic pots of the very best quality. There are few things more frustrating than a cheap skillet that doesn't cook food evenly or a hand-me-down pot with handles that get so hot that it's dangerous to lift. You may pay $100 for a pot but if you use it every day for the next 25 years, it's worth it.

And it certainly isn't necessary to buy a set of matching pots. Buy pots for the type of cooking you do—a large stockpot for making soups and cooking pasta, a sauté pan for cooking chicken and fish, a saucepan for vegetables, a roasting pan for the oven. Unfortunately, there is no one best material for pots; each has drawbacks but each also has good things going for it.

Nonstick pots are all the rage right now. Nonstick is important in a skillet or sauté pan when you want to cook with less fat, but not essential in a stockpot when it's going to be used for boiling water for pasta or in a saucepan used to steam vegetables. When buying a nonstick pot, check out the warranty and save your receipt. Find out if special utensils are required.

Basic Pan Shapes and Sizes

In some kitchens there is no difference between a skillet, a fry pan and a sauté pan because they basically do the same thing. There are, however, slight variations. A sauté pan has sloping sides and is relatively shallow, ranging from 8 inches to 14 inches in diameter. The word "sauté" comes from the French word meaning "to jump" and when sautéing small pieces of food that is literally what the food does. As you shake the pan back and forth, the food slides up the sides and turns over.

A skillet and a fry pan are pretty much the same—a round pan with slightly curved or straight sides, ranging in size from 5 inches to 12 inches in diameter with a long handle. Skillets and fry pans can be used for any kind of frying using a small amount of fat.

In most of Asia everyone owns a wok, and it's the only pot they own. It's used for everything: stir-frying, poaching, steaming, deep-frying, braising. They average 12 to 14 inches in diameter and come in a range of metals. You can also purchase an electric version. Once a wok is seasoned, it should not be scrubbed clean using soap or scouring pads, or it will lose its coating. Wash with water and a stiff brush or nylon scrubbie and dry immediately.

If you plan to cook pasta or make soup, you'll need a stockpot. It's taller than it is wide and is probably the largest pot in the kitchen. Sizes range from 4 quarts to 10 quarts for home use. Avoid buying a cheap enamel stockpot; it will chip and be unusable.

A saucepan is a straight-sided pan with a handle ranging from 1 quart to 5 quarts. Since this is one of the most used pots in the kitchen it should be of good quality.

Comparing Types of Cookware Materials

MATERIAL	PROS	CONS
Stainless steel	Strong; easy to clean; nonreactive	Not a good conductor of heat unless bottom is layered with copper or aluminum
Copper	Excellent conductor of heat	Expensive; heavy; difficult to clean; must be lined with tin or stainless steel
Aluminum	Good conductor of heat; low cost	Reacts with some foods and turns black; may discolor some food
Anodized aluminum	Scratch resistant; easy to clean	Expensive; cannot go in dishwasher
Enameled cast iron	Easy to maintain; nonreactive	Chips relatively easily; very heavy
Cast iron	Excellent conductor of heat; inexpensive	Cooks unevenly; must be seasoned

Pork with Honey and Walnuts

This is one recipe where I'm very particular about using the right pan. Sometimes you can substitute an ingredient in a recipe, but in this case there is no substituting pans. I will only use a cast-iron skillet. The cast iron holds a very high heat while the meat and peppers are seared, causing some very flavorful juices to develop in the pan. If you don't own a cast-iron skillet, borrow one from a family member or a friend. They won't refuse if you invite them to dinner.

1 tablespoon sesame oil or olive oil	2 tablespoons all-purpose flour
1 green and 1 red bell pepper, cut into ½-inch strips	¼ cup walnut halves
	¼ cup dry white wine
4 (6 ounce) boneless pork chops, about ½-inch thick	3 tablespoons honey
	½ teaspoon chili oil or Tabasco

Heat a cast-iron skillet until it becomes very hot. Add the sesame oil and the peppers and cook over high heat, tossing occasionally until they are light brown, about 2 minutes. You may want to cover the pan if the oil is spattering too much. Remove the peppers before they get soft and set aside. Lightly dredge the pork chops with the flour and add to the hot pan, searing them on both sides. Add the walnuts, white wine and honey. Cover the pan and cook over high heat 5 minutes longer. Add chili oil to taste. Serve the pork chops with the peppers.

Scallops with a Cornmeal Crust

Bay scallops found along the East Coast are the sweetest of all. Sea scallops are two to four times larger and slightly chewier. Calico scallops are bay scallops from the Florida coast and the Gulf of Mexico. They can be as small as pencil erasers but often resemble them in texture.

FOR THE MARINADE

1 cup milk

6 cloves Caramelized Garlic
   (page 186)

1 teaspoon dried basil

1 teaspoon dried parsley

½ teaspoon Tabasco

¼ teaspoon ground nutmeg

2½ pounds bay scallops

FOR DREDGING

1 cup finely ground cornmeal

½ cup all-purpose flour

FOR COOKING

2 tablespoons butter

2 tablespoons olive oil

Lemon wedges or Spicy Tomato
   Sauce (page 69) for serving

In a medium bowl combine the milk, garlic, basil, parsley, Tabasco and nutmeg and mix well. Add the scallops and marinate 2 hours, refrigerated.

In a shallow dish combine the cornmeal and flour and mix well. Drain the scallops and roll in the mixture, shaking off any excess.

Heat a large sauté pan over medium high and heat the butter and olive oil. Add the scallops and pan-fry until lightly brown on all sides. If your pan isn't large, you may have to do this in 2 or 3 batches. Serve the scallops with lemon or a spicy tomato sauce.

Tossed Crab Meat

This is an expensive dish to make unless you live in New Iberia, Louisiana, where they practically give crab meat away at the height of the season. Although it might be more fun to hop a plane and go to the source, rely on your fishmonger to supply you with fresh backfin crab when it's in season. Otherwise, buy pasteurized lump crab meat for that special occasion.

¼ pound butter

Juice of I lemon

2 teaspoons chopped fresh parsley

I teaspoon Tabasco

2 pounds fresh lump backfin crab,
  preferably in season

Heat a saucepan over medium heat and melt the butter. Just before the butter begins to brown, stir in the lemon juice, parsley and Tabasco. Add the crab meat and gently toss until it's steaming hot. Serve at once on warm plates with cold beer.

Sautéing

Pan-Seared Catfish

Farm-raised catfish fillets are milky white with a sweet taste and soft texture. Make sure the skin is removed before cooking because it can be quite tough. Catfish is versatile and can be steamed or poached, but I like it fried, especially when it has a crunchy coating.

¼ cup milk

1 tablespoon chopped Italian
  parsley

2 cloves Caramelized Garlic
  (page 186)

1 teaspoon Tabasco

Freshly ground black pepper to
  taste

Pinch nutmeg

2 pounds (2 to 3 ounces each)
  catfish fillets

¼ cup all-purpose flour

¼ cup cornmeal or corn flour

2 tablespoons olive oil

2 tablespoons butter

¼ cup dry white wine

4 thin lemon slices

2 tablespoons butter or 4 tablespoons chicken stock

In a shallow bowl combine the milk, parsley, garlic, Tabasco, nutmeg and black pepper and soak the catfish for 30 minutes.

In a shallow dish combine the flour and cornmeal. Drain the catfish fillets and dip them lightly into the flour mixture, shaking off any excess.

Preheat a large sauté pan over high heat. Add the olive oil and butter and, when they're hot, sear the catfish on one side for 2 minutes and turn. Add the white wine and lemon slices and cook until the fish is tender, 5 to 8 minutes. Remove the fish and swirl in the butter or stock and cook until the sauce thickens. Pour the sauce over the fish.

NOTE: If you choose to substitute the chicken stock for the butter, the sauce will not be as thick, but the fish will be moist.

Margarita Shrimp

During a visit to San Antonio on a warm summer's day, I was sipping Margaritas along the riverfront and I came up with the idea of using the drink as a marinade for shrimp. The ingredients are all there—the tequila, Grand Marnier, lime juice. But instead of serving a Margarita straight up or over ice, the ingredients marinate the shrimp and are reduced to make the sauce. Olé!

1 to 1½ pounds large shrimp	1 tablespoon cilantro, chopped
1 cup sweetened lemonade	1 teaspoon Tabasco
Juice of 2 limes	1 tablespoon olive oil if sautéing
¼ cup tequila	Warm flour tortillas
2 tablespoons Grand Marnier	
6 cloves Caramelized Garlic (page 186)	

Peel and devein the shrimp, leaving on the tail.

Combine the lemonade, lime juice, tequila, Grand Marnier, garlic, cilantro and Tabasco in a shallow nonreactive pan and marinate the shrimp 20 to 30 minutes.

Preheat the grill to high or heat a sauté pan.

If grilling the shrimp, place them on skewers and sear on all sides. Remove the shrimp from the skewers, place in a pan with the marinade and cook until opaque, 2 to 3 minutes longer. Remove the shrimp, boil down the marinade until it thickens and pour over the shrimp.

If sautéing the shrimp, heat the olive oil in the hot pan, add the shrimp and cook over medium high heat until light brown. Add the marinade and cook 2 minutes. Remove the shrimp, boil down the marinade until it thickens and pour over the shrimp.

Serve the shrimp with warm tortillas.

Sautéing

Golden Buck

Golden buck is Welsh rarebit with a poached egg on top. My version cooks the egg right in with the other ingredients and substitutes Parmesan for the Cheddar cheese. Welsh rarebit is traditionally served as part of a high tea, but Golden Buck can be eaten as a breakfast or brunch dish.

8 eggs	1 teaspoon prepared mustard
2 tablespoons butter	1 teaspoon Tabasco
1 onion, sliced thin	1 cup grated Parmesan cheese
¼ cup beer	Buttered toast
Juice of ½ lemon	

Break the eggs into a medium bowl and mix well.

Heat a nonstick sauté pan until hot and melt the butter. Add the onion slices and cook over low heat, until they caramelize. (See below.)

When the onion is fully browned, stir in the beer, lemon juice, mustard and Tabasco and raise the heat to very high. Add the cheese and stir well.

Add the eggs and cook over medium heat, stirring slowly until set, 3 to 4 minutes. Remove at once. Place the eggs on buttered toast and serve immediately.

Caramelizing Onions Caramelizing vegetables means to cook them slowly until their natural sugars turn brown, giving the vegetables a sweet taste. To caramelize onion, heat a nonstick pan until hot and melt the butter. Add thinly sliced onion and spread out the slices evenly in the pan. Reduce the heat and cook the onion, without stirring, until it begins to brown on the bottom. Stir the onion slices, spread them out evenly again and cook, without stirring, until they brown on the bottom. Keep repeating this procedure until the onion slices are golden brown.

This caramelizing can take anywhere from 10 to 20 minutes depending on the amount of sugar in the onion and the amount of moisture present.

Cauliflower Sauté

Mark Twain once said that "Cauliflower is nothing but a cabbage with a college education." Was he talking B.S., M.A. or Ph.D.? This is a two-step technique that leaves the cauliflower crisp yet tender while the garlic, lemon and olives create a sensational boost of flavor for the otherwise bland vegetable.

1 head cauliflower	2 tablespoons olive oil
¼ cup all-purpose flour	1 head Caramelized Garlic
Pinch of cayenne pepper	(page 186)
¼ teaspoon ground nutmeg	Juice of 1 lemon
¼ teaspoon dried thyme	3 tablespoons chopped green
¼ teaspoon freshly ground black	olives
pepper	1 tablespoon chopped fresh parsley

Trim any black spots from the cauliflower, remove the leaves and cut out the core with a small, sharp knife. Cut into florets, place in 3 quarts of boiling water and cook until crisp tender, about 10 to 15 minutes. (If the cauliflower is overcooked it will not hold up to the sautéing.) Drain well and pat dry with a paper towel.

In a medium bowl, combine the flour with the cayenne, nutmeg, thyme and black pepper. Toss the florets in the flour mixture and shake off any excess.

Heat a sauté pan until very hot. Heat the olive oil and sauté the cauliflower over high heat until brown on all sides. Stir in the garlic, lemon juice and green olives. Sprinkle with parsley and serve at once.

Roasting

Roasting is probably the oldest form of cooking. Before the development of enclosed roasting ovens, roasting was done on a spit over a roaring fire. Today, roasting is done in the oven in an open pan. This form of dry cooking produces a brown exterior and a moist interior. There has to be some sort of fat present, either in the food itself or added before it goes into the oven.

Roasting is used for tender cuts of meat; less tender cuts must be cooked with moist heat such as braising. Roasting vegetables intensifies their flavors and caramelizes their natural sugars. And there is nothing simpler to make, or more delicious, than a roasted chicken.

Roasting is the simplest of all the cooking techniques because once you place the food in the oven, you can almost walk away. The mother of a friend of mine used to say, "And God does the rest."

It isn't necessary to have a fancy oven like a Garland or a British Aga to roast properly, but an accurate thermostat is a must. When a recipe calls for a

350°F oven, it should be 350°F and not 325° or 375°F. If the dish doesn't turn out right, it's not always the recipe that didn't work. Often, an incorrect temperature is the culprit by causing the food to cook too slow or too fast.

The Convection Oven

The convection oven does the same job as a traditional oven but features a fan that is constantly blowing the air around. Because of this increased air circulation, a convection oven usually cooks a little hotter and a little faster, so set the oven 50°F lower and shorten the roasting time by about 15 minutes. Check the manufacturer's instructions.

Tips for Better Roasting

Whenever the oven door is opened, the temperature goes down 25°F, so open the door as little as possible. When short on time, it isn't necessary to preheat the oven when cooking a roast.

If your oven racks don't slide in and out easily, rub the edges with a little vegetable oil.

Keep the oven clean to avoid smoke in the kitchen and to prevent contamination of delicate baked goods like cake and pastry.

Where you place the rack will affect the look of the food. When food is placed on the rack in the middle position, it cooks more evenly. Placed on the highest rack, the food will brown more on the top; placed on the lowest rack the food will brown more on the bottom.

Always use the right size pan, not only in width and length, but also in depth. If the pan is too large, the drippings will probably burn. If the pan is too small, the meat can stick to the sides. A jelly roll pan with low sides is not suitable for roasting because hot fats can spatter out of the pan. Pans over three inches deep cause food to steam instead of roast.

Any roasting pan should be made of heavy-duty material so that it doesn't warp in a hot oven. Disposable aluminum pans are not suitable for roasting because they're too flimsy, they don't conduct any heat, and they bend under the weight of a chicken or roast. If you need to use one, put it on a baking sheet.

Invest in an instant-read thermometer, and you'll never have to guess when meat is done. Insert the thermometer in the *thickest* portion of the meat, avoiding bone and fat. Wait 10 seconds for it to register.

Always place roasts fat side up, so that the fat melts and bastes the meat as it cooks.

When roasting large pieces of meat, remove them from the refrigerator ½ hour before for a medium roast and 1 hour before for a large one. This allows the meat to come to room temperature and cook more evenly.

Make sure the meat you're cooking is completely defrosted, including the bone. Otherwise, the meat will cook on the outside and be uncooked near the bone. This is prone to happen with chicken.

Veal Roast with Potatoes and Onions

A veal roast can be very bland tasting but not this one. The sausage and rosemary add zip to the juices, which, in turn, flavor the potatoes. The sausages are supposed to be mixed in with the potatoes and onions, but who could blame you if you made a nice little snack out of them?

3-pound veal roast from the loin
   or leg

2 tablespoons olive oil

I head Caramelized Garlic
   (page 186)

2 tablespoons balsamic vinegar

I teaspoon Tabasco

2 stems fresh rosemary

3 sweet or hot Italian sausage links,
   about ¾ pound

6 russet potatoes

I onion, cut into wedges

2 tablespoons melted butter

½ teaspoon dried thyme

Freshly ground black pepper to
   taste

Preheat the oven to 350°F.

Rub the outside of the veal with the olive oil, garlic, vinegar and Tabasco. Place the roast in a pan and put the rosemary and sausage on top and secure with toothpicks. Place the roast in the oven for 30 to 40 minutes. Remove the sausage, and slice into ½-inch pieces and set aside.

Scrub the potatoes and cut lengthwise into wedges. Place the potatoes, onion, butter, thyme and pepper in a medium bowl and toss well. Scatter the potatoes around the roast, return the pan to the oven for about an hour and cook the roast until it registers 150°F on an instant-read thermometer. Remove the roast to a platter and keep warm. Raise the oven temperature to 400°F, and cook the potatoes until they're crisp, about 10 minutes. Add the sliced sausage to the potatoes and serve with the sliced veal.

Roasting

Herb Roast Chicken

Smearing the butter and seasonings under the skin acts like a natural basting machine and helps keep the breasts moist during the dry oven cooking. To further baste the birds, you can wrap the outsides with thin slices of pancetta or bacon before they go in the oven.

2 (2½ pound) chickens	1 teaspoon dried thyme
4 tablespoons butter, softened	1 teaspoon dried rosemary
1 head Caramelized Garlic	1 teaspoon dried sage
(page 186)	1 teaspoon Tabasco
Juice of 1 lemon	Freshly ground black pepper to
1 tablespoon dried parsley	taste

Preheat the oven to 350°F.

Wash the chickens and pat dry. Carefully place your fingers and then your hands between the skin and the meat beginning at the breast cavity opening. Loosen the skin, but do not remove it and be careful not to puncture the skin.

In a small bowl combine the butter with the garlic, lemon juice, parsley, thyme, rosemary, sage, Tabasco, and black pepper and mix well.

Smear half the butter mixture on the meat *under the skin* of each chicken and then rub the skin to smooth out the butter. Truss the chickens (see page 38), place in a roasting pan and cook until the chickens are golden brown, about 1 hour. An instant-read thermometer inserted in the leg, without touching a bone, should register 170°F.

Roasted Cornish Hen

Rather than roast the Cornish hens whole, this recipe calls for splitting them, but leaving the two halves attached. When the halves roast flat, the result is a crispier bird than a whole roasted one because the meat is placed on a rack which allows air to circulate all around.

2 (1 pound) Cornish hens   **Cornish Hen Marinade (page 60)**

Split the Cornish hens between the back and breast cavity, just behind the thigh. Pour the marinade over the Cornish hens and refrigerate 1 hour.

Preheat the oven to 375°F.

Remove the Cornish hens from the marinade and place on a rack inside a roasting pan. Place the hens in the oven for 30 minutes, basting occasionally with the marinade. Lower the oven temperature to 325°F and cook until they're done, about 15 to 20 minutes longer.

Roasted Vegetable Medley

Today's array of vegetables goes well beyond the ubiquitous peas and carrots of the sixties. Roasting vegetables intensifies their natural flavors as the heat caramelizes their natural sugars, including the garlic. (This is one instance when you'll want to use raw garlic.) Served with Stuffed Portobello Mushrooms (page 180) for a complete vegetarian meal. You won't even miss the meat.

2 sweet potatoes, peeled and
  quartered
I large onion, peeled and cut into 8
  pieces or 2 small onions,
  peeled and quartered
2 carrots, scrubbed and cut into
  finger-size pieces
I parsnip, peeled and cut into
  finger-size pieces
2 leeks, white part only, split and
  washed

6 cloves raw garlic
2 tablespoons olive oil
I teaspoon dried rosemary,
  crumbled
I teaspoon dried thyme
Freshly ground black pepper to
  taste
¼ cup dry white wine or chicken
  broth

Preheat the oven to 375°F.

Place the sweet potatoes, onion, carrots, parsnip, leeks and garlic into a large roasting pan, sprinkle with the olive oil, rosemary, thyme, and black pepper and toss lightly. Place the vegetables in the oven for 25 minutes or until they become light brown. Add the white wine, stir and cover with aluminum foil. Roast until the vegetables are tender, about 10 minutes longer.

Know Your Fire

Grilling

Grilling calls for cooking food over intense heat either outdoors over charcoal or gas or indoors on an electric grill or under the broiler. Since grilling does not tenderize food and tends to dry it out, most foods benefit from marinating first.

Know Your Fire

"Know your fire" is the key to cooking and to food. To think that the only heat source available for cooking is the stove or oven in the kitchen is being shortsighted. Once you understand the heat source and how it affects food, you have begun to learn the mysteries of food.

I found a classic example teaching students in one of my culinary classes. When browning beef bones for a beef stock, they had to roast the bones in the oven until golden brown, add a mirepoix (diced onions, carrots and celery) and allow it to brown, add some tomato sauce and allow the ingredients to color slightly.

On the surface, the process sounds very simple and, when done correctly, it produces a rich amber beef stock. When done incorrectly, it produces a weak and tasteless pot of cloudy water.

As a culinary student you need to answer these questions: How cold were the bones? Were the bones too crowded in the roasting pan, and did they steam instead of roast? Was the mirepoix added too early, causing the vegetables to steam? Did opening the oven door too often to check on the color of the bones prevent the oven from getting hot enough to brown the bones correctly? Were the bones and mirepoix the right shade of light golden brown when the tomato sauce was added?

So now you want to know what this all has to do with grilling. Making beef stock is the perfect example of understanding how heat affects food and how each step of the process is important. It all comes down to an understanding of what happens with food in terms of the temperature of your oven, grill, stovetop, smoker or whatever heat source you're using.

Turn Your Backyard into a Kitchen

When you think of grilling, most people think of burgers and hot dogs, but it's possible to cook anything on the grill that you can cook in your kitchen. Think of the grill as an extension of your stove, but when you grill outdoors, you keep the heat out of the kitchen. And frying outdoors relieves the kitchen of a greasy mess and lingering odors. Most of the newer grills come equipped with a side burner so that you can grill the ingredients for a sauce while you boil water for pasta.

Gas Versus Charcoal

I've cooked over just about every kind of grill made, both gas and charcoal.

Grilling with gas is versatile and convenient. Gas grills are easy to light and cheap to operate, and they allow you to begin cooking almost immediately. On the other hand, they cost more than charcoal grills.

By far, charcoal grilling gives more flavor, but you have to plan ahead. It takes 30 to 45 minutes for the charcoal to become hot enough to begin cooking.

Techniques of Lighting the Fire

A metal chimney is the safest and quickest way to light a fire for a charcoal grill. It's about the size of a large juice can, with holes around the bottom and a handle on the side. Place crumpled newspaper on the bottom of the chimney and fill to the top with charcoal. When you light the paper with a match through one of the bottom holes, the flame is drawn up to the charcoal and ignites it. In about 15 minutes, the coals are white and ready to dump onto the grill. Without the chimney, it can take up to 45 minutes for the coals to be hot enough. You can buy these chimneys in home centers and hardware stores.

Never use fuel to light charcoal. It isn't safe and the taste of the petroleum may taint the food.

Before you light a charcoal fire, you have to estimate how many pieces of charcoal to ignite. Think of how much room the food will take up on the grill. Use enough charcoal to make a single layer below that space and add a few more briquets.

When the briquets are covered with gray ash, spread them in a single layer. Arrange the briquets close together in the center, so that the fire will be hotter there and leave some space between the coals at the edge for a cooler fire.

Hold your hand, palm side down, 5 inches over the coals. If you can only hold your hand there for a second, the fire is very hot. If you can hold it there for 2 to 3 seconds, the fire is hot; 4 to 5 seconds, the fire is medium; and 6 seconds, the fire is low.

How to Avoid Flare-Ups

Flare-ups are caused by melting fat. The best way to avoid them is to trim off most of the visible fat or cook meat over indirect heat. Indirect heat means you're not cooking directly over the heat source. The heat source (gas or charcoal) is on one side of the grill and the food is placed on the other side with a tray beneath it to catch any fat so that it doesn't flare up. Indirect heat can also mean that the grill cover is lowered and you're using the grill like an oven.

Grilling

Should a flare-up occur, the quickest way to stop it is to cut off the oxygen supply by closing the grill cover.

Old fashioned gas grills came with lava rocks and when hot fat dripped down and hit them, it would flare up. Many newer models have replaced the lava rocks with metal bars. When hot fat hits these, it evaporates or slides off into a receptacle.

Steak and Fusilli Salad

Most pasta salads are side dishes but with the addition of grilled steak slices, this one becomes the main course. To cut down on fat calories, use the water from soaking the sun-dried tomatoes to replace part of the oil in the Herb Vinaigrette. Fusilli pasta are corkscrew-shaped pasta about 1½ inches long.

1 (20 ounce) strip, loin or flank steak	¼ cup sun-dried tomatoes
1 tablespoon olive oil	12 ounces fusilli pasta, cooked
9 to 10 cloves Caramelized Garlic (page 186)	1 cup Herb Vinaigrette (page 76)
1 teaspoon Tabasco	2 tablespoons grated Parmesan cheese
Freshly ground black pepper to taste	1 teaspoon red pepper flakes to taste
	Lettuce leaves

Preheat the grill to very high.

Rub the steak with the olive oil and season with the garlic, Tabasco and black pepper. Grill the steak for 3 minutes, turn and continue cooking until desired doneness. Cool the steak for about 5 minutes and cut into thin slices across the grain.

Place the sun-dried tomatoes into ¼ cup boiling water for 5 minutes, drain well and cut into strips.

Combine the cooked fusilli with the Herb Vinaigrette, sun-dried tomatoes, Parmesan cheese and pepper flakes and toss gently. Line a serving platter with lettuce leaves and arrange the fusilli in the center and the steak slices around it.

Grilling

Grilled Salmon with Tomato Dill Salsa

The abundance of farm-raised salmon has caused the price to go down and the availability to be more dependable. The flavor of farm-raised salmon is also milder than the wild variety. This especially appeals to people who don't like fish with a strong taste. If you don't like to wrestle with bones, purchase the fillet rather than the steak. The colorful salsa adds a nice crunch to the dish.

Juice of 2 limes

2 tablespoons olive oil

2 pounds salmon fillet or 2¼ pounds salmon steaks

FOR THE SALSA

4 plum tomatoes, seeded and chopped

1 green or red bell pepper, seeded and chopped

1 cucumber peeled, seeded, and chopped

1 scallion, chopped

1 tablespoon chopped fresh dill

1 tablespoon olive oil

1 tablespoon cider vinegar

Freshly ground black pepper to taste

Combine the lime juice and olive oil and marinate the salmon in this mixture for 30 minutes.

For the salsa: In a small bowl, combine the tomato, bell pepper, cucumber, scallion, dill, olive oil, vinegar and black pepper and marinate 30 minutes.

Preheat the grill to high.

Remove the salmon from the marinade and place it on the grill for a total of 8 to 10 minutes, turning the salmon once. The fish is cooked when it turns pink. Serve the salmon with the tomato dill salsa.

Shrimp with Lemon and Rosemary

Using rosemary stems as skewers not only makes a nice presentation, the rosemary imparts a subtle flavor to the shrimp. Watch the shrimp carefully so they don't overcook. To make Caramelized Garlic Olive Oil, combine 1 head Caramelized Garlic (page 186), 1 cup olive oil and 1 teaspoon Tabasco. Allow the oil to sit for *at least* 1 hour, but it will have more flavor if it sits overnight.

1 pound large shrimp

2 lemons, sliced thin

8 fresh rosemary stems (each at least 8" long), or skewers and 1 tablespoon dried rosemary

4 tablespoons Caramelized Garlic olive oil (see note above)

Freshly ground black pepper to taste

Preheat the grill to high.

Pierce holes in the shrimp and lemon slices with a metal skewer or the tip of a sharp knife. Alternately thread the shrimp and lemon slices onto the rosemary stems. If fresh rosemary stems are not available, use metal skewers and season the shrimp with dried rosemary. Brush the shrimp with the caramelized garlic olive oil and season with pepper. Sear the shrimp over high heat for 2 to 3 minutes and move to medium heat until cooked, about 3 to 4 minutes longer.

Grilling

Ham-Stuffed Shrimp

It may appear strange to stuff shrimp with meat, but the combination of shellfish and smoke-flavored foods works well. See discussion on shrimp sizes on page 141. Crab, clams or other grilled vegetables can be substituted for the ham.

1 (4 ounce) ham steak	½ teaspoon Tabasco
½ onion, thickly sliced	Freshly ground black pepper to
1 red bell pepper, halved and seeded	taste
Olive oil	12 rosemary sprigs, about 2 inches
12 extra-large shrimp	long, or toothpicks
4 cloves Caramelized Garlic	6 slices prosciutto, sliced very thin,
(page 186)	and cut in half lengthwise
½ cup fresh bread crumbs	3 tablespoons olive oil
¼ cup mayonnaise	¼ cup white wine
1 tablespoon chopped fresh basil	Juice of 1 lemon

Preheat the grill to medium.

Brush the ham steak, onion and bell pepper with olive oil. Grill the ham over medium heat for 4 to 5 minutes on each side and chop. Increase the grill temperature to high and grill the pepper for 2 to 3 minutes on each side and the onion 3 to 4 minutes on each side. Remove the pepper and onion and chop. If using a charcoal grill, grill the ham at the cooler edges and the vegetables over the hotter coals in the center.

Remove the shrimp shell down to the last ring above the tail. Remove the vein and butterfly the shrimp by splitting them down the outside curve *almost but not entirely* through. Spread the shrimp open like a butterfly.

Heat the grill to hot.

Combine the ham, onion, bell pepper, garlic, bread crumbs, mayonnaise, basil, Tabasco and black pepper in a medium bowl and mix well. Fill the shrimp with the stuffing, bring the two sides together and wrap a half slice of prosciutto around each shrimp. Secure with the rosemary sprigs or toothpicks and brush with olive oil. Quickly sear on a hot grill for 2 to 3 minutes on each side, turning once.

Combine the white wine and lemon juice in a medium-size heatproof casserole or skillet that can hold the shrimp in a single layer. Arrange the shrimp in the dish, place the pan on the grill and cook until the shrimp is done, about 2 minutes longer. Take care not to overcook the shrimp.

Chorizo and Pepper Stew

Grilling the chorizo and vegetables before they go into the pot is a good example of how browning the ingredients first adds to the flavor of the dish.

All chorizo sausages are not the same. The Spanish make it from smoked pork, while Mexican chorizo is made from fresh pork. To further confuse the issue, the flavor can differ depending on the variety of spices and the hotness of the chilies and the texture can range from styles made with chunks of meat to those made with ground meat.

I pound chorizo sausage	I teaspoon ground cumin
2 bell peppers, halved and seeded	I teaspoon dried oregano
I onion, peeled and thickly sliced	I teaspoon chopped fresh parsley
Olive oil	I teaspoon paprika
3 slices bacon, chopped	½ teaspoon Tabasco
I (16 ounce) can white beans, rinsed and drained	I cup red wine
6 cloves Caramelized Garlic (page 186)	

Preheat the grill to medium and light the side burner.

Grill the chorizo 7 to 8 minutes, turning occasionally. Remove, cool and slice into 1-inch pieces. Brush the bell peppers with olive oil, grill 2 to 3 minutes on each side and cut into thin strips. Brush the onion slices with olive oil, grill 3 to 4 minutes on each side and chop.

On the side burner or stovetop, cook the bacon in a soup kettle for 30 seconds over high heat. Add the grilled peppers and onion, beans, garlic, cumin, oregano, parsley, paprika and Tabasco and cook 2 minutes, stirring constantly. Lower the heat to medium, add the chorizo and cook 2 minutes longer. Stir in the wine and cook 5 minutes longer, stirring occasionally.

Smoking

Before you read this section of the book, lest you think that smoking is something either too complicated to consider or that it's a habit you've been trying to break for many years, let me introduce to you one of the simplest yet most flavor-enhancing ways to prepare a wide variety of foods.

There are two ways to smoke food: cold smoking and hot smoking, of which hot smoking is probably the most popular and accessible for the home cook.

In cold smoking, most food is brined (see page 285) and then "cold-smoked" at temperatures of between 195° and 205°F for long periods of time in a special three-part water smoker. This is an ideal way to prepare large pieces of meat such as brisket, pork butt and whole turkey.

The water smoker is a bullet-shaped container with three levels: the heat source (charcoal or electricity) is on the bottom, a pan filled with water or other liquid is in the center, and a rack upon which the food is placed is on top. Using liquids such as beer, wine, vinegar, fruit juice, cola or cider adds flavor and aroma to the food. Using this cold-smoking technique can remove most of the moisture from the food so there is considerable shrinkage in large pieces of meat. There is, however, so much moisture given up by the liquid in the smoker that the meat does not dry out. Hot smoking can also be done in the water smoker by leaving out the water pan and using a higher temperature.

Hot smoking is done on the grill using a commercially available smoker or a simple home-made device that holds liquid-soaked wood chips. These create the smoke that both cooks the food and imparts a nice smoky flavor. Smaller cuts of meat such as steaks, chops, poultry parts and all types of seafood are well suited to the hot smoking technique.

Creating the Hot Smoker

To transform your outdoor grill into a hot smoker, soak wood chips for 30 to 60 minutes in liquid (wine, beer, cider, etc.). Drain them and place in an *iron smoker box,* available at any home center or where grilling supplies are sold. Or improvise with a disposable aluminum pan. Poke a few air holes around the sides, fill with chips and cover with aluminum foil. Place the smoker box on the grid of a preheated grill, lower the grill lid and, in about 10 minutes, the wood will begin to smolder. Open the lid and quickly sear the food on the grid on both sides. Close the lid and cook the food until it is done following recipe instructions.

The most common woods used in a smoker are mesquite, especially in the Southwest, and hickory, especially in the Southeast. In the Northeast, fruit woods such as apple and cherry are favorites but, unfortunately, only trimmings and clippings, which don't burn as long as larger chunks, are available commercially. In certain areas, maple, oak and pecan are available, but they are expensive.

If you are using freshly cut wood from your own or a neighbor's property, it should be cut into small pieces and allowed to dry protected from the elements. You should ensure that the wood has not been sprayed with chemicals.

Chips for smoking can also come from other sources such as wineries who market their old oak barrels or sell vine clippings which can be used to flavor the smoke. The McIlhenny Company chops up and sells the barrels used to age their pepper mash. Or you can use the stems from herb plants like rosemary, basil or even fruit and vegetable peelings which still have flavor.

When smoking foods like fish, chicken parts, or duck breasts, soak the chips for about 30 minutes before they go into the smoker. When smoking whole chickens or larger roasts, soak the wood for about two hours.

Flavoring with wood is a major part of smoking but it is only part of the process. I like to use dry herb-and-spice rubs and marinades (see page 55) as well. Smoking alone will impart a particular flavor, but it may leave the food somewhat bland. Also, for some delicate foods such as seafood, marinating helps to keep them moist.

MAKES 4 SERVINGS

Cold-Smoked Trout

Trout has a mild, sweet, delicate flavor that's enhanced by the marinade. This distant relative of the salmon family is sold filleted or butterflied. Trout is relatively low in fat and has a soft, flaky texture when smoked. Serve with coarse brown bread and mugs of cold beer.

4 (18 to 20 ounce) fresh trout, gutted and scaled

Marinade for Cold-Smoked Trout (page 59)

1 (12 ounce) can beer

Mustard and horseradish for serving

Place the trout in the marinade and refrigerate for 24 hours. If the marinade does not cover the trout, turn them every 2 hours.

Prepare a cold water smoker, allowing about 45 minutes for it to heat up. Remove the trout from the marinade and place them on a greased rack. Pour the marinade into the water pan and add the can of beer. Place the water pan over the fire box. Place the trout in the smoker for approximately 2 hours. The temperature should remain between 195° and 205°F. The trout will wrinkle slightly. They're done when the meat shrinks away from the bone. Serve with mustard and horseradish.

Know Your Fire

Cold-Smoked Pork

Sometimes it's worthwhile waiting for food to cook if you wind up with something great. In this case, these pork tenderloins are worth the wait. If you have any left over, freeze it and use later in salad, pasta or soup. Chance are no one will be able to detect the flavor of the cola in the water pan. It will taste familiar, but will be hard to identify.

Caribbean Spice Rub (page 59)

2 (10 to 12 ounce) pork tenderloins

FOR THE SMOKER

Hickory or mesquite shavings
    soaked in water for 30 minutes

2 liters cola

2 cups vegetable peelings (from
    onion, celery and carrots)

1 cup rum

2 cinnamon sticks

4 bay leaves

Rub the Caribbean Spice Rub onto all sides of the pork and refrigerate 24 hours.

Build a charcoal fire in the cold smoker and add the soaked hickory or mesquite shavings on top. When the charcoal turns to white ash, place the water pan filled with the cola, vegetable peelings, rum, cinnamon sticks and bay leaves in the smoker. Place the tenderloins on the grid, close and smoke from 2 to 2½ hours or until the internal temperature of the meat is 165°F. Eat the tenderloins warm or cool and serve in the Pork Salad Roti (page 262).

Pork Salad Roti

Caribbean food is a good example of how many different cultures influence a cuisine. Seasonings such as chilies, peppers, citrus, ginger and garlic from Africa, China, Spain and the Netherlands are combined into foods that are unique to the Caribbean. This salad, wrapped in roti and eaten out of your hand, is a popular street food.

A roti wrapper is a very thin, flat, unleavened pancake or crêpe. It resembles a tortilla in texture and shape, but it has a fuller taste. The roti is made primarily with all-purpose flour, baking powder, milk or water, and salt. The dough is pressed thin and cooked on both sides on a griddle over an open flame. Sometimes puréed chick peas are added to the dough. Look for them at Caribbean markets.

2 cold-smoked pork tenderloins
   (page 259)
16 roti wrappers (see headnote) or
   16 (6- or 8-inch) flour tortillas
¼ cup hoisin sauce or other sweet
   seasoning sauce
2 cups green bok choy leaves,
   chopped

2 mangoes, peeled, seeded, and
   diced
1 red pepper, seeded and shredded
3 scallions, chopped
Juice of 2 limes

Slice the smoked pork tenderloins very thin.

Brush the inside of the roti wrapper with hoisin sauce. Top with slices of smoked pork, chopped bok choy, mango, red pepper and scallions. Sprinkle with lime juice. Fold the wrapper in half, then fold into quarters.

Center Cut Hot-Smoked Pork Chops

To my way of thinking, you're eating the best when you can enjoy center pork chops cut from the loin. Give them a little taste of Texas by adding some mesquite to the smoker box.

4 (1-inch) center cut pork chops

1 tablespoon Tabasco

1 head Caramelized Garlic
   (page 186)

2 tablespoons chopped cilantro

1 tablespoon chopped fresh thyme

1 tablespoon coarsely ground black
   pepper

1 teaspoon grated lemon peel (save
   the juice)

2 handfuls of mesquite chips

Juice from one lemon

Rub the pork chops on both sides with the Tabasco and garlic, then pat on the cilantro, thyme, black pepper and lemon peel. Marinate in the refrigerator for 1 hour.

Soak the mesquite chips in the lemon juice for about 30 minutes.

Preheat the grill to medium. Place the chips in a smoker box, place on the grill, and close the cover for 5 minutes for smoke to develop.

Place the chops on the grill, quickly sear 1 minute on each side and close the cover. After 5 to 6 minutes, turn the chops and cook until done, 8 to 10 minutes longer. An instant-read thermometer will read 150°F. Serve with Apple-Raisin Sauce (page 135).

Smoking

Smoked Ribs

Spareribs are the lower portion of the pig's rib and breastbone. I'm often asked how many different ways there are to cook ribs and which method is the best. Here's the answer.

3 racks of pork spareribs
Rib Rub (page 60)

FOR THE SMOKER
hickory chips

FOR THE WATER PAN
vegetable trimmings
1 cup cider vinegar
2 liters cola

Rub the Rib Rub onto both sides of the ribs. Refrigerate for at least 24 hours.

Soak the hickory chips in water for 30 minutes.

Following manufacturer's instructions, prepare the water smoker and place the vegetable trimmings, cider vinegar and cola in the water pan.

Place the ribs in the smoker and smoke at 195°F for approximately three hours. The ribs are done when an instant-read thermometer registers 150°F.

Know Your Fire

Smoked Turkey

Turkey roasted in a water smoker is incredibly moist, and the flesh takes on a rosy hue. It's better to smoke two small turkeys rather than one big one because small birds are more tender and a large turkey takes a long time to cook. You can also lessen the cooking time by cutting the turkey into parts and smoking them for 2 to 3 hours versus 6 to 8 hours for a 10- to 12-pound bird. The hickory smoke, the flavorful liquid in the water pan plus the zesty rub make it a turkey to remember.

The temperature of the smoker should remain between 195° and 205°F. It will be necessary to replenish the charcoal about every hour or so. Light a new batch of charcoal about 15 minutes before you need it in a charcoal chimney starter or 30 minutes on a separate grill. Wind, outside temperature and humidity will affect the cooking time.

1 (10 to 12 pound) turkey	2 cups vegetable peelings (carrots,
Smoked Turkey Rub (page 61)	onion, ginger and orange)
	Several chunks of hickory wood
FOR THE SMOKER	soaked in water for 1 hour
2 liters ginger ale, cola or lemon	
soda	

The day before smoking the turkey, wash the turkey inside and out, pat dry and truss. Rub the outside of the turkey with the Smoked Turkey Rub and refrigerate for 24 hours.

Prepare a charcoal fire in a charcoal smoker following the manufacturer's instructions, and when the ashes turn white, add the hickory wood. Place the liquid and vegetable peelings in the water pan and place it in the smoker. Place the turkey on the rack and cold smoke for 6 to 8 hours or until the turkey thigh meat registers 155°F on an instant-read thermometer.

Smoked Pineapple

Pineapples lend themselves to many different types of cooking. I probably wouldn't start the smoker for this recipe alone, but if the smoker is fired up, this is a good way to use it. The flavor will be very close to pineapple rings baked on smoked ham. If there's any leftover for dessert, a scoop of vanilla ice cream or a dollop of sweetened whipped heavy cream could only make it taste better.

I whole ripe pineapple

¼ cup brown sugar

¼ cup nuts (pecans, walnuts, etc.)

2 tablespoons granulated sugar

½ teaspoon allspice

2 tablespoons honey, corn syrup or cane syrup

Peel the pineapple and cut out all the "eyes." Leave the pineapple whole.

Combine the brown sugar, nuts, sugar and allspice in a small bowl and mix well. Brush the pineapple with the honey and rub with the brown sugar mixture.

Following the directions on pages 257 to 258, cold smoke the pineapple for 1½ hours or hot smoke for 15 minutes.

Baking

The Difference Between Baking and Roasting

Baking and roasting are both dry-heat methods of cooking in an enclosed oven, yet they're different. You would hardly say "I'm roasting a cake" or "I'm baking a leg of lamb." When roasting any kind of food, you need some kind of fat, which gives it a characteristic browning and crispness. This could either be natural fat, such as marbling in meat, or added fat, such as oil brushed on before roasting. In most cases roasting causes a physical change. When a roasted chicken comes out of the oven, its physical properties—color, texture, flavor—have changed but it still looks like a chicken.

Baking, on the other hand, can cause chemical changes. Take a cake, for instance. You mix together flour, sugar, milk and eggs and place them in the oven. Not only does their appearance change, but they have undergone a chemical change and become something new and different and we can't recognize the original ingredients.

These are not diehard rules, however, and there are exceptions. A baked potato or a baked bean casserole are said to be baked yet undergo the physical changes associated with roasting rather than chemical changes of baking.

Some Thoughts on Baking

Baking is probably the most scientific category of the culinary arts. You can add an extra potato, leave out the anchovy, double the amount of tomatoes in a cooked dish without risk of failure. But you can't do that when it comes to baking. Ingredients cannot be added and deleted indiscriminately. A cake that does not rise is not a cake; the wrong ratio of dry ingredients to wet often will spell disaster.

There are principles in baking that must be understood, scientific properties that contribute to the success of the baked dish.

Take, for example, a bread pudding, a combination of bread, eggs, milk and sugar. While the bread can be a combination of white, Italian, cinnamon-raisin, day-old Danish or coffee cake, these variations will alter only the taste and texture. The most important component of bread pudding, however, is the structure of the pudding or custard. The basic recipe is 8 eggs to 1 pint of milk. You can make more or less, but the ratio must remain the same. If you increase the eggs, there won't be enough milk, and the custard will be tough and chewy; if you decrease the eggs, there's too much milk, and the custard will be runny or too soft.

Sugar also plays an important role. When you use too little sugar, the custard tastes flat; use too much and it will be too sweet and the exterior of the bread pudding will become a dark brown. You can adjust the sugar by cutting down on the amount, but you have to replace it with corn syrup, cane syrup or maple syrup.

How to Measure

Measuring accurately is imperative. In professional kitchens, dry ingredients are always *weighed* for more accuracy. However, home cooks and bakers, not in the habit of having a scale on the kitchen counter, use measuring cups.

Dry ingredients should be measured in nested cups, a set of graduated measuring cups with the following sizes: 1 cup, ½ cup, ⅓ cup and ¼ cup. Spoon the dry ingredients into the cup and level it off with the flat edge of a knife.

It isn't necessary to sift flour before measuring, but it could have become compacted in the container, so it can be stirred with a fork before measuring.

Wet ingredients should be measured in a glass measuring cup. These range from 1 cup to 8 cups. Pour in the liquid, place the cup on a flat surface and measure it at eye level.

Use measuring spoons for dry ingredients such as baking powder and spices and for wet ingredients such as lemon juice and vanilla. The spoons are labeled 1 tablespoon, 1 teaspoon, ⅓ teaspoon and ¼ teaspoon.

Measurements and Equivalents

1 teaspoon	⅓ tablespoon
3 teaspoons	1 tablespoon
2 tablespoons	⅛ cup or 1 fluid ounce
4 tablespoons	¼ cup or 2 fluid ounces
5⅓ tablespoons	⅓ cup or 2⅔ ounces
8 tablespoons	½ cup or 4 fluid ounces
12 tablespoons	¾ cup or 6 fluid ounces
16 tablespoons	1 cup or 8 fluid ounces
2 cups	1 pint or 16 fluid ounces
4 cups	1 quart or 32 fluid ounces
16 cups	1 gallon, 4 quarts or 128 fluid ounces

Substituting Pan Sizes

Sometimes one pan can be substituted for another if it has the *same volume*. To measure the volume, fill each pan with water to the top and pour the water into a glass measuring cup. If the volume of the two are the same, they're interchangeable. However, there may be some adjustment necessary in the baking times. In other words, if you use a loaf pan rather than a cake pan, the cooking time would be increased because the loaf pan produces a denser cake.

To determine the size of a pan, measure across the top from inner edge to inner edge. Do not measure the bottom. To determine the height of the pan, measure straight up with a ruler. Do not hold the ruler on a slant if the pan sides flare.

Pan Sizes and Volume Equivalents

ROUND CAKE PANS

8" x 1½"	4 cups
9" x 1½"	6 cups
8" x 2"	6 cups
9" x 2"	8 cups

SQUARE CAKE PANS

8" x 8" x 2"	7 to 8 cups
9" x 9" x 2"	10 cups

LOAF PANS

8" x 4" x 3"	6 cups
9" x 5" x 3"	8 cups

RECTANGULAR PANS

7½" x 11¾" x 1¾"	8 cups
9" x 13" x 1¾"	12 cups

Pastry Cream

Pastry cream or crême patisserie is a flour-based custard used as a filling for cream puffs and eclairs. After it's cooked, place a sheet of plastic wrap on the surface or sprinkle with granulated sugar to prevent a "skin" from forming and refrigerate immediately.

1½ pints milk	4 egg yolks
2 tablespoons butter	½ cup granulated sugar
1 teaspoon vanilla	3 tablespoons all-purpose flour
2 eggs	½ teaspoon grated orange zest

Combine the milk, butter and vanilla in a saucepan and bring to a boil over medium heat, stirring occasionally.

In a separate bowl combine the eggs, egg yolks, sugar, flour and orange zest and whisk until smooth.

Whisk about a cup of the hot milk mixture into the egg mixture to warm it and then pour it all back into the saucepan, whisking constantly. Continue to cook the mixture, whisking continuously, until the cream coats a spoon, which it will do at about 190°F. (If you cook it to boiling, 212°F, the pastry cream will be watery and lumpy.)

Pour the cream into a bowl and place it in a larger bowl of ice water to cool it as quickly as possible. Pastry cream can be refrigerated for 2 days.

Skillet Cornbread Shortcake

This Southern version of strawberry shortcake is baked in a black iron skillet, which gives it a crunchy crust, the perfect foil for berries and sweetened whipped cream. Using cake flour will give the shortcake a lighter, more tender texture.

1 cup cornmeal	¼ teaspoon vanilla
1 cup cake flour or all-purpose flour	¼ teaspoon ground cinnamon
¼ cup granulated sugar	1 cup heavy cream
2 teaspoons baking powder	2 tablespoons confectioners' sugar
¼ teaspoon salt	
1 cup milk	1 pint strawberries
2 eggs, lightly beaten	Granulated sugar, if necessary
¼ cup melted butter	

Preheat the oven to 375°F.

In a medium bowl combine the cornmeal, flour, sugar, baking powder and salt. In a small bowl combine the milk, eggs, butter, vanilla and cinnamon and mix well. Pour the liquid ingredients into the dry ingredients and stir until no particles of the dry ingredients remain. Do not overmix.

Spoon the mixture into a well-greased, 8-inch, black iron skillet or cake pan and bake until a toothpick inserted in the center comes out clean, 25 to 30 minutes. Cool the bread 5 minutes in the pan; remove and cool completely on a rack.

Beat the heavy cream until soft peaks form. Add the confectioners' sugar and continue beating until peaks are stiff.

Wash the strawberries and pat dry gently with a paper towel. Cut half of the strawberries into slices and leave the rest whole. If the berries are not sweet, toss with 2 tablespoons sugar.

Slice the cornbread in half horizontally and spread the lower half with half the whipped cream and the sliced strawberries. Replace the top half and cover with the remaining whipped cream and the whole strawberries.

Know Your Fire

"Short" baking Technically, the word short is used to describe a pastry, cookie or cake that contains a high proportion of fat to flour. "Short" baked goods such as short pastry, shortbread and shortcake are rich, crumbly, tender and crisp.

Pâté à Choux (Cream Puff Pastry)

**MAKES 2 TO
3 DOZEN,
DEPENDING
ON SIZE**

Maybe because it has a French name, or maybe because it's a two-step process (first cooked on the stovetop and then in the oven) but many cooks avoid this recipe. Make it once and you'll be a convert. Cream puff pastry is versatile and, whether it's baked as cream puffs or eclairs, it freezes well. Since they defrost in minutes, they can be filled with ice cream and topped with chocolate sauce and served to unexpected guests or filled with chicken or lobster salad as a luncheon dish for someone special. Gougère of Ham (page 33) also makes use of this basic recipe.

1 cup water	½ teaspoon salt
4 tablespoons vegetable oil	1¼ cups all-purpose flour
3 tablespoons butter	4 eggs
2 tablespoons milk	

Preheat the oven to 450°F.

Combine the water, vegetable oil, butter, milk and salt in a medium saucepan over medium heat and bring to a boil, stirring occasionally. Add the flour all at once and stir with a wooden spoon until smooth. Cook the mixture over low heat until it dries slightly and leaves the sides of the pan, about 1 to 2 minutes. Remove the pan from the heat and add the eggs, one at a time, beating until each one is fully absorbed before adding the next one.

Cover a baking sheet, preferably one without sides, with parchment paper.

Place the paste in a pastry bag with a round tip with a ½-inch opening. To make cream puffs, hold the pastry bag at a 45 degree angle touching a paper-lined pan. Squeeze and lift the bag. Continue forming the puffs 1 to 2 inches apart. To make eclairs, squeeze the bag as you pull it toward you, making 3-inch long fingers.

Place the choux in the oven and, after 5 minutes, lower the temperature to 375°F. Depending on size, they will require 10 to 15 minutes total cooking time. If the oven door is opened before they're almost finished baking, they will collapse, so don't peek until 10 minutes have passed. To test for doneness, tap one on the bottom. It should sound hollow. Remove and cool on a rack.

Know Your Fire

How to fill cream puffs Wait until the puffs are cool and cut off the top third with a sharp knife. Fill the hollow bottom with a savory such as chicken or crab meat salad or a sweet such as pastry cream (page 271) or ice cream. Replace the top and serve. If the filling is a sweet one, dust the cream puffs with confectioners' sugar or pour chocolate sauce (page 136) over the top.

Apple Charlotte

In spite of its high sounding name, this is an extremely easy yet impressive dessert to make. A classic charlotte consists of layering ladyfingers, custard and whipped cream in a metal mold with sloping sides. Apple charlotte breaks the tradition because it's baked. It's also much lower in calories. The only way to improve this recipe is to add a dollop of whipped cream or a scoop of ice cream, and hang the saved calories! If you don't have a charlotte mold use any 2-quart metal pot with sloping sides.

8 slices day-old bread, such as white bread or raisin bread

½ cup melted butter

6 to 8 baking apples, peeled, cored and chopped

½ cup granulated sugar

2 tablespoons water

½ teaspoon ground cinnamon

Pinch ground nutmeg

2 tablespoons brandy

Grease an 8-inch charlotte mold.

Brush the sliced bread on both sides with the melted butter. Arrange the bread slices around the sides and the bottom of the mold, cutting the pieces to fit, if necessary.

Combine the apples, sugar, water, cinnamon and nutmeg in a saucepan and cook until it becomes a purée, about 20 minutes. Stir in the brandy.

Preheat oven to 375°F.

Fill the mold with the purée, cover the top with additional slices of bread and bake for 35 to 40 minutes. When the charlotte is finished, the bread will be well browned on the outside. Remove the pan from the oven and let it set 2 to 3 minutes. Place a flat dish on top, hold them both together and flip them over. Tap the outside of the mold and remove. Serve warm or cold.

Upside-Down Coffee Cake

Upside-down cakes were very popular years ago, and this version, which can also be made with apples, is an updated edition of that classic. Since your mother probably didn't tell you how really simple this cake is to make, let me remind you that the hardest part is resisting eating a second piece.

1 ⅓ cups granulated sugar

¼ cup water

5 slices canned pineapple, drained of all liquid, or 2 apples, cored, peeled and sliced

¼ cup walnut pieces

3 eggs

⅔ cup all-purpose flour

¼ cup melted butter

Preheat the oven to 375°F.

Combine 1 cup of the sugar with water in a saucepan and heat over low heat until the sugar liquefies and browns slightly. Pour this caramel mixture into a well-greased and floured 9-inch cake pan. Top with the pineapple or apple slices and walnut pieces.

Combine the remaining ⅓ cup sugar with the eggs and beat until light and creamy. Fold in the flour and the melted butter, alternating them, beginning and ending with the flour.

Pour the batter into the cake pan and bake until a toothpick inserted in the center comes out clean, about 30 to 35 minutes. Remove the cake and cool 2 minutes. Place a flat serving dish over the pan and, holding them together tightly, turn upside-down. Remove pan and cool the cake completely.

Baking

Apple Pecan Crumble

Here's a case when two apples are better than one. In this combination, the Granny Smiths add texture and the Macintosh add sweetness.

FOR THE FILLING

3 Granny Smith apples, peeled, cored and sliced

3 Macintosh apples, peeled, cored and sliced

Juice of 1 lemon

½ cup toasted pecans

2 tablespoons brown sugar

2 tablespoons granulated sugar

1 teaspoon cinnamon

¼ teaspoon nutmeg

FOR TOPPING

⅓ cup margarine, softened

6 tablespoons granulated sugar

1 teaspoon ground cinnamon

½ teaspoon vanilla

Pinch ground nutmeg

1 cup all-purpose flour

Preheat the oven to 375°F.

To make the filling, toss the apples together with the lemon juice in a medium bowl. This prevents them from browning. Add the pecans, both sugars, cinnamon and nutmeg and toss lightly. Place the mixture in a 9- by 1-inch pan without a removable bottom.

To make the topping, combine the margarine and sugar until light and creamy. Add the cinnamon, vanilla and nutmeg and mix well. Add the flour and blend the mixture with your fingers until crumbs form. Sprinkle the mixture evenly over the apples. Bake until the crumbs are light brown, about 25 to 30 minutes. Serve warm with caramel sauce or vanilla ice cream.

A crumble, a crisp and a cobbler A crumble is a baked fruit dessert topped with a crumbly pastry mixture. A crisp is very similar to a crumble but the pastry topping includes nuts or oatmeal, which makes it crunchy. A cobbler is a fruit dessert topped with a biscuit crust and baked. A betty is a baked pudding consisting of alternating layers of sweet spicy fruits and buttered bread crumbs.

Fruit Fool

I'm sure there's some culinary reason why cooked fruit combined with whipped cream is called a fool. Nonetheless, this version is baked, served over pound cake and garnished with whipped cream. Anyone would be a fool not to like it.

The fool has a puddinglike consistency. The cake crumbs give it body, and the egg whites bind the whole thing together. The fruit becomes soft and tender yet holds its shape.

I cup cubed firm fruit such as
  apples or pears
I cup cubed soft fruit such as
  peaches or plums
I cup pitted cherries or grapes
I cup cubed melon
¼ cup raisins, plumped in hot
  water for 5 minutes and
  drained

¼ cup brandy
½ cup crumbs from day-old cake,
  pound cake or muffins
¼ cup heavy cream
2 egg whites, lightly beaten
4 slices pound cake
Whipped cream for garnish

Preheat the oven to 400°F.

Combine the fruits in a medium bowl and stir in the brandy. Add the cake crumbs, cream and egg whites and mix well. Spoon mixture into a 9-inch ring mold or cake pan for 20 minutes. Serve over pound cake and garnish with whipped cream.

Banana Praline Custard

Here's a spinoff of crème brulée, a custard dessert with a crispy cara-melized top. The texture of the creamy filling made with mashed bananas and crunchy pecans is a delicious contrast to the caramel topping.

It may seem odd to use a propane torch to melt the sugar top-ping, but broilers often don't get hot enough and the propane brings the heat to the precise spot you want it. You can buy a small propane torch in any hardware store and some specialty food stores are selling them.

I cup mashed, ripe bananas	3 cups half-and-half
5 egg yolks, beaten slightly	Butter for greasing pan(s)
⅓ cup granulated sugar	½ cup light brown sugar
¼ cup lightly toasted pecans	2 tablespoons melted butter
½ teaspoon vanilla	I tablespoon heavy cream
¼ teaspoon ground nutmeg	Pinch ground cinnamon

Preheat oven to 325°F.

Combine the bananas, egg yolks, sugar, pecans, vanilla and nutmeg in a medium bowl and mix well. Stir in the half-and-half and combine thoroughly to make the "custard."

Butter a round 8- by 2-inch custard pan or six (6 ounce) individual ceramic souffle cups. Fill cups or pan with the custard to within ½ inch of the top. Set the oven rack in the center of the oven. Place the custard pan or souffle cups in a larger shallow pan without touching the sides and place on the oven rack. Pour in enough hot tap water to reach about halfway up the sides of the dishes. Bake the custard until it shimmers slightly in the center or until a toothpick or skewer inserted in the center comes out clean. This will take about 50 to 60 minutes for the larger dish or 25 to 30 minutes for the smaller ones. Remove from the water bath, allow the custard to cool to room temperature about 1 hour, cover and refrigerate until well chilled.

Preheat the broiler or propane torch.

Mix together the brown sugar, butter, cream and cinnamon. Pour the mixture over the tops of the custard and place under the broiler. In approximately 1 to 2 minutes, the sugar will begin to bubble and caramelize. If using a torch, adjust the flame to high and sweep it back evenly from side to side until the sugar melts. Serve immediately.

Cherry Cake

This is probably the easiest cake you will ever bake. And it couldn't be simpler—everything goes into one bowl. Peaches, plums, pears or nectarines can be substituted for the cherries.

Try getting out of bed 30 minutes earlier on a Sunday morning and surprising your family with a special breakfast treat for their coffee.

2 cups prepared biscuit mix   ½ cup sliced almonds
⅔ cup milk   Confectioners' sugar
1 cup pitted fresh black cherries

Preheat oven to 375°F.

Butter a 9-inch tart or cake pan.

Place the biscuit mix and milk in a medium bowl and stir until just combined. Stir in the cherries and almonds. Spoon into the prepared pan and dust the top heavily with confectioners' sugar. Place the pan in the oven and bake 15 to 20 minutes, or until a toothpick inserted in the middle comes out clean. Remove the cake from the oven, cool slightly on a rack and sprinkle a second time with confectioners' sugar.

Know Your Fire

Pizza Rustica

Originally pizza rustica was a way to use up any cheese or smoked meat leftovers. Here's a case where the whole is equal to more than the sum of its parts. Bits of cheese and smoked meats flavor the ricotta and egg filling and make it perfect picnic food served with a green salad and a glass of red wine. Or serve thin slices as part of an antipasto.

8 ounces pizza dough (see page 194)

2 tablespoons olive oil

FOR THE FILLING

½ cup ricotta, strained

¼ cup shredded fontina cheese

2 slices prosciutto, chopped

2 slices pancetta or bacon, chopped, cooked and drained

2 tablespoons grated Parmesan cheese

6 cloves Caramelized Garlic (page 186)

4 eggs, lightly beaten

1½ cups half-and-half

4 basil leaves, chopped

½ teaspoon Tabasco

1 teaspoon crushed black peppercorns

Preheat the oven to 375°F.

On a lightly floured surface, roll out the dough ⅛-inch thick and press it into the bottom and ½ inch up the sides of a 10-inch cake pan. Brush with olive oil, prick the dough with the tines of a fork and bake for 5 to 6 minutes. Remove and cool while making the filling.

In a medium bowl, combine the ricotta, fontina, prosciutto, pancetta, Parmesan cheese and garlic and mix well. Add the eggs and mix until thoroughly blended. Stir in the half-and-half, basil, Tabasco and peppercorns. Pour the mixture into the partially baked shell and bake at 375°F for 25 minutes, reduce the oven temperature to 350°F and bake until done, about 15 to 20 minutes longer. The pie is cooked when the top is set and does not shimmer when the pan is shaken. Cool slightly and cut into wedges.

Preserving

Preserving is a catch-all phrase that means preparing food so that it can be stored for an extended period of time. It includes making pickles, relishes, jams and preserves as well as smoking, freezing and dehydrating.

Preserving Fruits, Pickles, Relishes, Etc.

Not everyone gets excited about spending warm summer days in a hot kitchen surrounded by piles of fruits and vegetables, Mason jars and other canning paraphernalia. Today "putting by" is a luxury, not the necessity for survival it once was, but homemade jars of preserves or relish can brighten up a snowy day and make precious gifts for special friends.

What Is Pickling or Brining?

Pickling is preserving fruits or vegetables in a seasoned vinegar and/or salt solution.

The most common foods preserved in brine are pickles, a cinch to make and a delight to eat. The standard brining solution for pickles is one pound of Kosher salt to one gallon of water. Kirbys, small crispy cucumbers, placed in this brine will be ready for eating in two to four weeks. Add some garlic, fresh dill, peppercorns and mustard seeds and you have a great-tasting pickle. If you don't want to process them, pickles will keep for several months in the refrigerator. Some commercial pickles have nitrates added to extend their shelf life.

But don't stop at kirbys. Many vegetables such as eggplant, tomatoes, cauliflower, bell and hot peppers, corn and cabbage are suitable for pickling. Never use vegetables that have been treated with a waxy coating. When the days get shorter and tomatoes don't have time to ripen on the vine, I collect the green tomatoes and pickle them.

Vinegar

Vinegar is aptly named. It comes from the French "vin aigre" meaning sour wine but it can also be made from cider, beer or fruit juice. As the liquids ferment, yeast and bacteria turn the sugars to alcohol and the alcohol converts into acetic acid. Vinegars contain from 4 to 9 percent acetic acid.

White distilled vinegar is the most acidic of all vinegars. It is made from pure grain alcohol and diluted with water. It has the longest shelf life and is used in many commercial operations. (See page 73 for other types of vinegar.)

Making Wine Vinegar

In order to make vinegar at home you need a "mother," a slimy, gelatinous substance containing yeast and other bacteria that converts certain liquids into vinegar. You may already have one in a bottle of vinegar that has been sitting around for a long time in the back of a cool, dark cupboard. You can strain the mother out by using a fine-meshed sieve. Combine the mother with 2 cups red wine and place in a large, wide-mouth jar so that a large surface is exposed to air. A 2-quart mayonnaise jar is ideal. Cover the top with two layers of cheesecloth and secure with a rubber band. Set the jar aside in a warm, but not hot, spot and forget about it for several weeks. By that time, the aroma and taste should tell you it's vinegar.

Strain out the vinegar into a sterilized bottle and cork it. You can store the mother by placing it in a jar, covering it with wine or vinegar and capping well.

The better the quality of the wine you start out with, the better the vinegar will be. It's easier to make vinegar from red wine than it is from white wine. Because of its high acidity, white wine will take longer to turn to vinegar but you can hasten the time by cutting it with an equal amount of water before adding the mother.

Jams, Jellies and Preserves

A jam is a mixture of chopped or crushed fruit and sugar cooked until it's a thick purée. Depending on how much natural pectin is in the fruit, commercial pectin is sometimes added.

Jellies are made from fruit juice and sugar with pectin frequently added to thicken them. It's a two-step process: first you make the juice and then you make the jelly.

Preserves are chunks of fruit cooked with sugar and sometimes pectin, sometimes enhanced with liqueur. The consistency is jellylike with large pieces of fruit.

Marmalade is a preserve that includes pieces of fruit rind, the most popular being orange marmalade. The word "marmelada" means "quince jam" in Portuguese. Marmalade can also be made from vegetables (see recipe page 292).

A conserve is a combination of two or more fruits cooked with sugar and nuts until it thickens. Sometimes it's flavored with liqueur.

Fruit spreads are less dense than jams and preserves. Sometimes they're puréed, other times they contain small pieces of fruit. Fruit spreads are often sweetened with fruit juice.

Botulism

Botulism contamination is odorless and tasteless and you can't see it. It can be prevented in preserved foods by following directions carefully and by not taking short cuts such as reducing the processing time or the amount of salt or sugar. Botulism spores can be destroyed in low-acid foods by processing them in a steam pressure cooker for the correct time. If you have doubts about any processed food, empty the contents into a pan and boil for 15 minutes.

The Mason Jar

A Mason jar is a glass bottle that comes with a special two-part top consisting of a flat metal lid and a screw band. Each time you use the jar, the metal lid must be replaced, but screw bands can be reused many times unless they're dented. The jars should have solid edges without any nicks or cracks. During the cooking process, the jars are sealed by a vacuum that holds the lid down.

Before using the jars, wash them in hot soapy water, rinse well and place in very hot water until ready to use. Fill the jars with food using a wide-mouth funnel or ladle. If the food is in a liquid, make sure it completely covers the food and leave the required headroom (space between food and rim.) Trapped air bubbles can cause yeast and mold to form so remove air by running a knife, the handle of a wooden spoon, even a chopstick, between the food and the inside of the jar.

Wipe the top edge and threads of the jar with a clean wet cloth to insure a good seal. Place the lids on the jars and attach the screw bands loosely.

The Water Bath

Set the jars in a rack or on towels in a large deep pot half-filled with hot water. The jars should be at least 1 inch apart, and they should not touch the sides of the pot. Cover the jars with a minimum of two inches of hot water. Bring the water to a boil, and after it begins to boil, start the timer. Additional time will be required if you're canning at a high altitude. When the processing is complete, remove the jars. You might want to invest in jar tongs especially designed for removing the hot jars. Set the jars aside to cool away from drafts.

When the jars are cool, test the seal. Press the center of the lid. If it's down, it's sealed. If it's up and you can press it down and it stays down, it's sealed. If you press it down and it comes up, the jar isn't sealed. Refrigerate the jar and use the contents within a few days or reprocess the jar.

After the jars have cooled tighten the screw bands. Label the jars, indicate the date and store in a cool, dark spot and consume within the time restrictions in the recipe.

A Word About Nonreactive Pans

Acid ingredients such as tomatoes, salt and vinegar should always be cooked in a nonreactive pan, which means it is made from a substance that won't react with the acid. You don't want the pot to affect the color, flavor or texture of the food. Use a pot made of stainless steel, flameproof glass, porcelain-clad metal or one of the inert "space age" materials. Avoid aluminum and cast iron.

Kirbys are the cucumber of choice for pickles because they stay firm. As an alternative to processing the bottles in boiling water, the pickles can be refrigerated and used within 2 months.

3 pounds kirby cucumbers	4 (1 pint) canning jars with 2-piece
2 cups water	lids
2 cups white distilled vinegar	4 sprigs fresh dill
2 tablespoons dill seed	1 head Caramelized Garlic
1 tablespoon black peppercorns	(page 186)
1 teaspoon mustard seed	

Wash the kirbys, pat dry and pierce on all sides with a fork.

Combine the water, vinegar, dill seeds, peppercorns and mustard seed in a medium nonreactive pan and bring to a boil. Cover the pot, lower the heat and simmer for 20 minutes. Strain the liquid and discard seasonings.

Fill the jars evenly with the fresh dill, garlic and kirbys. Cover with the pickling liquid, leaving ½ inch headroom. Run a thin spatula or knife between the sides of the jars and the kirbys to remove any trapped air. Wipe the rims of the jars with a clean, dry cloth and place the lids on.

Place the jars on a rack or on a terry cloth towel in a large kettle. They should not touch each other. Add enough water so that the tops of the jars are covered by at least 2 inches. When the water comes to a rolling boil, begin timing. In 10 minutes, remove the jars with tongs or a jar lifter and place them out of drafts to cool. Store in a cool dark place for 4 to 6 weeks for the pickles to age.

Preserving

Bread and Butter Pickles

Bread and butter pickles are sweet-and-sour pickles and a favorite on hamburgers, but they taste just as good on any sandwich. Have the kids help with this recipe by measuring out the ingredients and in a few weeks they'll be overjoyed with their success. Never use waxed cucumbers.

2 pounds cucumbers, preferably kirbys	2 cups cider vinegar
3 onions, thinly sliced	1 tablespoon black peppercorns
1 red bell pepper, seeded and sliced into rings	1 tablespoon mustard seeds
4 tablespoons Kosher salt	1 teaspoon turmeric
3 cups granulated sugar	½ teaspoon Tabasco
	4 (1-pint) canning jars with 2-piece lids

Wash the cucumbers and slice ⅛-inch thick. Combine with the onion, bell pepper and salt in a large bowl and toss well so that the salt is evenly distributed. Refrigerate for 2 hours.

In a nonreactive pot combine the sugar, vinegar, peppercorns, mustard seeds, turmeric and Tabasco and bring to a boil. Rinse the salt from the vegetables and drain well. Add the vegetables to the vinegar mixture and place over heat until the mixture comes to a boil. Pack the hot vegetables into the pint jars and fill with the liquid, leaving ½-inch headroom. Run a thin spatula or knife between the sides of the jars and the vegetables to remove any trapped air. Wipe the edges of the jars with a clean, dry cloth and place the lids on.

Place the jars on a rack or on a terry cloth towel in a large kettle. They should not touch each other. Add enough water so that the tops of the jars are covered by at least 2 inches. When the water comes to a rolling boil, begin timing. In 10 minutes, remove the jars with tongs or a jar lifter and place them out of drafts to cool. Store in a cool dark place for 6 to 8 weeks for pickles to ripen.

Pickled Green Tomatoes

Sometimes I call this the September 15th recipe. It's a handy way to use up those tomatoes that don't get a chance to turn red before the days get shorter and the nights get colder. And this preserving recipe doesn't require the usual processing of jars, etc. These tomatoes are great with a roasted ham or with roast beef.

2 pounds green tomatoes, cut into
  wedges

1 red onion, cut into wedges

1 red bell pepper, cut into 2-inch
  strips

6 serrano peppers

6 jalapeño peppers

1 head Caramelized Garlic
  (page 186)

2 cups white distilled vinegar

2 cups cider vinegar

8 sprigs fresh thyme

1 tablespoon black peppercorns

Wash the vegetables (except the garlic) and pat dry.

Pack the green tomatoes, onion, bell pepper, serrano and jalapeño peppers and garlic evenly into two 1-quart mason jars.

In a nonreactive pan, combine the vinegars, thyme and peppercorns and bring to a boil, lower heat and simmer 2 to 3 minutes. Remove from heat and chill over a bowl of ice water. When the liquid is cool, pour over the vegetables and seal the jars. Store the jars in a cool, dark place for 2 weeks. This recipes does not require processing, but refrigerate the jars if the tomatoes are not consumed within 4 weeks. Of course, once a jar is opened, it should be stored in the refrigerator.

MAKES 2 QUARTS # Piccalilli

Piccalilli is a good way to use up those excess vegetables when your garden runneth over. Few preserves are as brightly colored and sparkling as piccalilli. Serve it with any kind of meat or poultry or as part of an American-style antipasto. It's commonly served with cold cuts and hamburgers in the Midwest and you'll find it on the table in New England when the menu offers baked beans.

The name piccalilli is thought to be a combination of the words pickle and chili. This spicy mustard-based relish originated in India and was brought to our shores by English seamen and army officers. Sometimes you'll see it called India relish or India pickle. Piccalilli is very similar to chow-chow, a mustard-flavored relish supposedly originating in China that combines vegetables with pickles.

4 cups cider vinegar	1 cup fresh or frozen corn kernels
2 cups granulated sugar	1 red bell pepper, cut into 1-inch
¼ cup all-purpose flour	strips
3 tablespoons dry mustard	1 green bell pepper, cut into 1-inch
2 teaspoons turmeric	strips
½ cup malt vinegar	1 small onion, chopped
2 cups cauliflower florets	1 cup sliced small zucchini
2 cups green beans, cut into 1-inch	2 (1-quart) canning jars with 2-part
pieces	lids
1 cup peeled and sliced carrots	

Combine the vinegar and sugar in a large nonreactive pot and bring to a boil. In a bowl combine the flour, mustard, turmeric and vinegar and blend well. Stir into the vinegar mixture and boil for 5 minutes.

Blanch the cauliflower and green beans by placing them in boiling water for 3 minutes. Immediately plunge into cold water to stop the cooking process. When the vegetables are cold, drain well. Cook the carrots in boiling water until tender, about 8 minutes. Immediately plunge into cold water. When cold, drain well.

Fill the jars with all the vegetables, arranging them evenly and fairly tight. Cover the vegetables with the hot vinegar solution, leaving ½-inch headroom. Run a thin spatula between the insides of the jars and the vegetables to expel any trapped air. Wipe the edges of the jars with a dry cloth and place the lids on.

Know Your Fire

Place the jars on a rack or on a terry cloth towel in a large kettle. They should not touch each other. Add enough water so that the tops of the jars are covered by at least 2 inches. When the water comes to a rolling boil, begin timing. In 10 minutes, remove the jars with tongs or a jar lifter and place them out of drafts to cool. Store in a cool dark place for 2 weeks for the piccalilli to ripen.

Tomato and Hot Pepper Marmalade

If you consider the tomato a fruit, you'll have no trouble calling this a marmalade. The hotness can be regulated by using less or more jalapeño peppers. Try it with cream cheese on crisp wheat crackers.

4 cups peeled, seeded, and chopped
    tomatoes
2 cups granulated sugar
2 oranges, thinly sliced
1 lemon, thinly sliced
¼ teaspoon ground cumin

¼ teaspoon dried thyme
4 fresh jalapeño peppers, sliced into
    rings
4 (1 pint) canning jars with 2-piece
    lids

Place the tomatoes and sugar in a 3-quart nonreactive pan and simmer over low heat for 15 to 20 minutes. Add the orange and lemon slices, cumin and thyme and simmer, stirring occasionally, until the mixture is thick and translucent, about 1 hour. Add the jalapeño slices and pack the mixture into the jars.

Run a thin spatula or knife between the insides of the jars and the marmalade to remove any trapped air. Wipe the tops of the jars with a clean, dry cloth and place the lids on.

Place the jars on a rack or on a terry cloth towel in a large kettle. They should not touch each other. Add enough water so that the tops of the jars are covered by at least 2 inches. When the water comes to a rolling boil, begin timing. In 10 minutes, remove the jars with tongs or a jar lifter and place them out of drafts to cool. Store in a cool, dark place for two weeks for marmalade to develop flavor.

Peach Mint Jam

It only takes a few ingredients and about an hour to make this jam. It's not much time and effort to put a smile on your face when you spread it on your breakfast toast on a particularly harried morning.

8 medium peaches

10 cups granulated sugar (about 5
   pounds)

⅓ cup fresh lemon juice

1 tablespoon chopped fresh mint
   leaves

¾ of a 6-ounce bottle of pectin

8 jelly jars or 8 jelly jars with
   2-piece lids

paraffin wax

Remove the peel from half the peaches by dipping them into boiling water for 1 minute and then plunging them into cold water. The peel should come off easily with a paring knife. Cut all the peaches in half, remove the pits and chop fine. There should be 6 cups. Place the peaches in a large pot with a heavy bottom. Add the sugar, lemon juice and mint leaves. Bring to a rolling boil, stirring constantly, and cook 5 minutes. Remove from the heat and stir in the pectin and mix until well blended. Remove from the heat and skim off any foam with a metal spoon. Immediately ladle the jam into hot sterilized jars leaving ½-inch headroom and cover with a thin layer of melted paraffin wax. The jam should be consumed within six weeks. Store the jars in the refrigerator.

For longer storage, use canning jars. Ladle in the jam, wipe off the tops of the jars with a clean cloth and place the lids on. Place the jars on a rack or on a terry cloth towel in a large kettle. They should not touch each other. Add enough water so that the tops of the jars are covered by at least 2 inches. When the water comes to a rolling boil, begin timing. In 10 minutes, remove the jars with tongs or a jar lifter and place them out of drafts to cool.

Preserving

Spiced Peaches

Freestone peaches, as opposed to clingstone peaches, are easy to pit. Use peaches that are ripe and without any blemishes. If you want to peel the peaches first, dip them into boiling water for 60 seconds and then plunge them into cold water. The skins should slip off easily with a knife. The lemon zest can be removed with a vegetable peeler.

Serve spiced peaches with smoked foods, duck, pork or lamb. If it's a very hot night, order a pizza, sit on the porch and enjoy the peaches with a scoop of vanilla ice cream.

12 Freestone peaches, peeled

1 cup water

1 cup granulated sugar

½ cup brown sugar

Juice of 1 orange and the zest cut into ½-inch pieces

Juice of 2 lemons

4 cinnamon sticks or 1 teaspoon ground cinnamon

¼ cup brandy

¼ teaspoon ground allspice

4 (1 pint) canning jars with 2-piece lids

8 mint leaves

Cut the peaches in half and remove the pits.

Combine the water, granulated and brown sugars, orange juice and zest, lemon juice and cinnamon sticks in a nonreactive pan and bring to a boil. Add the peaches and brandy, lower heat and simmer 10 minutes. Stir in the allspice. Pack the peaches into the jars, add 2 mint leaves to each jar, and cover with the syrup, leaving ¼ inch headroom. If using cinnamon stick, place 1 stick in each jar.

Run a thin spatula or knife between the insides of the jars and the peaches to remove any trapped air. Wipe the tops of the jars with a clean, dry cloth and place the lids on.

Place the jars on a rack or on a terry cloth towel in a large kettle. They should not touch each other. Add enough water so that the tops of the jars are covered by at least 2 inches. When the water comes to a rolling boil, begin timing. In 10 minutes, remove the jars with tongs or a jar lifter and place them out of drafts to cool. Store in a cool dark place for 2 to 3 days for peaches to develop flavor.

As an alternative to the hot-water bath, the peaches can be refrigerated for 2 to 3 days to absorb the flavors; they should be consumed within 1 month.

Index

acorn squash, and pumpkin, 181
allemande sauce, 126
allspice, 52
almond oil, 71, 72
almonds, to toast, 110
Anaheim peppers, 64
anchos, 64, 65
Angel Hair Pasta with Smoked Salmon, 85
anise seed, 52
anthocyanin, 168
Apple Charlotte, 276
Apple Pecan Crumble, 278
Apple-Raisin Sauce, 135
Arancini (rice balls), 104
arborio rice, 99
   croquettes, 106–7
aromatic rices, 98
arrowroot, 127
arugula, 118
asparagus, many ways, 172
aurora sauce, 126
Avery Island, Louisiana, 64–65

baby beef, 16
baking, 267–70
   of fish, 143
   of potatoes, 92
balsamic vinegar, 73
banana peppers, 63
barley, 100
basic recipes, 185
basil, 52
   cheese ravioli with pine nuts and, 88
basmati rice, 98–99
bass, poached, with sweet potato straws, 222
bay leaves, 52

bay scallops, 139, 234
beans, dried, 101–3
   black, jambalaya, red snapper with, 204
   pasta with, 115
   and steak soup, 163
béarnaise sauce, 126
béchamel sauce, 125
beef, 5–10
   Burgundy Pot Roast, 206
   fillet, grilled, 11
      with mushrooms and red wine sauce, 13
   Steak and Bean Soup, 163
   Steak and Fusilli Salad, 251
   stir-fried with cashews, 215
   stock, 191, 247–48
   Swiss Steak, 205
   tenderloin tips with curry sauce, 12
   Texas Chili, 14–15
beer
   batter, cod fried with, 214
   leg of lamb roasted with, 26
   and onion soup, 166
beet greens, 118
beets, 168
   in orange sauce, 173
Belgian endive, 118
Benedict, Mr. and Mrs. LeGrand, 226
benne seeds, 54
bercy sauce, 126
Bermuda onions, 170
bettys, 278
black beans, 102
   jambalaya, red snapper with, 204
black-eyed peas, 102
   Hoppin' John, 114
black pepper, 54

blue cheese
  and poached pear salad, 225
  salad dressings, 77, 78
boiling, 197
  of potatoes, 91–92
bolognese sauce, 127
bordelaise sauce, 126
botulism, 286
bouillabaisse, 148
braising, 41, 197, 199–201
  beef cuts for, 9
  of cabbage, 207
  lamb cuts for, 21
  pork cuts for, 29
  veal cuts for, 17
Brandy and Cheese Soup, 162
Bread and Butter Pickles, 290
Bread and Butter Sauce, 134
bread crumbs, to make, 106
breading, for frying, 211
bread pudding, 268
brining, 285
broccoli, pasta with garlic and, 89
broccoli rabe
  cavatelli with hot sausage and, 87
  couscous with, 174
broiling, 197–98
  beef cuts for, 9
  of fish, 142
  lamb cuts for, 21
  pork cuts for, 28
  veal cuts for, 17
brown rice, 98
Brussels Sprouts and Walnuts, 175
Bucatini with Spicy Tomato Sauce, 69
bulghur, 100
  ginger pilaf, 111
Burgundy Pot Roast, 206
butter, 71, 230
  to thicken sauces, 128
butters, flavored, 134
  See also Sauces

cabbage, 168, 169
  braised, 207
Calas, 218
calico scallops, 139, 234

cannellini beans, 102
  pasta with, 115
canning, 287
canola oil, 71, 210
capons, 35
capsaicin, 62
capsicum peppers, 62–65
Caramelized Garlic, 185, 186
caramelized vegetables, 190, 238
caraway seeds, 52
carbohydrates, 97
cardamom, 52
Careme, Antonin, 125
Caribbean Spice Rub, 59
carotenoid, 169
carrots, 169
cascabel peppers, 63
cashews, beef stir-fried with, 215
cast-iron cookware, 232, 233
catfish, pan-seared, 236
cauliflower, 169, 176
  with fontina sauce, 177
  sautéed, 239
Cavatelli with Hot Sausage and Broccoli
    Rabe, 87
cayenne peppers, 63
Celery Root Slaw, 124
champagne, eggs poached in, 221
charcoal grills, 248–49
chausseur sauce, 126
Chayote Stuffed with Chorizo, 178
Cheese, 128
  and brandy soup, 162
  Cauliflower with Fontina Sauce, 177
  Golden Buck, 238
  Poached Pear and Blue Cheese Salad, 225
Cheese Ravioli with Pine Nuts and Basil, 88
Cherry Cake, 272
cherry peppers, 63
chicken, 34
  en croûte, 44–45
  fingers, sautéed with linguine, 48
  fricassee, 43
  roasted, 38–39, 244
  stock, 188
  wood-smoked, 46, 59
Chicken Livers in Tomato Sauce, 47

Index

chick peas, 102
chicory, 118
chilaca peppers, 64
chile, 63
chili, 14–15, 63
chiltepin peppers, 64
Chinese cabbage, 176
chipoltes, 64
chives, 52
Chocolate Sauce, 136
chorizo
    chayote stuffed with, 178
    and pepper stew, 256
cider vinegar, 73
cilantro, 53
cinnamon, 52–53
clams, 138, 142
    chili-baked, 68
    fritters, 213
    with garlic and wine, 153
clarified butter, 150
cloves, 53
coatings for frying, 210–11
cobblers, 278
coconut oil, 71
cod, fried with beer batter, 214
coffee cake, upside-down, 277
cold-smoking of foods, 257–58
    pork, 59, 261
    trout, 59, 260
collards, hot and sour, 179
colored potatoes, 91
conserves, 286
convection ovens, 241
converted rice, 98
cookware. See pans
coriander seed, 53
corn, 169
    nacho, 66
    tortilla soup, 164–65
Cornish hens, 35
    marinade for, 60
    roasted, 245
corn oil, 71, 210
cornstarch, 127
cos lettuce, 118
court bouillon, poaching in, 221

couscous, 101
    with broccoli rabe, 174
    racks of lamb with, 23
crab meat, tossed, 235
cracked wheat, 100
cranberry beans, 102
Crayfish Omelet, 155
Cream Puff Pastry, 274–75
cream soups, 157–58
crisps, 278
croquettes, arborio rice, 106–7
crumbles, 278
crustaceans, 138
cubanelle peppers, 64
cucumbers, pickles, 289, 290
cumin seed, 53
curry powder, 12, 122
custard, banana praline, 280–81
cutting boards, 39–40

deep-fat frying, 208–9
defrosting of foods. See freezing of foods
desserts
    Apple Charlotte, 276
    Apple Pecan Crumble, 278
    Banana Praline Custard, 280–81
    Cherry Cake, 282
    Fruit Fool, 279
    poached pear, 228
    Skillet Cornbread Shortcake, 272–73
    Upside-Down Coffee Cake, 277
dill, 53
    pickles, 289
    and tomato salsa, grilled salmon with, 252
distilled vinegar, 73, 285
drawn butter, 150
dressings. See salad dressings
dried herbs, 50, 51
dry-heat cooking, 197–98
duck, 35, 37
    boneless roast, 42

eggs
    Crayfish Omelet, 155
    Golden Buck, 238
    and oysters, 156
    poached, 221, 227

eggs (*cont.*)

    yolks, to thicken sauces, 127

Eggs Benedict, 226

emulsions, 74

escarole, 118

espagnole sauce, 125

estragon sauce, 126

extra-virgin olive oil, 72

fats, 71–73, 210

    See also oils

fennel seed, 53

filé powder, 204

filleting of fish, 141–42

fillet mignon, 12, 13

filo dough, 45

fish, 137–44

    bass, poached, with sweet potato straws, 222

    Bouillabaisse, 148

    catfish, pan-seared, 236

    cod, fried in beer batter, 214

    flounder, stuffed and rolled, 145

    Halibut with Mustard Pepper Crust, 147

    Monkfish in Oyster Sauce, 146

    Red Snapper with Black Bean Jambalaya, 204

    salmon, smoked, with angel hair pasta, 85

    salmon grilled with tomato dill salsa, 252

    trout, cold-smoked, 260

fish sauce, 127

fish stock, 189

flavone, 169

flavorings, 49, 51

flounder, stuffed and rolled, 145

fowl, 34

fra diavolo sauce, 126

freezing of foods

    beef, 7–8

    herbs, 51

    lamb, 22

    pork, 28

    poultry, 36

    soups, 160

    veal, 17

French-frying, 209–10

fresh herbs, 51

fricassee, chicken, 43

frisee, 118

fritters

    clam or oyster, 213

    fruit, 219

    semolina, 112

frozen fish, 143–44

Fruit Fool, 279

Fruit Fritters, 219

fruits

    Apple Charlotte, 276

    Apple Pecan Crumble, 278

    Apple-Raisin Sauce, 135

    Banana Praline Custard, 280–81

    Cherry Cake, 272

    dressing, 80

    Peach Mint Jam, 295

    poaching of, 221

    sauces from, 129, 135

    Smoked Pineapple, 266

    Spiced Peaches, 296

    spreads, 286

    vinegars, 73

frying, 197, 208–11

    Beer Batter Cod, 214

    Calas, 218

    Clam or Oyster Fritters, 213

    of fish, 143

    Fried Grits and Mushrooms, 212

    Fruit Fritters, 219

    Hush Puppies, 217

    Sweet Potato Straws, 216

garlic

    caramelized, 186

        pasta with broccoli and, 89

    clams with wine and, 153

    and horseradish butter, 134

    and lemon butter, 132

garlic bread, 185, 187

garnishes for soups, 160

gas grills, 248

Gebhardt, Willie, 63

ginger, 53

Ginger Bulghur Pilaf, 111

Gnocchi, 95
Golden Buck, 238
goose, 35
Gorgonzola, 77
gougère of ham, 33
grading of meat, 6
grains, 100
gravy, to make, 128
Great Northern beans, 102
grillades, grits and, 202–3
grilling, 197–98, 247–50
  beef cuts for, 9
  Chorizo and Pepper Stew, 256
  of corn, 165
  of fish, 142
    salmon with tomato dill salsa, 252
  Ham-Stuffed Shrimp, 254–55
  lamb cuts for, 21
  pork cuts for, 28
  Shrimp with Lemon and Rosemary, 253
  Steak and Fusilli Salad, 251
  veal cuts for, 17
grills, smoking on, 258–59
grits
  fried, and mushrooms, 212
  and grillades, 202–3
ground beef, grades of, 8

habanero peppers, 64
Halibut with Mustard Pepper Crust, 147
ham, 29
  gougère of, 33
  and mushroom sauce, 132
  shrimp stuffed with, 254–55
hazelnut oil, 72
herbs, 49–56
  basil, ravioli with pine nuts and, 88
  roast chicken with, 244
  rosemary, shrimp with lemon and, 253
  tarragon tomato salad, 123
  vinaigrette, 76
  vinegars, 55, 73
hoisin sauce, 127
hollandaise, 125
honey, pork with walnuts and, 233
Honey and Onion Shrimp, 149

Hoppin' John, 114
horseradish
  and garlic butter, 134
  pork cutlets with, 31
  rub, 57
hot-smoking of foods, 257–59
Hungarian wax peppers, 63
Hush Puppies, 217

indirect grilling, 46
ingredients, 3–4
inspection of meat, 6
instant-read thermometers, 5, 241
Italian bacon, 29
Italian peppers, 64

jalapeño peppers, 64
Jalapeño Rolls, 70
jambalaya, black bean, red snapper with,
  204
jams, 286
  peach mint, 295
jellies, 286

ketchup, 129
kidney beans, 102
kirby cucumbers, 289
knives, 170–71
knowledge, for good cooking, xi–xii

lamb, 20–22
  leg, roasted with beer, 26
  peppers stuffed with, 24
  racks, with couscous, 23
  rubs for, 58
  shanks, in red wine, 25
lambs lettuce, 118
lard, 71, 210
leftovers, soups from, 159
lemon
  and garlic butter, 132
  shrimp with rosemary and, 253
lentils, 102
linguine, chicken fingers sautéed with, 48
Little Neck clams, 153
lobster coral, 151

lobsters, 138–39
  baked, stuffed, 152
  boiled, 150
  broth, 161
  grilled, 151
lolorosa, 118
long-grain rice, 98

mace, 54
mache, 118
McIlhenny, William, 65
malt vinegar, 73
Margarita Shrimp, 237
marguery sauce, 126
marinades, 55
  for Cornish hens, 60
  for smoked trout, 59
marinara sauce, 126
marjoram, 53
marmalade, 286
  tomato and hot pepper, 294
mashed potatoes, perfect, 93
Mason jars, 287
Maui onions, 170
mayonnaise, 74, 125
measuring for baking, 268–69
mesclun, 117–18
mint, 53
  and peach jam, 295
mirliton squash, 178
mizuna, 118
moist-heat cooking, 197–98
mollusks, 138
Monkfish in Oyster Sauce, 146
mornay sauce, 126
mushrooms
  beef fillet with red wine sauce and, 13
  fried grits and, 212
  and ham sauce, 132
  and pork stew, 32
  Portobello, stuffed, 180
mussels, 138, 142
  chilled, in pesto mayonnaise, 154
mustard, 129–30
mustard greens, 118
mutton, 21

Nacho Corn, 66
nantua sauce, 126
New Mexico chiles, 64
nutmeg, 54

oils, 71–73
olive oil, 71, 72, 210, 230
omelet, crayfish, 155
onions, 169, 170
  and beer soup, 166
  caramelized, 238
  and salmon salad, 121
  shrimp, with honey and 149
  veal roast with potatoes and, 243
  Vidalia, roasted, 182
orange sauce, beets in, 173
oregano, 54
Orzo and Peas, 86
oysters, 139–40
  eggs and, 156
  fritters, 213
  poached, on spinach salad, 224
oyster sauce, 127
  monkfish in, 146

palm oil, 71
pancetta, 29
  spinach and, 183
pan frying, 209
pan gravy, 128
pans, 230–32, 241, 269–70, 288
pan-seared catfish, 236
paprika, 54
Parma ham, 29
parsley, 54
parsnips, 169
pasillas, 64
pasta, 81–84
  angel hair, with smoked salmon, 85
  with beans, 115
  with broccoli and caramelized garlic, 89
  Bucatini with Spicy Tomato Sauce, 69
  Cavatelli with Hot Sausage and Broccoli
    Rabe, 87
  Cheese Ravioli with Pine Nuts and Basil,
    88

fusilli, and steak salad, 251
Orzo and Peas, 86
Pastry Cream 271
Pâté à Choux, 274–75
peaches
   and mint jam, 295
   spiced, 296
   sweet potatoes stuffed with, 185
peanut oil, 71, 72, 210, 230
pears, poached, 228
   and blue cheese salad, 225
peas, orzo and, 86
Peck, Paula, 116
pepper, black, 54
pepperoncini, 64
peppers:
   green, lamb-stuffed, 24
   hot, 62–65
      Chili-Baked Clams, 68
      Fiery Peppers, 67
      Jalapeño Rolls, 70
      Nacho Corn, 66
      and tomato marmalade, 294
   sweet
      Chorizo and Pepper Stew, 256
      and veal stew, 18
perciatelli, 69
perigueux sauce, 126
pesto, 133
   mayonnaise, chilled mussels in, 154
pickles, 285
   bread and butter, 290
   dill, 289
   green tomato, 291
   piccalilli, 292–93
Pierogi, 96
pilaf, 108
   ginger bulghur, 111
   wild rice, 109
pineapple, smoked, 266
pine nuts, cheese ravioli with basil and, 88
pinto beans, 103
pinwheels, turkey, 41
pizza dough, 185, 194
Pizza Rustica, 283
poaching, 41, 197, 220–21

bass with sweet potato straws, 222
Eggs Benedict, 226
Eggs in a Wink, 227
of fish, 143
oysters on spinach salad, 224
pear and blue cheese salad, 225
pear dessert, 228
poblano peppers, 64
pork, 27–29
   center cut chops, hot-smoked, 263
   cold-smoked, 59, 261
   cutlets with grated horseradish, 31
   with honey and walnuts, 233
   loin chops, sautéed with shrimp, 30
   and mushroom stew, 32
   ribs, smoked, 60, 264
   rubs for, 57, 59, 60
   salad, in roti wrappers, 262
Potato Bread, 192–93
potatoes, 90–92, 169
   Gnocchi, 95
   perfect mashed, 93
   Pierogi, 96
   and rutabaga mash, 94
   veal roast with onions and, 243
poultry, 34–40
   poaching of, 221
preserves, 286
preserving of foods, 284–88
prosciutto, 29
pumpkin, and acorn squash, 181
puttanesca sauce, 127

radicchio, 118
red oak leaf lettuce, 118
Red Snapper with Black Bean Jambalaya,
   204
red wine, lamb shanks in, 25
rémoulade sauce, 126
rice, 97–100
   Arborio Croquettes, 106–7
   balls (arancini), 104
   pilaf, 108, 109
   Tomato Risotto, 105
   See also Wild rice
rice vinegar, 74

roasting, 197, 240–42, 267
  beef cuts for, 9
  of chile peppers, 65
  lamb cuts for, 21
  pork cuts for, 28
  of potatoes, 92
  of poultry, 37–39
    Herb Roast Chicken, 244
    Cornish hens, 245
  veal, with potatoes and onions, 243
  veal cuts for, 17
  vegetable medley, 246
romaine, 118
Roquefort cheese, 77
rosemary, 54
  shrimp with lemon and, 253
roti wrappers, pork salad in, 262
rouille sauce, 126
roux, 127, 157–58
rubs, 56
  Caribbean spice, 59
  grated horseradish, 57
  hickory, dry, 59
  for lamb, 58
  pork seasoning, 57
  for smoked ribs, 60
rutabaga, 169
  and potato mash, 94

safflower oil, 71, 210, 230
sage, 54
salad dressings, 74
  creamy blue cheese, 78
  fruit, 80
  smoky ranch, 79
  thousand island, 79
  vinaigrettes, 75–77
salads, 116–19
  Celery Root Slaw, 124
  hearty green, 120
  poached oysters on spinach, 224
  poached pear and blue cheese, 225
  pork, roti, 262
  salmon and onion, 121
  shrimp curry, 122
  steak and fusilli, 251

tomato tarragon, 123
turkey and walnut, 223
wild rice, 110
salmon
  grilled, with tomato dill salsa, 252
  and onion salad, 121
  smoked, angel hair pasta with, 85
salmonella, 39
salsa, 126
salt, 52
sauces, 125
  apple-raisin, 135
  bread and butter, 134
  chocolate, 136
  fruit, 135
  Garlic and Lemon Butter, 132
  Garlic Horseradish Butter, 134
  grilled tomato, 131
  ham and mushroom, 132
sausage, hot, cavatelli with broccoli rabe and,
    87
sautéeing, 198, 229–32
  beef cuts for, 9
  lamb cuts for, 21
  pork cuts for, 29
  veal cuts for, 17
scallops, 138, 139
  with a cornmeal crust, 234
  to poach, 143
Scotch bonnets, 64
seafood, 137–44
  See also fish; shellfish
sea scallops, 139, 234
seasonings, 49
Semolina Fritters, 112
serrano peppers, 64, 68
sesame oil, 71, 72–73
sesame seeds, 54
shellfish, 138
  Clam or Oyster Fritters, 213
  clams, chili-baked, 68
  Clams With Garlic and Wine, 153
  crab meat, tossed, 236
  Crayfish Omelet, 155
  mussels, chilled, in pesto mayonnaise, 154
  oysters, eggs and, 156

oysters, poached, on Spinach Salad, 224
Scallops with a Cornmeal Crust, 234
shrimp, ham-stuffed, 254–55
shrimp, Margarita, 237
Shrimp Curry Salad, 122
Shrimp with Lemon and Rosemary, 253
shopping tips
   for beef, 7
   for herbs and spices, 50
   for lobsters, 138–39
   for pork, 27
   for poultry, 35–36
   for seafood, 137–38
shortcake, cornbread, 272–73
shrimp, 140
   curry salad, 122
   ham-stuffed, 254–55
   honey and onion, 149
   with lemon and rosemary, 253
   Margarita, 237
   to poach, 143
   pork loin chops sautéed with, 30
Sicilian sauce, 127
simmering, 197
Skillet Cornbread Shortcake, 272–73
slaw, celery root, 124
slurry, 128
smoking of foods, 257–59
   pineapple, 266
   pork chops, 263
   spareribs, 264
   turkey, 265
Smoky Ranch Dressing, 79
soubise sauce, 126
soups, 157–60
   brandy and cheese, 162
   corn tortilla, 164–65
   Lobster Broth, 161
   onion and beer, 166
   pastas for, 82
   steak and bean, 163
soybean oil, 71, 210
soy sauces, 127
Spanish onions, 170
spices, 49–56
spinach, 119

and pancetta, 183
   salad, poached oysters on, 224
spit-roasted poultry, 46
split peas, 103
Spoon Bread, 113
spring lamb, 20–21
Steak and Bean Soup, 163
steaming of vegetables, 168
stews
   Bouillabaisse, 148
   Chicken Fricassee, 43
   chorizo and pepper, 256
   pork and mushroom, 32
   veal and pepper, 18
Stilton cheese, 77
stir-frying, 198, 210
   beef with cashews, 215
stocks, 158, 185
   beef or veal, 191, 247–48
   chicken, 188
   fish, 189
   vegetable, 190
storage of foods
   beef, 7–8
   herbs and spices, 50
   lamb, 22
   pork, 28
   potatoes, 91
   poultry, 36
   salad greens, 119
   veal, 17
   vegetables, 168
strawberries, cornbread shortcake, 272–73
substitutions for oils, 73
sweating of vegetables, 159
sweet potatoes, 169
   stuffed with peaches, 185
Sweet Potato Straws, 216
   poached bass with, 222
Swift, Jonathan, 139
Swiss chard, 119
Swiss Steak, 205

Tabasco peppers, 64–65
tarragon, 54
Texas Chili, 14–15

Texmati rice, 98
thickeners, 127–28, 157–58
Thousand Island Dressing, 79
thyme, 55
tofu, 111
tomalley, 151
tomatoes
  and dill salsa, grilled salmon with, 252
  green, pickled, 291
  Grilled Tomato Sauce, 131
  and hot pepper marmalade, 294
  risotto, 105
  and tarragon salad, 123
tomato sauce, 125
  chicken livers in, 47
  spicy, bucatini with 69
trichinosis, 29
trout, cold-smoked, 59, 260
turkey, 35
  pinwheels, 41
  roasting of, 37–38
  smoked, 61, 265
  and walnut salad, 223
turmeric, 55
turnips, 169

Upside-Down Coffee Cake, 277

veal, 9, 16–17
  and pepper stew, 18
  rib chop, grilled, 19
  roast with potatoes and onions, 243
  stock, 191
vegetables, 167–71
  asparagus, 172
  Beets in Orange Sauce, 173
  broccoli, pasta with garlic and, 89
  broccoli rabe, couscous with, 174
  broccoli rabe, pasta with sausage and, 87
  Brussels Sprouts and Walnuts, 175
  cabbage, braised, 207
  Cauliflower Blanc, 176
  Cauliflower Sauté, 239
  Cauliflower with Fontina Sauce, 177
  Chayote Stuffed with Chorizo, 178
  Chinese Cabbage, 176

collards, hot and sour, 179
Corn Tortilla Soup, 164–65
peas and orzo, 86
Portobello mushrooms, stuffed, 180
Pumpkin and Acorn Squash, 181
roasted, 240, 246
  Vidalia onions, 182
Spinach and Pancetta, 183
Sweet Potatoes Stuffed with Peaches, 185
Sweet Potato Straws, 216
See also beans, dried; peppers, hot; potatoes
vegetable stock, 190
velouté sauce, 125
Vidalia onions, 170, 182
vinaigrettes, 75–77, 125
vinegars, 55, 73–74, 285

Walla Walla onions, 170
walnut oil, 73
walnuts
  brussels sprouts and, 175
  pork with honey and, 233
  and turkey salad, 223
watercress, 119
Waters, Alice, 167–68
water smokers, 257–58
Wehani rice, 99
Welsh rarebit, 238
wild rice, 99
  pilaf, 108, 109
  salad, 110
wine, cooking with, 32
  Burgundy Pot Roast, 206
  clams with garlic and, 153
  red, beef fillet with mushrooms and, 13
wine vinegar, 73, 285–86
winter squash, 169
Wood-Smoked Chickens on a Spit, 46

yams, 169
yellow onions, 170
yogurt, to thicken sauces, 128

zest of citrus fruits, 80

Dear Friends:

Thank you for choosing *Know Your Fire*. I hope that it becomes a much used addition to your cookbook library. And because it's important to hear from my readers and viewers, I encourage you to contact me with questions or comments.

Also, if you want to receive more information about Know Your Fire products, please send your name and address to:

Know Your Fire
PO Box 655
King's Park, New York 11754

or contact me at my web page:
http://chefghirsch.com

—CHEF GEORGE HIRSCH